SERIES

6

PASS TRAK

Questions & Answers

Investment Company/

Variable Contracts

Limited Representative

*14*th Edition

Dearborn
Financial Publishing, Inc.

At press time, this 14th edition of PassTrak Series 6 contains the most complete and accurate information currently available for the NASD Series 6 license examination. Owing to the nature of securities license examinations, however, information may have been added recently to the actual test that does not appear in this edition.

Dearborn Financial Publishing, Inc.

While a great deal of care has been taken to provide accurate and current information, the ideas, suggestions, general principles and conclusions presented in this book are subject to local, state and federal laws and regulations, court cases and any revisions of same. The reader is thus urged to consult legal counsel regarding any points of law—this publication should not be used as a substitute for competent legal advice.

Executive Editor: Kimberly K. Walker-Daniels
Project Editor: Nicola Bell
Cover Design: Vito DePinto

©1990 by Dearborn Financial Publishing, Inc.
Published by Dearborn Financial Publishing, Inc.

Printed in the United States of America.

90   91   92   10   9   8   7   6   5   4   3   2   1

Library of Congress Cataloging-in-Publication Data

PassTrak series 6, Investment company/variable contracts limited
   representative. Questions & answers.—14th ed.
     p. c.m.
   ISBN 0-7931-0144-1
    1. Mutual funds—Examinations, questions, etc. 2. Stockbrokers—
Examinations, questions, etc. I. Dearborn Financial Publishing.
II. Title: PassTrak series six, Investment company/variable
contracts limited representative. III. Title: Investment
company/variable contracts limited representative.
HG4530.P352 1990   90-3921
332.63'27—dc20   CIP

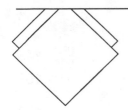

Contents

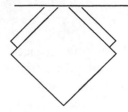

Introduction to PassTrak Series 6

Welcome to PassTrak Series 6. Because you probably have a lot of questions about the course and the exam, we have tried to anticipate some of them and provide you with answers to help you on your way.

The Course

How is the course structured?

PassTrak Series 6 is divided into two volumes: a textbook and an exam book. The textbook, titled *Principles & Practices*, consists of four chapters, each devoted to a particular area of investment company/variable contract products (IC/VC) trading and regulation that you will need to know to pass the IC/VC Limited Representative Qualification Exam (Series 6). Each chapter is subdivided into study sections devoted to specific areas with which you need to become familiar.

The exam book, titled *Questions & Answers*, contains 14 review exams that correspond to the sections in the four chapters in the textbook. The book concludes with three final exams composed of questions similar to those you will encounter on the actual Series 6 exam.

What topics does this course cover?

The information you need to pass the Series 6 exam is covered in PassTrak Series 6 through the following chapters:

Chapter 1: Securities, Securities Markets and Investment Risk
Chapter 2: Investment Companies
Chapter 3: Variable Contracts and Retirement Plans
Chapter 4: Securities Regulation

How much time should I spend studying?

You should plan to spend approximately 40 hours reading the material, working through the questions and studying the books. Your actual time, of course, may vary from this figure depending on your reading rate, comprehension, professional background and study environment.

Spread your study time over the two to three weeks prior to the date you are scheduled to take the Series 6 exam. Select a time and place for studying that will allow you to concentrate your full attention on the material at hand. You have a lot of information to learn and a lot of ground to cover. Be sure to give yourself enough time to learn the material.

What is the best way to approach the exams in this book?

Approach each exam as if you were taking the actual test. Read each question carefully, and write down your answers. Then check your answers against the key, and read the rationale that follow. Making yourself go through all of these steps (rather than simply reading each question and skipping directly to the rationale) will greatly increase your comprehension and retention of the information.

Do I need to take the final exams?

The final exams contain questions that test the same knowledge you will need to answer the questions on the NASD Series 6 exam. By completing these exams and checking your answers against the answers and rationale, you should be able to pinpoint any areas with which you are still having difficulty. Review those questions you missed, paying particular attention to the rationale for those questions. If any subjects still seem troublesome, go back and review the chapter(s) covering those topics.

If you consistently achieve scores of 80% or higher on the review and final exams in *PassTrak Series 6 Questions & Answers*, you should be well prepared to pass the Series 6 exam.

The Exam

Why do I need to pass the Series 6 exam?

Your employer is a member of the National Association of Securities Dealers, Inc. (NASD) or another self-regulatory organization (SRO) that requires its members to pass a qualifications exam in order to become registered. To be registered as a representative qualified to sell investment company and variable contract products, you must pass the Series 6 exam.

What can I sell after I pass this exam?

Upon passing the NASD Series 6 exam for investment company and variable contract products, you will be able to sell mutual funds, variable annuities and variable life products (assuming you have also passed applicable state exams and are registered to sell these products within the state in which you do business).

You *cannot* sell with this registration:

- closed-end investment company shares
- real estate investment trusts (REITs)
- stocks
- bonds
- other individual securities

If you have a question as to which securities you are registered to sell or which additional registrations you may require, contact your firm for further information.

What is the Series 6 exam like?

The Series 6 is a 2-hour-and-15-minute exam, administered by the NASD. It is offered at various testing sites around the country.

How do I enroll for the exam?

To obtain an admission ticket to the Series 6 exam, you must complete either a U-10 form (if your firm is a non-NASD member) or a U-4 form (if your firm is an NASD member) and file it with the NASD along with the appropriate processing fees. The NASD will then send you an entrance ticket that is valid for 90 days. To take the exam during this 90-day period, you must make an appointment with a Control Data Center at least two weeks before the date on which you would like to sit for the test.

What topics will the exam cover?

This course covers the wide range of topics the NASD has outlined as being essential to the IC/VC limited representative. The NASD exam is divided into four broad topic areas as follows:

Securities, Securities Markets and Investment Risk	20%
Investment Companies	35%
Variable Contracts and Retirement Plans	20%
Securities Regulation	25%

How long does the exam take?

You will be allowed 2 hours and 15 minutes in which to finish the exam. If you are taking the computerized version of the exam, you will be given additional time before the test to become familiar with the PLATO® terminal.

What score do I need to pass?

You must answer correctly at least 70% of the questions on each part of the Series 6 exam in order to pass and become eligible for NASD registration as a representative.

What is PLATO®?

The Series 6 exam, like many other professional licensing examinations, is administered on the PLATO® computerized testing system. PLATO® is an interactive computer network developed by Control Data as an educational and testing service.

Included with your notice of enrollment from the NASD, you will receive a directory of Control Data Learning Centers and a brochure describing how the exam is formatted and how to use the computer terminal to answer questions. When you have completed the exam, the PLATO® system promptly scores your answers and within minutes displays a grade for the exam on the terminal screen.

How well can I expect to do on the exam?

The examinations administered by the NASD are not easy. You will be required to display considerable understanding and knowledge of the topics presented in this course in order to pass the exam and qualify for registration. If you study and complete all of the sections of this course, you will have the foundation you need to pass the NASD Series 6 exam.

1 Equity Securities

1. If interest rates are increasing and the market price of bonds is decreasing, what would happen to the value of preferred stock during this same time period?

   A. The value of stock would increase.
   B. The value of stock would decrease.
   C. The value of stock would remain the same.
   D. Interest rates and the value of bonds have no impact on the value of stock.

2. If a corporation wanted to offer stock at a given price for the next five years, it would issue

   A. rights
   B. warrants
   C. callable preferred stock
   D. put options

3. The XYZ Company has outstanding a 5% cumulative preferred stock and a $2.40 participating preferred stock. Last year, XYZ Company paid no dividends. This year, XYZ Company has excess earnings to distribute. If a dividend is declared, in which order will the dividend be paid?

   I. The dividend in arrears to the cumulative preferred stockholders
   II. The stated dividend to the cumulative preferred stockholders
   III. The excess earnings to the participating preferred stockholders
   IV. The stated dividend to the participating preferred stockholders

   A. I, II, III, IV
   B. I, III, II, IV
   C. II, IV, I, III
   D. III, II, IV, I

4. If ABC Company's dividend decreases by 5% and its stock's market value decreases by 7%, the current yield of the stock will

   A. decrease
   B. increase
   C. remain at 5%
   D. not be affected by price fluctuations

5. Stock rights (which are also called subscription rights) are

    I. short-term instruments that become worthless after the expiration date
    II. most commonly offered in connection with debentures to sweeten the offering
    III. issued by a corporation
    IV. traded in the securities market

    A. I and II
    B. I and III
    C. I, III and IV
    D. II, III and IV

6. An owner of common stock has which of the following rights?

    I. The right to determine when dividends will be issued
    II. The right to vote at stockholders' meetings or by proxy
    III. The right to receive a predetermined fixed portion of the corporation's profit in cash when declared
    IV. The right to buy restricted securities before they are offered to the public

    A. I, III and IV
    B. II
    C. II, III and IV
    D. II and IV

7. Limited liability means that

    I. investors are not liable to the full extent of their investment in a corporation
    II. creditors have recourse to the assets of the corporation but not to the personal assets of the individual owners
    III. a business cannot go into bankruptcy
    IV. the stockholder would lose only the amount of his or her investment in the corporation if it went bankrupt

    A. I and II only
    B. II and IV only
    C. III only
    D. I, II, III and IV

8. Equity ownership of a corporation is split into two types. These types are commonly referred to as

    A. stocks and bonds
    B. common stocks and preferred stocks
    C. preferred stocks and bonds
    D. common stocks and convertible bonds

9. The legal privilege to maintain your proportionate ownership in a corporation is called a

    A. preemptive right
    B. voting right
    C. call right
    D. preferred right

10. A preferred stock that offers the new owner the privilege to receive any skipped or missed dividends is called

    A. straight preferred
    B. participating preferred
    C. convertible preferred
    D. cumulative preferred

11. You have been given the privilege to buy stock at $35 per share. You may buy up to 1,000 shares at any time within the next ten years. The stock is currently trading at $24 per share. You have

    A. a preferred stock
    B. a stock right
    C. a stock warrant
    D. something of no value

12. The current market value of a stock is determined by

    A. the board of directors
    B. what individuals are willing to pay
    C. a vote of the stockholders
    D. the company's financial condition

13. Dividends on common stock are paid only if

   A. preferred stockholders vote and approve such payment
   B. common stockholders vote and approve such payment
   C. book value is sufficient to warrant such payment
   D. the board of directors declares a dividend

14. Mr. Latka owns cumulative preferred stock (par value of $100) that pays an 8% dividend. The dividend has not been paid this year or for the last two years. How much must the company pay Mr. Latka per share before it can pay dividends to the common stockholders?

   A. $0
   B. $8
   C. $16
   D. $24

15. If a corporation wanted to raise capital and offer stock at a given price for the next 45 days, it would issue

   A. rights
   B. warrants
   C. callable preferred stock
   D. put options

16. The ABC Company has outstanding a 5% preferred stock and a $2.40 participating preferred stock. Last year, ABC Company paid dividends. This year, ABC Company had a poor year and will not declare a dividend. In which order will the dividend be paid this year?

   I. The dividend in arrears to the cumulative preferred stockholders
   II. The stated dividend to the cumulative preferred stockholders
   III. The stated dividend to the participating preferred stockholders
   IV. No dividend will be paid.

   A. I, II, III
   B. I, III, II
   C. II, I, III
   D. IV

17. If XYZ Company's dividend increases by 5% and its stock's market value increases by 7%, the current yield of the stock will

   A. decrease
   B. increase
   C. remain at 5%
   D. not be affected by price fluctuations

18. Which of the following best describe warrants?

   I. Short-term instruments that become worthless after the expiration date
   II. Most commonly offered in connection with debentures to sweeten the offering
   III. Issued by a corporation
   IV. Traded in the securities market

   A. I and II
   B. I and III
   C. I, III and IV
   D. II, III and IV

19. An owner of preferred stock has which of the following rights?

   I. The right to determine when dividends will be issued
   II. The right to vote at stockholders' meetings or by proxy
   III. The right to a predetermined fixed portion of the corporation's profit in cash when declared
   IV. The right to buy restricted securities before they are offered to the public

   A. I, III and IV
   B. II, III and IV
   C. II and IV
   D. III

20. Ownership of a corporation is evidenced by

   A. stocks and bonds
   B. common stocks and preferred stocks
   C. preferred stocks and bonds
   D. common stocks and convertible bonds

21. The prerogative of the shareholders to elect the board of directors in a corporation is called a

   A. preemptive right
   B. voting right
   C. call right
   D. preferred right

22. A preferred stock which states that the new owner could receive dividends in excess of the amount on the stock's face is called

   A. straight preferred
   B. participating preferred
   C. convertible preferred
   D. cumulative preferred

23. You have been given the privilege to buy stock at $35 per share. You may buy an amount of shares equal to the number of shares you presently own within the next 45 days. The stock is currently trading at $24 per share. You have

   A. preferred stock
   B. stock rights
   C. a stock warrant
   D. something of no value

24. The price of a stock is determined by

   A. the board of directors
   B. what individuals are willing to pay for it
   C. a vote of the stockholders
   D. the company's financial condition

25. Common stock pays a dividend if

   A. preferred stockholders vote and approve such payment
   B. common stockholders vote and approve such payment
   C. book value is sufficient to warrant such payment
   D. the board of directors declares a dividend

26. Mr. Jones owns preferred stock (par value of $100) that pays an 8% dividend rate. The dividend has not been paid this year or for the last two years. How much must the company pay Mr. Jones per share before it can pay dividends to the common stockholders?

   A. $0
   B. $8
   C. $16
   D. $24

27. Mr. Schroeder owns 100 shares of ABC Company. A dividend is declared on August 30th. The dividend will be paid to stockholders of record on Thursday, September 15th. When will the stock sell ex-dividend?

    A. September 9th
    B. September 11th
    C. September 12th
    D. September 15th

28. The ex-dividend date is the

    I. date on and after which the buyer is entitled to the dividend
    II. date on and after which the seller is entitled to the dividend
    III. fourth business day prior to the record date
    IV. fourth business day after the record date

    A. I and III
    B. I and IV
    C. II and III
    D. II and IV

29. The Internal Revenue Service permits dividend exclusion on the first

    A. $100 of dividend income annually
    B. $500 of dividend income annually
    C. $1,000 of dividend income annually
    D. The dividend exclusion has been repealed.

30. Amalgamated Corporation manufactures electronic components. It wants to incorporate new laser technology into its manufacturing process. This change requires a large expenditure of capital. The board of directors has decided that Amalgamated must conserve cash. If a dividend is declared, in light of Amalgamated's current situation, what decision might the board of directors have made?

    A. To authorize preemptive rights
    B. To declare a cash dividend instead of a stock dividend
    C. To declare a stock dividend instead of a cash dividend
    D. To buy outstanding shares of stock

31. The market value of stock is determined by

    A. the board of directors
    B. a vote of the stockholders
    C. what individuals are willing to pay for the stock
    D. the company's financial condition

32. A common stockholder's voting rights apply to which of the following?

    I. The election of the board of directors
    II. The declaration of dividends
    III. The authorization or issue of more common shares

    A. I only
    B. I and III only
    C. II and III only
    D. I, II and III

33. Every corporation must issue

    A. cumulative stock
    B. preferred stock
    C. callable stock
    D. common stock

34. Mary Folkman wants to invest in Amalgamated common stock. She knows that the company has recently declared a cash dividend. She should

    A. act quickly to become a stockholder of record so that she can receive the dividend
    B. not be concerned because the common stock will trade at a price reduced by the dividend amount after the ex-dividend date
    C. make sure her order is received before the payable date so that she can receive the dividend
    D. make sure her order is received after the record date so that she can pay the dividend

35. Which of the following characteristics describe participating preferred stock

    I. Carries voting rights
    II. Represents a form of ownership in the corporation
    III. Gives owners the right to share in earnings above the stated rate
    IV. Allows owners to convert the shares into common stock?

    A. I, II and III
    B. I, III and IV
    C. II and III
    D. II and IV

36. Which of the following statements describe preferred stocks?

    I. They are equity securities.
    II. They attract income-oriented investors.
    III. They have a fixed rate of return.
    IV. They may be callable.

    A. I, II and IV only
    B. I and III only
    C. II and III only
    D. I, II, III and IV

37. Hall Manufacturing has issued both common and 6% cumulative preferred stock ($100 par value). The preferred dividends paid for the previous four years were: $4, $3, $0 and $6. If the company pays a dividend to common stockholders this year, what amount must the preferred shareholders receive per share?

    A. $6
    B. $11
    C. $17
    D. $19

38. When a warrant is issued, the exercise price is usually

    A. higher than the current market value of the stock
    B. lower than the current market value of the stock
    C. the same as the current market value of the stock
    D. none of the above

39. Amalgamated has 1.2 million shares of stock outstanding and issues an additional 500,000 shares. The corporate charter grants preemptive rights. How many rights will Amalgamated issue with this offering?

    A. One right to each shareholder
    B. 500,000
    C. 1.2 million
    D. The number declared by the board of directors

40. Amalgamated declared a dividend on June 2nd. The board of directors chose June 30th as the record date and July 15th as the payment date. The ex-dividend date was June 24th. What is the first date on which an investor could purchase the stock but not receive the dividend?

    A. June 23rd
    B. June 24th
    C. June 25th
    D. June 30th

41. Which of the following statements describes the record date?

    A. It is fixed by the NYSE for determining which investors own stock.
    B. It indicates when the public offering of new issues can legally be made.
    C. It is set by the issuing corporation to determine which stockholders will receive a declared dividend.
    D. It is set by the issuing corporation as the mailing date for distribution of stock rights.

42. Which of the following is not a feature of common stock?

    A. The right to sue the board of directors if it is negligent
    B. Preemptive rights
    C. The right to part of the assets if the corporation should liquidate
    D. A guaranteed dividend

43. Which of the following would be paid a minimum dividend if common stockholders were paid a dividend?

    I.   Cumulative preferred
    II. Convertible preferred
    III. Participating preferred
    IV. Preferred

    A. I only
    B. I and II only
    C. II and III only
    D. I, II, III and IV

44. A company in which you own stock is about to have a stock rights offering. You do not plan on subscribing to the offer. Your proportionate interest in the company will be

    A. reduced
    B. left the same
    C. increased
    D. More information is needed to answer this question.

45. A contract that gives you the privilege of investing in a company stock at a predetermined price at any time for the next five years is called a

    A. right
    B. coupon
    C. bond
    D. warrant

46. A 75-year-old company is about to remodel its plant. In order to raise the necessary money, it will sell new shares of stock. This will be referred to as

    A. primary issue
    B. secondary issue
    C. agency issue
    D. refunding

47. A preemptive right is

    A. the right to be the first to buy new shares of stock in the company and thus maintain proportionate ownership
    B. the right to vote someone else's stock
    C. the right to sell someone else's stock
    D. all of the above

48. The record date for a stock is Tuesday, January 13th. What is the ex-dividend date?

    A. Wednesday, January 7th
    B. Friday, January 9th
    C. Saturday, January 17th
    D. Monday, January 19th

49. Fred Meyer bought stock in ABC Company. ABC has paid a dividend every quarter for the past 20 years. The price of ABC stock has increased dramatically this past quarter, but the dividend ABC has declared for payment this quarter has remained the same. If Fred were to purchase more ABC stock, he would notice that

    A. current dividend yield has gone up
    B. current dividend yield has gone down
    C. current dividend yield has remained the same
    D. dividend yield to maturity has gone down

50. A similarity between common and preferred stock is

    A. the dividend is fixed
    B. they have an equal vote
    C. the dividend must be declared by the board of directors
    D. None of the above are similarities.

51. You bought stock in ABC Company last year. ABC's stock has been paying a nice dividend every quarter for the last several years. The price of ABC's stock has gone down since you bought it, but the dividend amount per share has stayed the same. If you were to buy additional shares now, you would notice that

   A. current yield has gone up
   B. current yield per share has gone down
   C. current yield per share was unaffected
   D. yield to maturity has gone up

52. The last date before the buyer would be entitled to receive a declared dividend being paid by a corporation would be the

   A. record date
   B. declaration date
   C. ex-dividend date
   D. payment date

53. The ex-dividend date of a stock is Tuesday, January 13th. When is the record date?

   A. Wednesday, January 7th
   B. Friday, January 9th
   C. Saturday, January 17th
   D. Monday, January 19th

54. XYZ Corporation has outstanding 10,000 shares of common ($100 par) and 10,000 shares of 5% preferred ($100 par). At the end of 1990, it has net earnings of $200,000. The preferred stockholders, who have received no dividend payments during 1989

   A. may receive $5 per share
   B. must receive $5 per share
   C. may receive $10 per share
   D. must receive $10 per share

55. The record date is the

   A. date on which a transaction is made between two parties
   B. day on and after which the buyer of a common stock is not entitled to the dividend previously declared
   C. day on which a list is compiled of stockholders who will receive dividends from a corporation
   D. day on which a dividend is paid

56. An investor buys stock for $100 per share (100 shares). The total value of the outstanding stock is $10,000,000. The company loses $6,000,000 a year for three years. For what amount is the investor liable?

   A. Only his or her original $10,000
   B. The full $10,000,000
   C. The full $18,000,000
   D. The balance sheet must be provided to answer this question.

57. If the current dividend distribution of a company stock has increased by 5% while the offering price has increased by 7%, the current yield of this stock has

   A. increased
   B. decreased
   C. stayed the same
   D. More information is needed to answer this question.

58. A cumulative preferred stockholder could have all the following rights EXCEPT the right to

   A. receive skipped dividends
   B. receive a stated dividend
   C. vote on the issue of more preferred stock
   D. vote on the issue of more common stock

59. When the underlying stock price increases, the premium of a call option will generally

   A. increase
   B. decrease
   C. remain the same
   D. fluctuate rapidly

60. Which of the following investors will purchase stock if the option is exercised?

    I. Owner of a call
    II. Owner of a put
    III. Writer of a call
    IV. Writer of a put

    A. I and II
    B. I and IV
    C. II and III
    D. III and IV

61. Which of the following investors will sell stock if the option is exercised?

    I. Owner of a call
    II. Owner of a put
    III. Writer of a call
    IV. Writer of a put

    A. I and II
    B. I and IV
    C. II and III
    D. III and IV

62. Which of the following option investors arc bearish?

    I. Buyer of a call
    II. Writer of a call
    III. Buyer of a put
    IV. Writer of a put

    A. I and II
    B. I and IV
    C. II and III
    D. III and IV

63. Belle tells her broker that she thinks the price of ABC is going to go up, but she doesn't have the money to buy 100 shares right now. Which way could she use options to profit from a rise in the stock's price?

    I. Buy calls on ABC
    II. Write calls on ABC
    III. Buy puts on ABC
    IV. Write puts on ABC

    A. I and II
    B. I and IV
    C. II and III
    D. II and IV

64. Which one of the following investors has the greatest potential risk if the price of XYZ goes up?

    A. Angus, long ten calls on XYZ
    B. Karen, short ten calls on XYZ
    C. Adam, long ten puts on XYZ
    D. Belle, short ten puts on XYZ

65. Which two of the following objectives are suitable for a put writer?

    I. To generate a large return
    II. To seek maximum capital gains
    III. To speculate that a stock will decline in price
    IV. To seek to buy a stock at a lower price

    A. I and II
    B. I and IV
    C. II and III
    D. III and IV

66. All of the following are objectives of call buyers EXCEPT

    A. speculating for profit on the rise in price of stock
    B. delaying a decision to buy stock
    C. hedging a long stock position against falling prices
    D. diversifying holdings

67. Which of the following options positions is riskiest?

    A. Covered call writing
    B. Uncovered call writing
    C. Writing puts
    D. Buying puts

68. The OEX and major market indexes are examples of which of the following?

    A. Broad-based indexes
    B. Narrow-based indexes
    C. Foreign currency indexes
    D. Debt security indexes

69. Income from which of the following qualifies for the 70% corporate dividend exclusion?

    I. Common stock
    II. Preferred stock
    III. Convertible bonds
    IV. Municipal bonds

    A. I and II
    B. I, II and III
    C. II and IV
    D. III and IV

70. Which is the earliest date a customer can sell a stock and still receive a previously declared dividend?

    A. Ex-date
    B. Payable date
    C. Record date
    D. Next business day

71. In order to be paid a dividend, an owner's name should be recorded on the stock record book of the issuer's transfer agent by the

    A. ex-date
    B. payable date
    C. record date
    D. next business day

72. The issuer mails out dividend checks on the

    A. ex-date
    B. payable date
    C. record date
    D. next business day

73. Which of the following is(are) actively traded?

    I. Warrants
    II. Nondetachable rights
    III. Common stock
    IV. Options on stock

    A. I, III and IV only
    B. II only
    C. II and IV only
    D. I, II, III and IV

74. Which of the following statements is(are) true regarding rights and warrants?

    I. Warrants are issued with an exercise price higher than the underlying stock.
    II. Rights are issued with an exercise price lower than the underlying stock.
    III. Warrants are long lived, may even be perpetual and may be issued to anyone.
    IV. Rights are short lived and issued only to present shareholders.

    A. I only
    B. I and II only
    C. I, II and III only
    D. I, II, III and IV

75. A corporation's capitalization includes $1,000,000 of 7% preferred stock and $1,000,000 of 7% convertible debentures. If all the convertible debentures were converted into common stock, what would happen to the company's earnings?

    A. They would increase.
    B. They would decrease.
    C. There would be no change.
    D. It cannot be determined.

◆ Answers & Rationale

1. **B.** Preferred stocks are interest rate sensitive as are other fixed interest rate investment vehicles such as bonds. Because the dividend amount is fixed, if interest rates are increasing, the return provided by the dividend may be less than the return provided by other investments. The value of preferred stock will decrease.

2. **B.** A warrant is a purchase option for stock for a long period of time. The warrant allows the holder to purchase common stock for a set price. Rights and options have a short life.

3. **C.** Preferred dividends in arrears are paid before a dividend may be paid to common stockholders. However, if dividends are declared, payment of the stated dividend for preferred issues in the current year takes precedence. The dividends in arrears would be the next in priority for distribution with the participating preferred sharing in excess earnings (with the common) paid last.

4. **B.** Because the dividend rate decreased at a rate less than the market value of the stock, the current yield will be greater.

5. **C.** Warrants are commonly used as a sweetener in debenture offerings. Rights are issued by the corporation giving the subscriber the right to purchase stock within a short period of time at a reduced price from the stock's current market price. The right does not have to be exercised but may be traded in the secondary market.

6. **B.** The stockholder has the right to vote and the right to dividends if and when declared (although not to a fixed dividend). A restricted security is one that has prescribed limits on resale generally requiring registration.

7. **B.** Limited liability means that stockholders are liable only for amounts invested in the corporation; creditors cannot attach personal assets.

8. **B.** Equity ownership comes with two types of securities. These are common and preferred stocks.

9. **A.** Existing shareholders may be given preemptive rights that will allow them to maintain their proportionate ownership in a corporation.

10. **D.** Preferred stock comes in all the listed types, but only cumulative preferred allows the holder the right to receive skipped or missed dividends.

11. **C.** Warrants are given for a long period of time, while rights are for a short time and for existing stockholders only.

12. **B.** Market value of stock is determined by supply and demand.

13. **D.** The board of directors determines and votes on stock dividends.

14. **D.** If the company is going to pay a common stock dividend, it must pay the preferred dividends first. A cumulative preferred stockholder must also receive all dividends in arrears. There is $16 in back dividends due in addition to $8 this year for a total of $24.

15. **A.** A right is a purchase option for stock for a short period of time. The right allows the holder to purchase common stock for a set price. Warrants have a long life.

16. **D.** If no dividend is declared, no one gets paid a dividend.

17. **A.** Because the dividend rate increased at a rate less than the market value of the stock, the current yield will be less.

18. **D.** Warrants are commonly used as a sweetener in debenture offerings and carry a long life. Rights are issued by the corporation giving the subscriber the right to purchase stock within a short period of time at a reduced price from the stock's current market price. The warrant does not have to

be exercised, but may be traded in the secondary market.

19. **D.** The preferred stockholder generally has no right to vote, but carries a prior right to dividends if and when declared. A restricted security is one that has prescribed limits on resale generally requiring registration.

20. **B.** Equity ownership in a corporation is evidenced by common and preferred stock.

21. **B.** The right to vote on matters concerning the operation of the company is a stockholder's voting right.

22. **B.** Preferred stock comes in all the listed types, but only participating preferred allows the holder the right to receive dividends in excess of the rate (coupon) stated in a year.

23. **B.** Rights are given for a short period of time, while warrants are for a long time and offered to existing stockholders only.

24. **B.** Market value (price) of stock is determined by supply and demand.

25. **D.** The board of directors determines and votes on stock dividends.

26. **B.** If the company is going to pay a common stock dividend, it must pay the preferred dividends first. Only a cumulative preferred stockholder is entitled to receive dividends in arrears. The dividend declared would be 8% or $8 only.

27. **A.** The ex-dividend date is always four business days before the record date. The record date is Thursday, September 15th, so the ex-dividend date will be Friday, September 9th.

28. **C.** Stocks sold on the ex-dividend date entitle the seller to the dividend. Stocks sell ex-dividend four business day before the record date.

29. **D.** The dividend exclusion has been repealed (Tax Reform Act of 1986).

30. **C.** Amalgamated decided to declare a dividend, but finds it necessary to conserve cash. A stock dividend would allow Amalgamated to reward its shareholders without having a cash outlay. To buy outstanding stock requires cash, as for preemptive rights; this is an alternative for raising capital, but because the question refers to dividends, the best answer is C.

31. **C.** Market value of stock reflects what people are willing to pay for the stock. The company's financial situation will affect what people are willing to pay.

32. **B.** Common stockholders may elect the board of directors (indirectly influencing the policy on payment of dividends) and may vote on issues concerning the company's capitalization (such as the issuance of more common stock).

33. **D.** A corporation, according to its charter, must issue voting common stock. Thereafter, the company is free to issue other securities.

34. **B.** The value of stock declines by the amount of the dividend declared on the ex-dividend date. A shareholder who purchases stock just before the ex-dividend date will receive the dividend, but will also see a loss in value of that stock. Because the dividend is a taxable yield, making a purchase just to receive the dividend is not a recommended practice.

35. **C.** Preferred stock represents ownership, or equity, in the corporation, but unlike common stock, it is not considered a voting interest in the company. Participating preferred may share in excess earnings with common stockholders over and above the fixed rate stated on the issue.

36. **D.** Preferred stock is issued with a stated dividend rate and thus appeals to income-oriented investors. Preferred stock is an ownership interest and may be issued with a call provision.

37. **C.** Because common stockholders were paid, all dividends in arrears plus the current dividend for the cumulative stock must be paid. A total

$11 of dividends in arrears plus the current $6 dividend was paid to the cumulative shareholder.

38. **A.**   Generally when a warrant is issued, the exercise price is at a price that is higher than the current market value of the stock.

39. **C.**   When rights are issued, one right is issued for each share of stock outstanding. In this case, 1.2 million rights will be issued.

40. **B.**   The ex-dividend date is the date on which the purchaser of a stock buys it "ex," or without a dividend.

41. **C.**   The record date is the date set by the corporation, at which time a list is compiled of those stockholders who will receive a dividend.

42. **D.**   Common stock is entitled to receive profits as a dividend, if and when the dividend is declared by the board of directors. The amount of the dividend is left to the discretion of the directors; it is not a guaranteed or stated amount.

43. **D.**   Because preferred stock is a senior equity issue compared to common stock, if common stockholders received a dividend, then all preferred issues would have to receive at least the dividend stated on the issue prior to any dividend distribution to common shareholders.

44. **A.**   A preemptive right enables the stockholder to maintain a proportionate share of ownership in the corporation. Because the shares have already been authorized, should the stockholder decline to participate in the rights offering, the stockholder's interest is reduced.

45. **D.**   An equity purchase option that exists for longer than a year is called a warrant.

46. **A.**   The initial sale of stock from which the company receives the proceeds is a primary offering. Even though the company has been in existence for 75 years, it is selling "new" shares of stock, thus called a primary offering.

47. **A.**   A preemptive right allows the existing stockholder the right to maintain his proportionate interest in a corporation. If the company authorizes and sells additional stock, existing shareholders have the right to be the first to purchase shares to maintain their percentage of ownership.

48. **A.**   The ex-dividend date is four business days prior to the record date, so answers C and D are incorrect. Saturday and Sunday are not considered business days, so counting backwards, the ex-date was Wednesday, January 7th.

49. **B.**   Price up, yield down.

50. **C.**   Before a dividend may be paid, it must first be declared by the corporation's board of directors.

51. **A.**   Because the price of ABC stock has gone down while the dividend has remained the same, the current yield or percentage return on ABC stock has increased. For example, if ABC stock was at $10 per share and paid a $1 dividend, ABC's current yield would be 10%. If the price of ABC's stock subsequently dropped to $5 per share while still paying a $1 dividend, ABC's current yield would now be 20%.

52. **C.**   To receive a previously declared dividend, the stock would have to be purchased prior to the ex-dividend date. The stockholder purchasing the stock on or after the ex-dividend date would purchase the stock "ex" or without the dividend.

53. **D.**   The record date is four business days after the ex-dividend date.

Tue	Wed	Thu	Fri	Sat	Sun	Mon
EX-	1	2	3	X	X	RECORD

54. **A.**   Because the question does not say a dividend has been declared, a dividend may be paid. Additionally, the question does not say the stock is cumulative; therefore, if a dividend is paid, it will be the stated amount only, or 5% equals $5.

55. **C.** The record date is the day stockholders are listed in the company's record books as owners. Shareholders of record may receive dividends when declared.

56. **A.** A stockholder of a corporation, although an owner, is liable only for the amount of money contributed to the corporation (limited liability).

57. **B.** The price of the stock has increased to a greater extent than the distribution. Price up, yield down, the current yield on the stock has decreased by 2%.

58. **D.** Only common stockholders have the right to vote on the issuance of common stock.

59. **A.** As the price of the underlying stock increases, so does the premium of a call option. The more the market price exceeds the exercise price, the more intrinsic value the option has. Because intrinsic value is part of the premium (Premium equals Intrinsic value plus Time value), the premium goes up with the intrinsic value.

60. **B.** A call owner has the right to purchase stock from a call writer. A put writer has the obligation to purchase stock if a put buyer chooses to exercise the option.

61. **C.** A put owner acquires the right to sell stock by exercising the option. A call writer undertakes the obligation to sell stock if a call owner exercises the option.

62. **C.** Remember that diagonal positions (those positions that are total opposites, such as buys versus sells and puts versus calls) are on the same side of the market.

63. **B.** The bullish strategies are buying calls and writing puts.

64. **B.** The answer has to be either B or C because only bearish investors are at risk if the stock price, goes up. The bearish options are short calls and long puts. Short calls are the riskiest

position. Put buyers stand to lose the premium paid, but call writers have an unlimited risk. They can be required to deliver stock at the strike price, and to do so, they will have to purchase stock at the market price, no matter how high.

65. **B.** Put writers receive the premium, so the strategy generates a return. The put writer's profit is limited to the premium, however, so writing puts is not a means of getting maximum capital gains. Puts may be exercised in a down market to sell stock at the relatively high exercise price. Writing puts, therefore, is not a good bear strategy. It is, however, a way to buy stock at a lower price—the exercise price minus the premium received.

66. **C.** Buying a call does not hedge a long stock position. A hedge is a position on the opposite side of the market; in case the investor is wrong, the hedge position will provide a consolation prize. A long stock position is bullish; so is a long call position. Long put positions, on the other hand, are bearish. So buying a put hedges a long stock position. If the stock price drops, causing the investor to lose money, the put will increase in value. The investor can sell the put at a profit or use it to sell the stock above the market price.

67. **B.** Uncovered calls are the riskiest option strategy.

68. **A.** Broad-based indexes attempt to reflect the status of the market as a whole, not the status of particular market segments.

69. **A.** The dividend exclusion rule has changed within the last few years. It currently states that the exclusion is 70% unless the holder has 20% or more of the company's stock. If the holder qualifies by owning 20% or more, the exclusion is still 80%. Because it is a dividend exclusion, only securities that issue dividends (common stock and preferred stock) would be included.

70. **A.** If the customer is holding the stock and wishes to sell the stock yet still receive the dividend, he must wait until the ex-date to sell.

Remember that the ex-date is four business days prior to the record date, and the regular way settlement is five business days before. If the customer sells on the ex-date, the transaction will settle the day after the record date. The record date is the date that the corporation determines who gets the dividend by who is a holder of record on that day.

71. **C.**   To receive a dividend, the buyer must be the bona fide owner (in other words, the buyer has to be on the books of the issuer as the owner) on or by the record date.

72. **B.**   The payable date is the day the issuer actually mails or pays the dividend. On the payable date, the issuer's current assets (cash) and current liabilities (dividends payable) change on the balance sheet.

73. **A.**   Warrants, common stock and options all have an active secondary market.

74. **D.**   Warrants are usually issued as a sweetener to a deal. For example, if a company wants to issue bonds at an interest rate lower than general market rates, it could throw in some warrants to make the bonds more attractive. Warrants are usually issued with a very long life and give the holder the right to purchase stock above the current market price. When a corporation has common stock outstanding and wants to issue more common stock, it must offer the shares to the current shareholders first (preemptive rights).

75. **A.**   Bond interest is an expense of the firm, and when it is paid, it reduces the earnings of the firm. If the bonds were to convert, there would be no more interest payments; therefore, the company would have higher earnings. There will be more shares of common stock outstanding, and this will normally translate to lower earnings per share for the common. Interest costs would be reduced, earnings would increase and the number of shares would increase.

2 Debt Securities and Yield

1. An investor has purchased convertible bonds issued by the ABC Company. The investor has decided to convert the bonds. He will convert them into

   A. preferred stock
   B. mortgage bonds
   C. common stock
   D. equipment trust certificates

2. A 12% corporate bond issued by the XYZ Company is due in ten years. The bond is convertible into XYZ common stock at a conversion price of $20 per share. The XYZ bond is quoted at 120. Parity of the common stock is

   A. $20
   B. $24
   C. $50
   D. $60

3. The securities put up as collateral for a collateral trust bond would be held by which of the following in case of default?

   A. Bondholder
   B. Bond issuer
   C. SEC
   D. Trustee

4. The market price of a convertible bond will depend on

   A. the value of the underlying stock into which the bond can be converted
   B. current interest rates
   C. the rating of the bond
   D. all of the above

5. Under which of the following circumstances would an investor expect to receive the greatest gain on an investment in a corporate bond?

   A. By purchasing long-term bonds when interest rates are high
   B. By purchasing long-term bonds when interest rates are low
   C. By purchasing short-term bonds when interest rates are high
   D. By purchasing short-term bonds when interest rates are low

6. Corporate unsecured long-term borrowing would be evidenced by which of the following securities?

   A. Debenture
   B. Mortgage bond
   C. Commercial paper
   D. Common stock

7. An individual calculating taxable income received from a municipal bond fund investment for this year would consider that

   A. part of the income distribution received as a dividend is taxable at ordinary income tax rates
   B. all of the income distribution received as a dividend is taxable at ordinary income tax rates
   C. any capital gains distributions received from the fund are taxable at ordinary income tax rates
   D. all distributions received from the fund, both income and gains, are exempt from federal income tax

8. At maturity of a 52-week Treasury bill is-sued by the federal government, any gain received by the investor would be taxed as

    A. short-term capital gain
    B. long-term capital gain
    C. ordinary income
    D. There would be no tax on this transaction.

9. Rank the following government securities according to the length of their maturities, from longest to shortest.

    I. Notes
    II. Bills
    III. Bonds

    A. I, II, III
    B. I, III, II
    C. III, I, II
    D. III, II, I

10. Which type of nonmarketable security pays semiannual interest?

    A. Series II bonds
    B. Treasury bonds
    C. Series HH bonds
    D. Agency issues

11. Which of the following statements about debentures are true?

    I. They are secured by a mortgage or a lien.
    II. They are secured by the good faith of the issuing corporation.
    III. They are considered to be a safer invest-ment than preferred stock.
    IV. They have a senior claim to the corpo-ration's assets when compared to com-mon stock.

    A. I and III only
    B. II, III and IV only
    C. II and IV only
    D. I, II, III and IV

12. Which of the following statements about a bond selling above par value is(are) true?

    I. The nominal yield is lower than the cur-rent yield.
    II. The yield to maturity is lower than the nominal yield.
    III. The yield to maturity is lower than the current yield.
    IV. The nominal yield always stays the same.

    A. I and IV only
    B. II, III and IV only
    C. IV only
    D. I, II, III and IV

13. Which of the following corporate bonds are usually backed by other investment securities?

    A. Mortgage bonds
    B. Equipment trust certificates
    C. Collateral trust bonds
    D. Debentures

14. Which of the following would be the best time for an investor to purchase long-term fixed-interest rate bonds?

    A. When short-term interest rates are high and are beginning to decline
    B. When short-term interest rates are low and are beginning to rise
    C. When long-term interest rates are high and are beginning to decline
    D. When long-term interest rates are low and are beginning to rise

15. A corporation has a 9% bond issue maturing within three weeks. The corporation does not have the capital to meet that deadline. In order to meet the maturity date, the company issues a 12% bond, the proceeds of which will be used to pay off the old debt. This is called

    A. hypothecation
    B. commingling
    C. parity
    D. refunding

16. Interest rates have been rising the past few days. What would you expect would be happening to the price of bonds traded in the bond market during the same period of time?

    A. Prices will increase.
    B. Prices will decrease.
    C. Prices will stay the same.
    D. Prices are not affected by interest rates.

17. A debt backed by the income generated from a municipal project such as a toll road, toll bridge or port facilities is called what type of bond?

    A. General obligation
    B. Revenue
    C. Industrial development
    D. Convertible

18. Which of the following statements is(are) true of Treasury bills?

    I. They are sold at a discount.
    II. They pay a fixed rate of interest semiannually.
    III. They mature in one year or less.
    IV. They mature in ten years or more.

    A. I, II and III
    B. I and III
    C. II and IV
    D. III

19. All the following U.S. government securities are marketable EXCEPT

    A. Treasury bills
    B. Treasury notes
    C. Treasury bonds
    D. Series EE bonds

20. The interest from which of the following bonds is exempt from federal income tax?

    I. State of California bonds
    II. City of Anchorage bonds
    III. Treasury bonds
    IV. GNMA bonds

    A. I and II only
    B. I, II and IV only
    C. III and IV only
    D. I, II, III and IV

21. Baa rated bonds may yield more than Aaa rated bonds because

    A. Baa rated bonds are more secure than Aaa rated bonds
    B. Baa rated bonds are debentures, whereas Aaa rated bonds are secured by collateral
    C. Aaa rated bonds are less marketable
    D. Baa rated bonds carry more investment risk than Aaa rated bonds

22. Which of the following are money market instruments?

    I. Repurchase agreements
    II. Treasury bills
    III. Commercial paper
    IV. Treasury bonds maturing in six months

    A. I and II only
    B. I, II and III only
    C. II, III and IV only
    D. I, II, III and IV

23. An investor has purchased convertible bonds issued by the ABC Company. The price of the bonds will reflect the current market value of the company's

    A. preferred stock
    B. mortgage bonds
    C. common stock
    D. equipment trust certificates

24. If a bond is purchased at a premium, the yield to maturity would be

    A. higher than the nominal yield
    B. lower than the nominal yield
    C. the same as the nominal yield
    D. none of the above

25. A 10% corporate bond issued by the ABC Company is due in ten years. The bond is convertible into ABC common stock at a conversion price of $25 per share. The ABC bond is quoted at 90. Parity of the common stock is

    A. $22.50
    B. $25
    C. $36
    D. $100

26. If interest rates are increasing and the market price of bonds is decreasing, what would happen to the value of preferred stock during this same time period?

    A. Value would increase
    B. Value would decrease
    C. Value would remain the same
    D. Interest rates and the value of bonds have no impact on the value of stock.

27. The security put up as collateral for a mortgage bond is typically

    A. stock from an affiliate company
    B. stock of another issuer
    C. real estate
    D. equipment of the issuer

28. The current market price of a debenture will depend on

    A. the value of the company's common stock
    B. current interest rates
    C. the debenture's par value
    D. all of the above

29. Corporate secured long-term borrowing would be evidenced by which of the following securities?

    A. Debenture
    B. Mortgage bond
    C. Commercial paper
    D. Common stock

30. An investor is looking into the purchase of Series EE bonds through payroll deduction at his place of employment. If the investor decides to purchase the Series EE bonds, he would receive the interest earned

    A. monthly
    B. semiannually
    C. annually
    D. at redemption

31. Rank, from shortest to longest, the following government securities according to the length of their maturities.

    I. Notes
    II. Bills
    III. Bonds

    A. I, II, III
    B. II, I, III
    C. III, I, II
    D. III, II, I

32. A municipal bond is quoted at 6 1/4%. Currently its yield to maturity is 6 3/4%. From this information it can be determined that the municipal bond is trading

    A. flat
    B. at par
    C. at a discount
    D. at a premium

33. Which type of marketable security pays semiannual interest?

    A. Series II bonds
    B. Treasury bonds
    C. Series HH bonds
    D. Series EE bonds

34. Which of the following statements about mortgage bonds are true?

    I. They are secured by a mortgage or a lien.
    II. They are secured by the good faith of the issuing corporation.
    III. They are considered to be a safer investment than preferred stock.
    IV. They have a senior claim to the corporation's assets when compared to common stock.

    A. I and III only
    B. II, III and IV only
    C. II and IV only
    D. I, II, III and IV

35. Which of the following statements about a bond selling below par value is(are) true?

    I. The nominal yield is lower than the current yield.
    II. The yield to maturity is lower than the nominal yield.
    III. The yield to maturity is lower than the current yield.
    IV. The nominal yield always stays the same.

    A. I and IV only
    B. II, III and IV only
    C. IV only
    D. I, II, III and IV

36. Which of the following corporate bonds are usually backed by machinery, aircraft or railroad boxcars?

    A. Mortgage bonds
    B. Equipment trust certificates
    C. Collateral trust bonds
    D. Debentures

37. Which of the following would be the best time for an investor to purchase short-term fixed-interest rate bonds?

    A. When short-term interest rates are high and are beginning to decline
    B. When short-term interest rates are low and are beginning to rise
    C. When long-term interest rates are high and are beginning to decline
    D. When long-term interest rates are low and are beginning to rise

38. A corporation has a 9% convertible bond issue maturing within three weeks. The current value of the corporation's stock is $20 per share. The bondholder may convert the bond into 50 shares of the company's stock. This is called

    A. hypothecation
    B. commingling
    C. parity
    D. refunding

39. Interest rates have been declining the past few days. What would you expect would be happening to the price of bonds traded in the bond market during the same period of time?

    A. Prices will increase.
    B. Prices will decrease.
    C. Prices will stay the same.
    D. Prices are not affected by interest rates.

40. A debt issued by the City of Chicago that is backed by the rents received from a corporation leasing industrial park facilities is likely to be what kind of bond?

    A. General obligation
    B. Revenue
    C. Industrial development
    D. Convertible

41. Which of the following statements is(are) true of Treasury bonds?

    I.   They are sold at a discount.
    II. They pay a fixed rate of interest semian-nually.
    III. They mature in one year or less.
    IV. They mature in ten years or more.

    A. I, II and III
    B. I and III
    C. II and IV
    D. III

42. All the following are considered U.S. government agency issues EXCEPT

    A. GNMA (Ginnie Mae) bonds
    B. TVA (Tennessee Valley Authority) bonds
    C. Sallie Mae (Student Loan Marketing Association) bonds
    D. Series EE bonds

43. The interest from which of the following bonds is exempt from state income tax?

    I.   State of California bonds
    II. Michigan Toll Authority bonds
    III. Treasury bills
    IV. Treasury bonds

    A. I and II only
    B. I, II and IV only
    C. III and IV only
    D. I, II, III and IV

44. Aaa rated bonds may yield more than Treasury securities because

    A. Aaa rated bonds are more secure than Treasury securities
    B. Treasury securities are debentures, whereas Aaa rated bonds are secured by collateral
    C. Aaa rated bonds are more marketable
    D. Aaa rated bonds carry more investment risk than Treasury securities

45. Which of the following would not be considered money market instruments?

    I.   A debenture rated Aaa
    II. Treasury notes
    III. Commercial paper
    IV. Treasury bonds maturing in six months

    A. I and II only
    B. I, II and III only
    C. II, III and IV only
    D. I, II, III and IV

46. If a bond is purchased at a discount, the current yield would be

    A. higher than the nominal yield
    B. lower than the nominal yield
    C. the same as the nominal yield
    D. none of the above

47. An investor has bonds maturing in two weeks. The investor plans to purchase new bonds with a 10% coupon rate. If interest rates decline in the period before the investor can purchase the new bonds, the investor would expect the income to be received from the new bonds to

    A. increase
    B. decline
    C. stay the same
    D. do none of the above

48. A municipal bond is quoted at 7%. The bond's nominal yield is 7 3/4%. From this information it can be determined that the municipal bond is trading

    A. flat
    B. at par
    C. at a discount
    D. at a premium

49. Rank the following in ascending order of their claims against a corporation's assets when it is forced to liquidate. Start with the lowest claim on assets.

    I. General creditors
    II. Preferred stockholders
    III. Bondholders
    IV. Common stockholders

    A. II, III, IV, I
    B. III, I, II, IV
    C. IV, I, III, II
    D. IV, II, I, III

50. Rank the following in descending order (from high to low) of their claims against assets upon liquidation of a corporation.

    I. General creditors
    II. Secured bondholders
    III. Cumulative preferred stockholders
    IV. Common stockholders

    A. I, II, III, IV
    B. II, I, III, IV
    C. II, III, I, IV
    D. III, IV, II, I

51. Which of the following ten-year bonds would involve the lowest risk if held to maturity?

    A. A rated corporate bond
    B. Aaa rated debenture
    C. B rated mortgage bond
    D. Baa rated corporate bond

52. A conversion feature on a corporate bond allows

    A. bondholders to convert the bond into shares of common stock
    B. common stockholders to convert bonds into shares of common stock
    C. bondholders to convert the bond into shares of preferred stock
    D. corporations to call the bond prior to maturity in order to issue new bonds at lower interest rates

53. If all of the following bonds were issued at the same time and for the same maturities, which would probably entail the highest risk?

    A. Bond paying 8 1/4% interest
    B. Bond paying 10% interest
    C. Bond paying 11 1/2% interest
    D. Cannot be determined with the information given

54. Which of the following statements about corporate bonds are true?

    I. They represent ownership in the corporation.
    II. They generally involve less investment risk than common stock.
    III. They pay a variable rate of income.
    IV. They usually mature ten or more years after issue.

    A. I and III only
    B. II and III only
    C. II and IV only
    D. I, II, III and IV

55. If a $1,000 bond is priced at 102 5/8, how much is this bond selling for?

    A. $102.58
    B. $1,000
    C. $1,025.80
    D. $1,026.25

56. Collateral trust bonds may be secured by

    I. real property of the issuing corporation
    II. equity and debt securities of a subsidiary corporation
    III. equity and debt securities of another corporation
    IV. installment payments based on the corporation's accounts receivable

    A. I only
    B. II only
    C. II or III only
    D. II or IV only

57. Eight-percent bonds due in 1990 are selling at 102. The bonds are currently selling at

    A. par value
    B. face value
    C. a discount
    D. a premium

58. A $1,000 bond with a nominal yield of 6% and a current price of 98 1/2 has a current yield of

    A. 5.91%
    B. 6.09%
    C. 6.12%
    D. 6.21%

59. A 7 1/2% Amalgamated bond is selling at 97. Which of the following statements is(are) true?

    I. The current yield is greater than the nominal yield.
    II. The yield to maturity is less than the current yield.
    III. The current yield is less than the yield to maturity.

    A. I
    B. I and II
    C. I and III
    D. II and III

60. All of the following pay semiannual interest EXCEPT

    A. Series HH bonds
    B. Treasury notes
    C. Treasury bills
    D. Treasury bonds

61. Which of the following securities are backed by the full faith and credit of the U.S. government?

    A. Savings bonds
    B. Treasury bills
    C. Treasury bonds
    D. All of the above

62. Joan Clausen owns several Series EE bonds. She wishes to redeem them after three years. She would

    I. pay federal income tax on the interest she has earned
    II. sell them through her broker
    III. receive the same rate of interest as she would had she held the bonds to maturity

    A. I only
    B. I and II only
    C. II and III only
    D. I, II and III

63. Interest earned on U.S. Treasury bills is subject to

    A. state tax
    B. local tax
    C. federal tax
    D. all of the above

64. Which of the following statements about general obligation municipal bonds are true?

    I. They are second only to U.S. government bonds in safety of principal.
    II. They are backed by the taxing power of the municipality.
    III. They are nonmarketable.
    IV. They pay higher interest rates than corporate debt securities.

    A. I and II
    B. II and III
    C. II, III and IV
    D. I, II and IV

65. Colleen Boyle is in the 33% tax bracket and is considering investing in a 6% municipal bond. What yield would she need on a corporate bond for the investment to yield an equivalent return?

   A. The corporate yield would have to be higher than the municipal yield of 6%.
   B. The corporate yield would have to be less than the municipal yield of 6%.
   C. The corporate yield would have to be the same as the municipal yield of 6%.
   D. Equivalent yields between corporate and municipal securities depend on the par value of the bonds.

66. Municipal general obligation bonds are most often issued to finance

   A. operating expenses of the municipality
   B. salaries of municipal employees
   C. capital expenditures of the municipality
   D. investments of the municipality

67. Which of the following characteristics describes a general obligation municipal issue?

   A. Backed by the full faith and credit of the issuer
   B. Redeemed only if there is enough income generated by the project financed from the sale of the issue
   C. Will pay interest using rental payments from corporations using leased municipal property
   D. Exempt from state and local taxes of the municipality, but not from federal income tax

68. Commercial paper and certificates of deposit are both

   A. instruments of the capital market
   B. guaranteed by the federal government
   C. issued by corporations with questionable credit ratings
   D. unsecured promissory notes

69. The major difference between the money market and the capital market is that money market instruments

   A. represent short-term financing
   B. represent long-term financing
   C. pay the highest yields
   D. are not issued to the public

70. If a $1,000 par value 8% bond is quoted at 102, the bond would sell for

   A. $102
   B. $816
   C. $1,000
   D. $1,020

71. Which of the following securities is the most senior?

   A. Mortgage bond
   B. Debenture bond
   C. Common stock
   D. Participating preferred stock

72. The U.S. government is the largest issuer of debt in the country. Which of the following government issues carries no set rate of interest and matures in the shortest time?

   A. T bonds
   B. T bills
   C. T certificates
   D. T notes

73. A client is interested in investing in a municipal bond. His interest in this is probably due to the fact that

   A. these bonds offer great appreciation potential
   B. these bonds are guaranteed against loss by the federal government
   C. any interest received from these bonds is free from federal income tax
   D. There are no advantages to investing in a bond of this type.

74. An investor purchases a corporate bond at 98 5/8. He sells the bond at 101 3/4. How much money did he make or lose on this transaction (excluding commissions, etc.)?

   A. Profit of $3.125
   B. Profit of $31.25
   C. Profit of $312.50
   D. Loss of $3.125

75. During an inflationary period, coupled with rising interest rates, what would happen to the market value of existing bonds?

   A. Increase
   B. Decrease
   C. Stay the same
   D. The nominal yield would increase.

76. Owners of each of the following are creditors EXCEPT those owning

   A. preferred stocks
   B. savings accounts
   C. government bonds
   D. corporate bonds

77. When a company liquidates assets, in which order are claims satisfied?

   A. Secured bondholders, preferred stock-holders, common stockholders, general creditors
   B. Secured bondholders, general creditors, preferred stockholders, common stock-holders
   C. General creditors, secured bondholders, common stockholders, preferred stock-holders
   D. Common stockholders, preferred stock-holders, secured bondholders, general creditors

78. Which of the following companies is using the most leverage?

   A. One financed mostly by the sale of com-mon stock
   B. One financed mostly by the sale of bonds and other debt issues
   C. One financed by equal amounts of com-mon stock and bonds
   D. None of the above

79. A client has invested in a U.S. Treasury bond. The interest received from these bonds is subject to

   A. federal income tax
   B. state income tax
   C. both A and B
   D. neither A nor B

80. Corporate bonds are considered safer than corporate stock issued by the same company because

   I. bonds represent equity in the corpora-tion
   II. the company is more likely to back the original investors
   III. bonds are senior to common stock
   IV. the holder of a corporate bond is a debtor to the company

   A. I and II
   B. II, III and IV
   C. III
   D. III and IV

81. Which of the following securities is(are) issued with a fixed rate of return?

   I. Bonds
   II. Preferred stock
   III. Common stock
   IV. Convertible preferred stock

   A. I, II and IV only
   B. III only
   C. IV only
   D. I, II, III and IV

82. Municipal bonds are issued as either revenue bonds or general obligation bonds. The characteristics of a revenue bond are

    I. interest from a revenue bond is exempt from federal income taxes
    II. interest is payable only from the revenue of the facility being financed
    III. these bonds do not have to carry a legal opinion of counsel
    IV. the principal of these bonds is backed by the full faith and credit of the issuing municipality

    A. I and II only
    B. I, II and IV only
    C. I and IV only
    D. I, II, III and IV

83. John Jones is in the 30% tax bracket and is earning 7% interest on a municipal bond. What rate of interest would he have to earn on a corporate bond to receive the same return?

    A. 6.7%
    B. 7%
    C. 10%
    D. 15%

84. The standard denomination of a corporate bond is

    A. $100
    B. $500
    C. $1,000
    D. $5,000

85. Cities and states issue both revenue bonds and general obligation bonds. Which of the following characteristics regarding a revenue bond would we notice?

    I. Interest from a revenue bond is exempt from federal income taxes.
    II. Interest is payable only from the revenue of the facility being financed.
    III. These bonds do not carry legal opinion of counsel.
    IV. The principal of these bonds is payable only from the revenue of the facility being financed.

    A. I and II only
    B. I, II and IV only
    C. I and IV only
    D. I, II, III and IV

86. A 9% corporate bond is quoted at 120. What is the current yield?

    A. 7 1/2%
    B. 9%
    C. 108%
    D. $90

87. Which of the following bonds would qualify as a municipal bond?

    I. General obligation bond of the City of Denver
    II. Revenue bond issued by the City of Detroit to build the Joe Louis Arena
    III. Sewer bond issued by Cook County, Illinois
    IV. Highway bond issued by the State of New Mexico

    A. I only
    B. I and II only
    C. I, II and III only
    D. I, II, III and IV

88. In a market of changing interest rates (both up and down), you would expect the yield to maturity and the current yield to

    A. move in the same direction
    B. move in the opposite direction
    C. never change
    D. There is no relationship.

89. Bond trust indentures are required for which of the following?

    A. Corporate debt securities
    B. Municipal general obligation bonds
    C. Municipal revenue bonds
    D. Treasury securities

90. What is the advantage of a Treasury receipt over a Treasury bill?

    A. An investor doesn't have to pay taxes on accrued interest.
    B. All interest is paid at maturity.
    C. There is less of a capital requirement.
    D. Interest is taxed as it accrues yearly, whether or not it has been received.

91. Which of the following is issued with a maturity of twelve months or less?

    A. T bills
    B. T notes
    C. T bonds
    D. T stock

92. Which of the following is considered as having an intermediate maturity?

    A. T bills
    B. T notes
    C. T bonds
    D. T stock

93. Which of the following is considered as having long-term maturity?

    A. T bills
    B. T notes
    C. T bonds
    D. T stock

94. Which of the following is the issuer of government securities?

    A. Federal Reserve Banks
    B. Federal Reserve Board
    C. Treasury Department
    D. Commerce Department

95. All of the following are true of a negotiable CD EXCEPT that

    A. yields are quoted for no shorter than a 14-day time period
    B. interest is paid at maturity
    C. it is guaranteed by the issuing bank
    D. it is registered

96. Which of the following does not trade in the secondary market?

    A. Bankers' acceptances
    B. Certificates of deposit
    C. Repurchase agreements
    D. Treasury bills

97. Which of the following debt instruments pays no interest?

    A. Treasury STRIP
    B. Treasury note
    C. Treasury bond
    D. Treasury stock

98. Which of the following statements is(are) true of a Treasury STRIP?

    I. The rate of return is locked in.
    II. There is no reinvestment risk.
    III. The interest is taxed as a capital gain.
    IV. The interest is realized at maturity.

    A. I
    B. I, II and III
    C. I, II and IV
    D. I and IV

99. Securities issued by which of the following are backed by the federal government?

   A. Federal National Mortgage Association
   B. Federal Home Loan Mortgage Corporation
   C. Government National Mortgage Association
   D. Federal Intermediate Credit Bank

100. Which of the following statements is true of GNMA mortgage-backed securities?

   A. They are backed by the Federal National Mortgage Association, which may borrow from the Treasury to pay principal and interest.
   B. They are backed by a pool of mortgages.
   C. Interest payments are exempt from federal income taxes.
   D. The minimum purchase is $25,000.

101. All of the following pay semiannual interest EXCEPT

   A. GNMAs
   B. Treasury bonds
   C. Treasury notes
   D. Public utility bonds

102. T bills are issued with all of the following maturities EXCEPT

   A. one month
   B. three months
   C. six months
   D. twelve months

103. Which of the following tenders for the 90- and 180-day T bills is always filled at the auction?

   A. Competitive
   B. Noncompetitive
   C. Negotiated
   D. Firm commitment

104. All of the following are true of a Treasury receipt EXCEPT

   A. it may be issued by a securities broker-dealer
   B. it is backed by the full faith and credit of the federal government
   C. the interest coupons are sold separately
   D. it may be purchased at a discount

105. Which of the following does not issue commercial paper?

   A. Commercial bank
   B. Finance company
   C. Service company
   D. Broker-dealer

106. A newly issued bond has call protection for the first five years after it is issued. This feature would be most valuable if, during this five-year period, interest rates are generally

   A. fluctuating
   B. stable
   C. falling
   D. rising

107. The newspaper indicates that T bill yields have gone down. This means that T bill prices

   A. are up
   B. are down
   C. are mixed
   D. cannot be determined

108. A 5% bond is purchased with an 8% yield to maturity. After the capital gains tax is paid, the effective yield is

   A. less than 5%
   B. 5%
   C. between 5% and 8%
   D. 8%

109. Each of the following four bonds has a 6.10% coupon rate. A five-basis-point change in each bond would have the greatest effect on the dollar price of which bond?

    A. 1 year to maturity, 6.10 basis
    B. 2 years to maturity, 6.50 basis
    C. 2 1/2 years to maturity, 7.25 basis
    D. 2 3/4 years to maturity, 7.35 basis

110. All of the following settle in federal funds EXCEPT

    A. municipals
    B. T bills
    C. government bonds
    D. government notes

111. All of the following trade flat or with accrued interest EXCEPT

    A. a bond in default of interest
    B. a zero-coupon bond
    C. if the settlement date and the interest payment date are the same
    D. a registered industrial revenue bond

112. All of the following are true of taxable zero-coupon bonds EXCEPT

    A. the discount is accreted
    B. tax is paid annually
    C. interest is paid semiannually
    D. bonds are purchased at a discount

113. Which of the following statements about a bond quoted as GMA Zr 12 would be true?

    A. The bond pays $12 interest annually.
    B. The bond pays $120 interest annually.
    C. The bond pays no interest until maturity.
    D. None of the above statements is true.

114. Where does a customer get the information needed to determine the amount of accretion on an original issue discount bond?

    A. Investor
    B. Underwriter
    C. IRS
    D. Issuer

115. The yield on a bond with 20 years to maturity decreases by ten basis points. The price of the bond will approximately

    A. decrease by $1
    B. increase by $1
    C. decrease by $10
    D. increase by $10

◆ Answers & Rationale

1. C. A convertible bond is converted into common stock issued by the company.

2. B. The bond is quoted as 120; therefore, it is selling for $1,200. Parity of the stock in which the holder of the bond can convert is equal to $24 as follows: The bondholder would be able to convert the bond into 50 shares of stock (face amount of the bond is $1,000 divided by $20 per share which equals 50 shares), because the bond has a current price of $1,200; dividing this amount by 50 equals the parity price of the underlying stock.

3. D. Securities for a collateral trust bond are held in the name of a trustee until the collateral trust bonds are repaid.

4. D. All of these factors affect the price of a convertible bond. The rating of a bond reflects the issuing company's health and therefore indirectly affects the value of the investment.

5. A. By purchasing bonds when interest rates are high, any attendant drop in interest rates will lead to a corresponding increase in value of the bond. Long-term debt instruments will fluctuate to a greater degree than short-term interest rates; thus, long-term debt offers the greater chance at gain.

6. A. A debenture is a long-term unsecured debt obligation issued by a corporation. Commercial paper is a short-term obligation. Common stock is not debt, and a mortgage bond is secured by real estate.

7. C. Interest in the form of dividends paid from a municipal bond fund would be exempt from federal income tax. Gains from the sale of portfolio securities would be subject to ordinary income tax.

8. C. Interest on Treasury bills, even though the bill is purchased at a discount from face value, is taxed as ordinary income (interest).

9. C. Treasury bills mature in less than a year, notes mature in from one to ten years and bonds mature in more than ten years.

10. C. EE bonds are sold at a discount and mature to face value; T bonds and agency issues are marketable debt. The HH bond is non-marketable and pays interest semiannually.

11. B. Debentures are secured by the good faith and credit of the issuing corporation. They are senior to stock ownership, have a senior claim to assets and are considered a safer investment.

12. B. Nominal yield is fixed and stays the same on all bonds. A bond selling above par is selling at a premium so the current yield and yield to maturity will be less than the nominal yield.

13. C. Collateral trust bonds are backed by other securities, while mortgage bonds are backed by real estate and equipment trust certificates are backed by equipment. Debentures are secured by the companies' promise to pay.

14. C. The best time to buy long-term bonds is when long-term interest rates have peaked. In addition to the high return, as interest rates fall the value of existing bonds will rise.

15. D. Replacing a debt with a debt is called refunding.

16. B. When interest rates rise, bond prices fall.

17. B. Revenue bonds are used to finance municipal projects that generate revenues.

18. B. T bills are sold at a discount and have maturities of up to one year. Although they mature at face value it is not considered interest.

19. D. Series EE and HH bonds are examples of nonmarketable government securities.

20. A. Municipal bonds are exempt from federal income tax. Treasury bonds are exempt from state tax. GNMAs are subject to federal and state income tax.

21. **D.** Baa bonds carry a greater investment risk and therefore will likely pay greater interest to induce investors to purchase them.

22. **D.** Money markets are made up of short-term high-yield debt issues. All of the items listed here are considered short term, even the bonds because they will mature in less than one year.

23. **C.** A convertible bond is converted into common stock issued by the company. Therefore, the stock's current price will impact the price of the convertible bond.

24. **B.** A bond purchased at a premium is purchased for an amount greater than the face amount of the bond at maturity. The premium paid reduces the yield of the bond if held until maturity.

25. **A.** The bond is quoted as 90; therefore, it is selling for $900. Parity of the stock in which the holder of the bond can convert is equal to $22.50 as follows. The bondholder would be able to convert the bond into 40 shares of stock (face amount $1,000 ÷ $25 per share = 40 shares) because the bond has a current price of $900; dividing this amount by 40 equals the parity price of the underlying stock.

26. **B.** Preferred stocks are interest rate sensitive as are other fixed-interest rate investment vehicles such as bonds. Because the dividend amount is fixed, if interest rates are increasing, the return provided by the dividend may be less than the return provided by other investments. The value of preferred stock will decrease.

27. **C.** Security for a mortgage bond is typically real estate, plant or other long-term assets held by the firm.

28. **B.** Although the value of the underlying stock may reflect the health of the company, current interest rates will have the greatest impact on the price of an unsecured debt issued by a corporation.

29. **B.** A debenture is a long-term unsecured debt obligation issued by a corporation. Commercial paper is a short-term obligation. Common stock is not debt, and a mortgage bond is secured by real estate.

30. **D.** Interest on Series EE bonds is received at redemption of the bonds.

31. **B.** *Ascending* means increasing. Treasury bills mature in less than a year, notes mature in one to ten years, and bonds mature in more than ten years.

32. **C.** The YTM is greater than the nominal yield, meaning the price must be less than par. The bond is selling at a discount.

33. **B.** EE bonds are nonmarketable, are sold at a discount and mature at face value; T bonds are marketable debt and pay interest semiannually. The HH bond is nonmarketable and pays interest semi-annually.

34. **D.** Mortgage bonds are secured by the good faith and credit of the issuing corporation evidenced by a pledge of real estate or a similar asset. They are senior to stock ownership, have a senior claim to assets over other debt issues and are considered a safer investment.

35. **A.** Nominal yield is fixed and stays the same on all bonds. A bond selling below par is selling at a discount, so the current yield and yield to maturity will be greater than the nominal yield.

36. **B.** Collateral trust bonds are backed by other securities, while mortgage bonds are backed by real estate. Equipment trust certificates are backed by equipment, such as railroad cars or aircraft. Debentures are secured by a promise to pay.

37. **A.** The best time to buy short-term bonds is when short-term interest rates have peaked. In

addition to the high return, as interest rates fall the value of existing bonds will rise.

38. **C.** Parity is when a convertible bond and the common stock for which it can be converted is equal in value (par of $1,000 ÷ 50 = $20 per share; CMV of stock = $20 per share).

39. **A.** When interest rates decline, bond prices increase.

40. **C.** Industrial development revenue bonds (IDRs) are used to finance municipal projects such as industrial parks that are in turn leased to private corporations. The lease payments serve as security for the note.

41. **C.** T bonds are sold at par and pay interest semiannually. The bonds have long maturities of ten or more years.

42. **D.** Series EE bonds are nonmarketable government securities issued by the Treasury. An agency bond is debt issued by a U.S. governmental jurisdiction other than the Treasury.

43. **D.** Municipal bonds are exempt from federal income tax and are exempt from state tax within the state of issue. U.S. Treasury issues are subject to federal income tax, but would be exempt from state taxes.

44. **D.** Aaa bonds carry a greater investment risk than Treasury securities, which are considered the safest long-term security that can be purchased.

45. **A.** Money markets are made up of short-term high-yield debt issues. Because the Treasury bond is maturing in less than a year, it is also considered a money market instrument. The debenture and Treasury note are long-term instruments.

46. **A.** A bond purchased at a discount is purchased for an amount less than the face amount of the bond at maturity. The discount received increases the current yield of the bond.

47. **C.** Fluctuations in interest rates may affect the price of a bond, but will not affect the income payable from the bond. The percentage interest payable for use of the money is stated on the face of a bond and is part of the bond indenture, a legal obligation on the part of the issuing company.

48. **D.** The nominal yield is greater than the quoted yield, meaning the price must be greater than par. The bond is selling at a premium.

49. **D.** Common stock has the last claim on assets, preceded by preferred stock and general creditors. Bondholders would have the greatest claim to company assets in the event of dissolution.

50. **B.** Secured bondholders have an immediate claim to a stated asset in the event of default; general creditors would be next in line, followed by owners of the corporation. Preferred stockholders have a prior claim to corporate assets over common stockholders who retain only a residual claim to corporate assets. Common stockholders are the last to be paid.

51. **B.** The higher the rating, the lower the risk, even if the debt is unsecured.

52. **A.** A convertible bond allows the bondholder, at his or her discretion, to convert the bond into a prescribed number of shares of common stock of the issuer. A call provision allows the issuer to redeem the bond prior to maturity.

53. **C.** Generally a bond issued at a higher rate of interest, when compared to equivalent bonds of the same maturity, carries the higher rate because of a lower rating or a higher risk of default.

54. **C.** Bonds represent a creditor relationship; stock represents an ownership interest. Normally bonds are issued with a stated rate of interest and mature in ten or more years.

55. **D.** Bonds are quoted as a percentage of par value ($1,000). Therefore, a bond quoted at 102 5/8 is actually selling for 102.625% of par, or $1,026.25.

56. **C.**   A collateral trust bond is backed by securities of a subsidiary corporation or another company's securities. A mortgage bond is backed by real property.

57. **D.**   A bond quoted at 102 is selling at $1,020 (102% of par). The bond is selling for an amount that is greater than its face amount of $1,000, or at a premium.

58. **B.**   A bond with a nominal yield of 6% will pay $60 in interest annually. The interest payment is fixed. The bond is selling at 98 1/2, or $985 (98.5% of par). An individual purchasing the bond for $985 would still receive $60 in interest; therefore the current yield of the bond is the $60 return divided by the current price of $985, or 6.09%.

59. **C.**   The Amalgamated bond is selling at a discount (97% of par, or $970). When prices are down, yields are up. The nominal yield of the bond does not change, but current yield will be greater than nominal yield, and the yield to maturity will be greater than the current yield.

60. **C.**   Treasury bills are purchased at a discount from face value. The difference between purchase price and face value represents the interest earned at maturity of the bill.

61. **D.**   Treasury securities (bills, notes and bonds) and U.S. savings bonds (EE and HH) are backed by the full faith and credit of the U.S. government.

62. **A.**   A Series EE bond is a nonnegotiable instrument. The bond is redeemed by the government (usually through a bank). The interest received by the bondholder will be less if the bond is redeemed prior to maturity. The difference between purchase price and redemption value represents interest, which is taxable at the federal level.

63. **C.**   Direct government debt is taxable only at the federal level. (Direct debt includes Treasury debt and savings bonds.)

64. **A.**   General obligation bonds are backed by the general taxing authority of the municipal issuer. As such, they are often considered very safe investments. Municipal issues are marketable and are bought and sold in the secondary marketplace. Because interest received on municipal debt is exempt from federal taxation, yields offered on municipal debt are lower than yields offered on corporate debt.

65. **A.**   Because a corporate yield is taxable at the federal level and because Colleen is in a 33% tax bracket, to receive the same aftertax yield as offered by the municipal issue, the corporate yield would have to be at least 33% higher than the 6% offered by the municipal bond.

66. **C.**   Municipal general obligation bonds are most often issued to fund municipal projects requiring capital outlays, such as sidewalks, new school buildings and so on.

67. **A.**   A general obligation bond is also called a full faith and credit bond because it is backed by the taxing power of the municipality. A revenue bond is backed by income to be received from a revenue-producing project. An industrial development bond will be backed by lease or rental payments on property developed by the municipality. All interest received on municipal issues is exempt from federal income tax.

68. **D.**   Commercial paper is an unsecured short-term corporate promissory note, and a certificate of deposit is a short-term bank promissory note. Both securities are issued in the money market.

69. **A.**   The capital market is for long-term financing; the money market is for short-term (less than a year) financing. Generally the shorter the maturity, the lower the yield.

70. **D.**   Bonds are quoted as a percentage of par. Therefore, 102% of $1,000 equals $1,020.

71. **A.**   Because a mortgage bond is a form of secured debt, the bondholder would have a prior

right to the secured asset before any other creditor or stockholder.

72. **B.** Treasury bills are short-term debt issued by the government at a discount from face value. The interest earned is the difference between purchase price and face value.

73. **C.** Interest received from a municipal issue is exempt from federal income taxation. The interest may or may not be exempt from state or city income taxation depending on the state of issue.

74. **B.** Bond quotes are a percentage of the issue's face value. The difference between the purchase price and sale price of the bond was .03125 times 1,000 equals a profit of $31.25. If you answered B, you were on the right track; however, these were bond quotes, not stock quotes.

75. **B.** The yield to price relationship of bonds is an inverse relationship. As interest rates increase, the market price for bonds declines.

76. **A.** A creditor is someone who has lent money; a debt is payable. Preferred stock is equity or ownership in a firm. The company has no obligation whatsoever to the equity owner.

77. **B.** The order of priority during the liquidation of assets is secured creditors first, then unsecured creditors, and finally stockholders. Common stockholders are the *last* in line to receive distributions from the company.

78. **B.** Leverage is the use of borrowed funds for investment. A highly leveraged company is one that depends on the sale of bonds or other forms of borrowing for capitalization. Equity financing is the sale of stock, and ownership interest is transferred.

79. **A.** Interest received from U.S. government issues is exempt from taxation on the state level, but is fully subject to federal income tax.

80. **C.** A bond represents a legal obligation to repay principal and interest by the company. The holder of a corporate bond is a *creditor* of the company.

81. **A.** Bonds and preferred stock are typically issued with a stated payment, either in interest or dividends. Common stockholders are entitled to receive a variable distribution of profits if and when a dividend is declared.

82. **A.** All municipal bonds must carry a legal opinion of counsel affirming that the issue is a municipal issue and interest is exempt from federal taxation. Interest and principal of a revenue bond will be paid only if the facility financed produces the revenue necessary to pay. AGO is a municipal issue backed by the full faith and credit of the municipality.

83. **C.** First of all, because a corporate yield is taxable and the interest rate would have to be greater than 7%, answers A and B can be eliminated. Answer D is more than twice the yield of 7%, and because John is only in a 30% bracket, the answer is too high, leaving answer B as the answer. The formula would be municipal rate (7%) divided by the complement of the tax bracket (100% − 30% = 70%), or 7% divided by 70% equals 10%.

84. **C.** Most corporate bonds are issued with a face amount (principal) of $1,000.

85. **B.** A revenue bond is a municipal issue sold to raise funds for the purpose of constructing a revenue-producing facility. All municipal bonds require an opinion of specialized bond counsel stating that the issue does indeed represent a municipal obligation and that interest payments are exempt from federal taxation. The interest and principal payments are backed to the extent the facility produces enough revenue to make payments.

86. **A.** A bond quoted at 120 is selling at a price of $1,200. Because the price of the bond is

up, the current yield is less than the nominal yield. In this instance the current yield would be 7.5%.

87. **D.** Any bond issued by a state, municipality or governmental unit other than the federal government is categorized as a municipal issue.

88. **A.** Yield to maturity and current yield move in the same direction inversely to movements in price.

89. **A.** Nonexempt issuers of debt securities (such as corporations) are required to include a bond contract by the Trust Indenture Act of 1939. Exempt issuers (such as municipalities and the U.S. government) are not required to enter into a trust indenture, although most municipalities do anyway.

90. **C.** The Treasury receipt is a creation of a broker-dealer. The broker-dealer buys Treasury bonds and "strips" them of their coupons. The broker-dealer sells the coupons separately and creates a pool with the bonds. The investor will purchase a piece of the pool and receive a receipt for his or her purchase (called a Treasury receipt). Because the customer can purchase a unit of the pool instead of an actual stripped bond, the capital requirement could be less.

91. **A.** T bills have maturities of three, six and twelve months.

92. **B.** T notes are intermediate-term securities having one- to ten-year maturities.

93. **C.** Treasury bonds are long-term securities, having maturities of 10 to 30 years.

94. **C.** The Treasury Department is the issuer of government securities.

95. **D.** Because certificates of deposit are issued by banks, they are exempt from registration under the act of 1933.

96. **C.** Repurchase agreements are not as much a security as they are a contract between two parties. Although one party may transfer its obligations or rights to a third party, there really isn't an active secondary market for repos.

97. **A.** The rate of return is locked in, and the interest is realized at maturity. There is no reinvestment risk because you are not receiving anything over the life of the bond to reinvest. The interest is taxed as ordinary income and must be accreted annually.

98. **C.** A STRIP has no reinvestment risk because there are no interest payments to have at risk in regards to reinvestment. Because there is no reinvestment risk, the total rate of return is locked in or set at issuance. The interest on the bond is paid at maturity, but it is taxed as interest income over the life of the bond.

99. **C.** GNMAs are guaranteed by the government. These are the only agency issues backed directly by the government. The other answers listed here are indirect federal debt.

100. **D.** GNMAs are issued in minimum denominations of $25,000.

101. **A.** The GNMA issues monthly checks that include both principal and interest payments.

102. **A.** T bills are issued with three-, six- and twelve-month maturities.

103. **B.** For T bill auctions there are only two types of bids: competitive and noncompetitive. All noncompetitive bids are filled at the average price of the winning bids. Noncompetitive bids are generally placed by individual investors; competitive bids are placed by financial institutions such as government securities dealers.

104. **B.** Although the Treasury securities underlying Treasury receipts are backed by the full faith and credit of the federal government, the stripped securities are not.

105. **A.** Commercial paper is not issued by commercial banks. The CP market was developed to circumvent banks so that corporations could lend to and borrow from each other more economically. CPs are unsecured corporate IOUs.

106. **C.** In this case *call protection* means that the bonds cannot be called by the issuer for at least five years. If interest rates are falling, the issuer would have reason to want to call the bonds in and, perhaps, issue new bonds at a lower interest rate. Therefore, the call feature protects the investor for a specific period of time.

107. **A.** If the yields have gone down, that means that the discount has been reduced; therefore, the dollar cost of bills has gone up.

108. **C.** This bond, because the yield is above the coupon, is trading at a discount. Therefore, if it is held to maturity, the customer will realize a return on the bond of 8% and have a capital gains tax. Because the tax paid will reduce the return on the customer's investment, the effective yield will be less than 8%.

109. **D.** The change in yields must be made up over a longer period, so the yield change results in a greater change in price for a longer-term bond.

110. **A.** Government securities settle in federal funds. Municipal bonds generally settle in clearinghouse funds.

111. **D.** Like most bonds, industrial revenue bonds trade with that accrued interest. If a bond is in default, it means the bond is not paying interest payments; therefore, interest would not accrue. If the settlement day is the first day of the new interest period, the seller would be entitled to receive the entire six months' payment and the bond will trade without accrued interest. Zeros are stripped bonds; therefore, there is no interest.

112. **C.** A portion of the original issue discount on taxable zero-coupon bonds must be declared as income and taxed annually until the bond matures. This is known as accreting the discount.

113. **C.** The GMA is a zero-coupon bond maturing in 2012. Zero-coupon bonds are bought at a discount and mature at face value. If held to maturity, the difference between the purchase price and the maturity price is considered interest.

114. **D.** The issuer determines the amount of accretion and will be entitled to an interest deduction for that year.

115. **D.** Remember the inverse relationship of bond yields to price. As bond yields decline, prices increase. Therefore, the choice is between increasing by $1 or $10. Because the bonds mature in 20 years, it is reasonable to assume that the bond will increase by $10 because prices on long-term bonds change more than prices on short-term bonds for a given change in yield.

3 Securities Markets

1. When a broker-dealer is holding money and/or securities in its own account, it is

   A. underwriting
   B. hypothecating the securities
   C. taking a position
   D. doing none of the above

2. Which of the following statements about the underwriting of a new issue is(are) true?

   A. In a best-efforts offering, the underwriters will not be held financially liable for any unsold portion of the offering.
   B. In a firm commitment underwriting, the underwriters pay the issuer for the full amount of the offering and retain any unsold shares.
   C. In an all-or-none underwriting, the issuer agrees to cancel the offering if all the shares are not sold.
   D. All of the above are true.

3. ABC stock is quoted at 67 3/4 bid—67 7/8 ask. An investor wishes to purchase one round lot from the broker-dealer. Excluding commissions, the investor would pay

   A. $6,775
   B. $6,787.50
   C. $6,789
   D. More information is needed to answer this question.

4. When trading common stock, either at an exchange or over the counter, the typical size of the trading unit is

   A. 10 shares
   B. 50 shares
   C. 100 shares
   D. not standardized

5. When dealing with a market maker, he or she may tell you the price of a stock is 22 bid—23 ask firm. This means the market maker

   A. is ready to buy the stock at $23 and is willing to sell at $22
   B. is ready to sell the stock at $23 and is willing to buy at $22
   C. will always buy the stock at $23 regardless of the current price of the stock
   D. is sharing information about the current price of the stock but is not ready to trade

6. Which of the following actions is(are) the responsibility of an investment banker?

   I. Distributing large blocks of stock to the public and to institutions
   II. Buying previously unissued securities from an issuer and selling them to the public
   III. Raising long-term capital for corporations by underwriting new issues of securities
   IV. Lending money to corporate clients who require debt financing

   A. I, II and III only
   B. I, II and IV only
   C. III only
   D. I, II, III and IV

7. Mr. Schroeder owns 100 shares of ABC Company. A dividend is declared on August 30th. The dividend will be paid to stockholders of record on Thursday, September 15th. When will the stock sell ex-dividend?

   A. September 9th
   B. September 11th
   C. September 12th
   D. September 15th

8. The over-the-counter market could be characterized as which of the following?

   A. Auction market
   B. Double-auction market
   C. Negotiated market
   D. None of the above

9. The ex-dividend date is the

   I. date on and after which the buyer is entitled to the dividend
   II. date on and after which the seller is entitled to the dividend
   III. fourth business day prior to the record date
   IV. fourth business day after the record date

   A. I and III
   B. I and IV
   C. II and III
   D. II and IV

10. XYZ stock is quoted at 10 bid—10 1/4 ask. An investor wishes to purchase one round lot from the broker-dealer. How many shares would the investor receive?

   A. 10
   B. 100
   C. 1,000
   D. More information is needed to answer this question.

11. Marjorie and Harry Kellog are tenants in common in a joint account. Which of the following statements is(are) true?

   A. If one of them dies, the survivor will not automatically assume full ownership.
   B. They need not have equal interest in the account.
   C. They have an undivided interest in the property in the account.
   D. All of the above are true.

12. Concerning a primary offering for the Ajax Company, the underwriter has agreed to sell all the shares and accepts liability for any shares that remain unsold. The underwriting agreement between Ajax and the issuer is a(n)

   A. best-efforts offering
   B. firm commitment underwriting
   C. all-or-none underwriting
   D. All of the above describe the agreement.

13. When trading common stock, either at an exchange or over the counter, an odd lot is a trade in quantities of fewer than how many shares?

   A. 10
   B. 50
   C. 100
   D. 1,000

14. When you purchase stock from a market maker, you pay the

   A. bid price
   B. ask price
   C. bid price minus commission
   D. ask price plus commission

15. Which of the following is(are) the responsibility of a selling group member?

    I. Managing the distribution of large blocks of stock to the public and to institutions

    II. Selling a predetermined share of an offering to its customers

    III. Raising long-term capital for corporations by assisting in the distribution of a corporation's outstanding securities

    IV. Lending money to corporate clients that require debt financing

    A. I, II and III only
    B. I, II and IV only
    C. II only
    D. I, II, III and IV

16. The third market could be characterized as which of the following?

    A. Auction market
    B. Double-auction market
    C. Negotiated market
    D. None of the above

17. Mike Scarpelli is seeking an investment that could protect him from inflation. What type of investment risk is Mike attempting to avoid?

    A. Financial risk
    B. Market risk
    C. Interest rate risk
    D. Purchasing power risk

18. You have learned that Mr. and Mrs. Cantwell's objective is long-term growth. They are willing to accept a reasonable amount of risk to obtain this objective. Which of the following investment vehicles would be a suitable choice?

    A. Money-market instruments
    B. Blue chip common stock
    C. Preferred stock
    D. Municipal bonds

19. Which of the following characteristics describe(s) a highly leveraged corporation?

    I. high net worth
    II. high debt-to-equity ratio
    III. Stable earnings

    A. I and II only
    B. II only
    C. II and III only
    D. I, II and III

20. If purchasing power of the dollar is declining, what is the consequence for the current yield of a 20-year 10% bond?

    A. Current yield is increasing.
    B. Current yield is declining.
    C. Current yield stays the same.
    D. This cannot be determined with the information given.

21. An investor makes a purchase of common stock at a cost of $1,000. He holds the stock for one year and sells it for $1,500. During the same time, the consumer price index increased from 100 to 125. At the time he liquidates his investment, the value of his investment in constant dollars is

    A. less than $1,000
    B. $1,000
    C. greater than $1,000 but less than $1,500
    D. $1,500

22. A stock exchange uses

    A. an auction method to trade stock
    B. a network of market makers to trade stock
    C. the NASDAQ and pink sheet system to enter orders
    D. a first come, first served method for handling all orders

23. When you accept an order to sell stock, that order

    A. must be in writing
    B. must be approved by the NASD or the DBCC
    C. shall be reviewed by the branch manager, or partner
    D. is cancelable at any time

24. A client buys 500 shares of Amalgamated Horse Manure at $50 per share. He deposits with his broker $23,500, leaving a $1,500 balance, which he intends to pay on the fifth full business day following the trade date. But one day after the trade date, the market price drops to $40 per share. This change

    A. increases his equity by $5,000
    B. increases his debt balance by $5,000
    C. will cause a margin call
    D. will not change his balance due the broker-dealer

25. The ex-dividend date of a stock is Tuesday, January 13th. When is the record date?

    A. Wednesday, January 7th
    B. Friday, January 9th
    C. Saturday, January 17th
    D. Monday, January 19th

26. Which of the following would constitute a wash sale?

    A. Securities sold at a long-term loss and bought back within 30 days after the sale
    B. The purchase of an option to buy the same shares being sold if within 30 days before the long position is sold at a long-term loss
    C. The purchase of an option to buy the same shares being sold if within 30 days after the long position is sold at a long-term loss
    D. All of the above

27. In a due diligence meeting, the

    A. issuer and underwriter determine the price of the issue and the profit margin
    B. issuer prepares the prospectus
    C. issuer and underwriter conduct a final review of the registration statement to be sure all material information is correct and disclosed
    D. certificates of the issue are engraved

28. J&P, a brokerage firm, has agreed to a firm commitment underwriting of Amalgamated stock. Some of the shares remain unsold and result in a loss. The loss is borne by

    A. J&P and Amalgamated
    B. J&P only
    C. Amalgamated only
    D. New shareholders

29. An investment banker performs which of the following functions?

    I.   Lending money to corporate clients requiring debt financing
    II. Buying securities from an issuer and reselling them to the public
    III. Raising long-term capital for corporations by underwriting new issues of securities

    A. I and II only
    B. I and III only
    C. II and III only
    D. I, II and III

30. Which of the following activities are characteristic of a primary offering?

    I.   Raising additional capital for the company
    II. Selling previously issued securities
    III. Increasing the number of shares or bonds outstanding

    A. I and II only
    B. I and III only
    C. II and III only
    D. I, II and III

31. When a client gives a broker-dealer an order to buy securities, the broker-dealer may

    I.   act as the client's agent by finding a seller and arranging the sale
    II. buy the securities, mark up the price and resell them to the client on a dealer basis
    III. sell the shares from its own inventory to the client if it has the security in inventory

    A. I only
    B. I and II only
    C. II and III only
    D. I, II and III

32. Which of the following statements describe a securities exchange?

    I.   The highest bid and the lowest offer prevail.
    II. Only listed securities can be traded.
    III. Minimum prices are established.

    A. I and II only
    B. I and III only
    C. II and III only
    D. I, II and III

33. The New York Stock Exchange is a

    A. negotiated market
    B. third market
    C. primary market
    D. none of the above

34. The over-the-counter market is

    A. an auction market
    B. the first market
    C. a negotiated market
    D. all of the above

35. J&P Brokerage acts as a dealer when filling a client's order to purchase 300 shares of Amalgamated. J&P makes its profit from a

    A. markup on the offering price of the securities
    B. markup on the offering price plus a commission on the sale
    C. markdown on the bid price of the securities
    D. commission

36. Broker A has an order to sell stock at 23 1/2; broker B has an order to sell at 23; and broker C has an order to sell at 24 1/4. Which broker would sell the shares first?

    A. Broker A
    B. Broker B
    C. Broker C
    D. This cannot be determined from the information given.

37. A stock is quoted at 97 1/8 bid—97 7/8 ask. A purchaser of this stock would pay (disregarding commissions)

    A. $97.12 1/2
    B. $97.75
    C. $97.87 1/2
    D. $97.87 1/2 plus the difference between the prices

38. When checking the newspaper for the daily bid and ask prices of over-the-counter stocks, you notice that two stocks in which you are interested have dramatically different spreads. You could conclude that

    A. typically the stock with the narrower spread is more active than the stock with the wider spread
    B. typically the stock with the wider spread is more active than the stock with the narrower spread
    C. the stock with the narrower spread will always be less expensive in the long run
    D. No conclusion may be drawn from this information.

39. An example of a secondary distribution would be

    A. the sale of authorized stock
    B. the placement of a block of newly issued securities with one buyer
    C. the distribution of a new issue by an underwriter
    D. a large block of outstanding securities being redistributed in smaller blocks

40. When referring to the third market, transactions occur through

    A. major stock exchanges (New York, American, etc.)
    B. the over-the-counter market
    C. over-the-counter trading of listed securities
    D. the government bond market

41. A broker-dealer is participating as an underwriter in an all-or-none underwriting for a new issue. The broker-dealer

    A. must be sure all the shares are sold
    B. must be sure that the shares remaining after a preemptive rights offering are sold
    C. must inform customers that no sales are final unless the entire offering is sold
    D. is participating in a form of firm commitment underwriting

42. A customer confirmation must

    I. contain all relevant information concerning the trade
    II. be sent within 24 hours of the trade
    III. be sent by settlement of the trade
    IV. accompany the delivery of the stock certificate

    A. I
    B. I and II
    C. I and III
    D. I and IV

43. What is the function of NASDAQ?

    I. It is a computerized system available to market makers allowing the subscriber to access bid and ask quotations and quotation sizes for all market makers in the OTC market.
    II. It is a computerized system available to market makers allowing them to complete trades in the OTC market.
    III. It is a computerized system allowing OTC market makers to complete transactions on the floor of the NYSE.
    IV. It is a computerized system allowing clients to trade directly with OTC market makers.

    A. I only
    B. I and II only
    C. I, II and III only
    D. I, II, III and IV

44. A broker-dealer is participating in a best-efforts underwriting. The broker is acting as

    A. an agent for the issuer
    B. a principal for the issuer
    C. the issuer
    D. none of the above

45. When an individual buys stock, the individual is

    A. a broker-dealer
    B. underwriting
    C. taking a long position
    D. taking a short position

46. A client in a cash account purchases 100 shares of XYZ stock. Under federal law the client must settle the transaction within how many days from the trade date?

    A. Five business days
    B. Seven business days
    C. Seven calendar days
    D. Ten business days

47. The essential difference between a primary and a secondary transaction is that the secondary transaction

   A. can be only new bond issues while the primary distribution can be only new stock
   B. involves the sale of outstanding securities
   C. must be resold at the public offering price
   D. is when $50,000 or less in value is being sold

48. An underwriter who is selling mutual fund shares under a best-efforts agreement is acting in the capacity of a(n)

   A. agent
   B. dealer
   C. manager
   D. trader

49. An underwriter is participating in selling unsold shares after a preemptive rights offering has been made to the shareholders. This underwriter is participating in a(n)

   A. all-or-none underwriting
   B. standby underwriting
   C. preemptive underwriting
   D. none of the above

50. A person who is vested with legal rights and powers to be exercised for the benefit of another is known as a

   A. dealer
   B. fiduciary or trustee
   C. broker
   D. sponsor

51. An NASD member quotes 32 1/4 — 32 1/2 on an over-the-counter stock. The client wishes to sell at that price. The client informs the broker-dealer of this, and the trade is completed. The client delivers the stock the next day, but now the price is 28 3/4. According to the rules, the trade will be

   A. completed at 28 3/4
   B. completed at 32 1/4
   C. completed at 32 1/2
   D. canceled

52. Which of the following investments would produce the least market risk?

   A. Stocks
   B. Fixed-income debentures
   C. Treasury bills
   D. Zero-coupon bonds

53. Government securities settle on the

   A. ex-date
   B. payable date
   C. record date
   D. next business day

54. A customer owns 100 shares of ABC at a cost basis of $25 per share. ABC distributes a 5% stock dividend. Under the Internal Revenue Code, what is the customer's basis in his stock?

   A. 100 shares at a cost of $25 and five shares at a cost of $0
   B. 100 shares at a cost of $25 and five shares at a cost of $21.75
   C. 105 shares at an average cost of $23.81 per share
   D. 105 shares at an average cost of $25 per share

55. The *broker* part of the term *broker-dealer* indicates which of the following?

    A. Acting for others in both purchase and sale
    B. Acting for others in purchase and sale and selling from inventory
    C. Acting for the firm and acting for others in purchases and sales
    D. None of the above

56. George has $300,000 worth of securities with ABC brokerage, his spouse has $300,000 in securities, and they have a joint account with $400,000 in securities. ABC filed for bankruptcy. What is George and his wife's SIPC coverage?

    A. $300,000
    B. $600,000
    C. $700,000
    D. $1,000,000

57. An investor is in a low tax bracket and wishes to invest a moderate sum in an investment that will provide her with some protection from inflation. Which of the following would you recommend?

    A. Municipal unit investment trust
    B. Specialized mutual fund
    C. Money-market mutual fund
    D. Ginnie Mae fund

58. If the Federal Reserve Board changes the reserve requirement, the effect of the change on the economy will most likely be

    A. regressive
    B. nonregressive
    C. multiplied
    D. The change will have no effect.

59. An economic downturn that lasts for six months is called

    A. a recession
    B. a depression
    C. progressive
    D. regressive

60. Which of the following statements best describes the federal funds rate?

    A. It is the average rate for short-term bank loans last week.
    B. It is the rate charged by major New York City banks.
    C. It is a rate that changes daily and that banks charge each other.
    D. It is the rate major New York City banks charge broker-dealers.

61. Each of the following terms would be associated with an underwriting of corporate securities EXCEPT

    A. stabilization
    B. matched orders
    C. blue-sky
    D. due diligence

62. The settlement for a government bond trade in a cash account is

    A. the same day
    B. the next business day
    C. five business days after the trade date
    D. seven business days after the trade date

63. Under the SEC customer protection rule, broker-dealers must deliver to other broker-dealers no later than

    A. 5 business days after trade date
    B. 10 business days after settlement date
    C. 30 business days after settlement date
    D. 30 calendar days after settlement date

64. A customer is buying 800 shares of OTC stock. The trader responds to the firm's request for an 800-share quote with 15 bid—15 1/2 ask. The trader must sell

    A. 100 shares at 15
    B. 100 shares at 15 1/2
    C. 800 shares at 15
    D. 800 shares at 15 1/2

65. The federal funds rate has been increasing for a long time. Which of the following is likely to occur?

    A. The FRB will increase bank reserve requirements.
    B. Member banks' deposits at Federal Reserve Banks will decrease.
    C. Money market interest rates will decrease.
    D. The prime rate will decrease.

66. An improvement in the business cycle is indicated by an increase in all of the following EXCEPT

    A. industrial production
    B. inventory
    C. S&P index
    D. consumer orders

67. An investor's portfolio includes ten bonds and 200 shares of common stock. If both positions increase by 1/2 of a point, what is the gain?

    A. $50
    B. $105
    C. $110
    D. $150

◆ Answers & Rationale

1. C. When a dealer is holding securities for its own account, it is considered to be taking a position.

2. D. Firm commitment places the underwriter at risk; with best-efforts the issuer is at risk; with all-or-none, no sales are final unless the entire issue is sold.

3. B. An investor purchases stock at the ask price, or in this question at $67.875. Because the investor is purchasing a round lot, or 100 shares, the amount payable is $6,787.50 (100 × $67.875).

4. C. Common stock trades in round lots of 100 shares.

5. B. The bid price is the price at which the market maker is willing to buy the stock, while the ask price is the price at which the market maker will sell. *Firm* means that the quote is good for a round lot (100 shares).

6. A. *Investment bankers* is another term for broker-dealers. They do everything listed except lend money to corporate clients that require debt financing.

7. A. The ex-dividend date is always four business days before the record date. In this case the record date is Thursday, September 15th, so the ex-date will be Friday, September 9th.

8. C. The New York Stock Exchange is an auction market, and the OTC market is a negotiated market.

9. C. Stocks sold on the ex-dividend date entitle the seller to the dividend. Stocks sell ex-dividend four business days before the record date.

10. B. An investor buying a round lot will purchase 100 shares.

11. D. Under joint tenants in common, owners may have a fractional interest in the undivided ownership of an asset. The interest passes to the decedent's estate at death, unlike JTWROS wherein the survivor succeeds to the interest.

12. B. Firm commitment places the underwriter at risk for any shares that remain unsold.

13. C. An odd lot is considered any trade of fewer than 100 shares of stock.

14. B. The bid price is the price at which the market maker is willing to buy the stock, while the ask price is the price at which it will sell. Because the individual is purchasing, the price will be the ask price.

15. C. A selling group member is part of the underwriting group, but does not manage the offering. The selling group member is liable only for shares sold and is typically given a quota of shares to sell to its clients.

16. C. The third market is the trading of New York Stock Exchange securities in the OTC market. Because the transaction occurs in the OTC market, the third market is also a negotiated market.

17. D. The ability of an investment to provide for income that maintains purchasing power in terms of constant dollars in an inflationary environment would avoid purchasing power risk.

18. B. A blue chip stock would allow for reasonable appreciation with a minimum of risk.

19. B. Leverage is the use of debt. Therefore, a company with a high ratio of debt to equity would be highly leveraged. Because debt requires a fixed payment of interest that is a legal obligation of the firm, swings in earnings would have a greater impact on the leveraged firm than on a firm financed primarily through stock.

20. A. If purchasing power is declining, then inflation and interest rates are rising. The price of a bond would decrease, but the current yield of the bond would increase.

21. **C.** The value of the individual's investment will be greater than $1,000, but less than $1,500 in terms of constant dollars. Even though the gain was $500, at the same time the cost of goods increased by 25% as measured by the consumer price index. In constant dollars the return on investment was something less than $500.

22. **A.** Exchanges use the auction method to trade stock. Orders to buy and sell are made by open outcry for all to hear.

23. **C.** All orders received by a registered representative shall be reviewed by a principal of that firm.

24. **D.** As of the trade date, the terms of a transaction are fixed. Regardless of what events occur before settlement, the terms of the trade remain as stipulated at the time of the trade.

25. **D.** The record date is four business days after the ex-dividend date.

Wed	Thur	Fri	Sat	Sun	Mon	Tues
EX-	2	3	X	X	4	RECORD

26. **D.** The purchase of an asset sold for a loss either 30 days before or after the claimed loss constitutes a wash sale; the loss will be disallowed.

27. **C.** During a due diligence meeting, the underwriter must be diligent that all material information concerning the proposed offering is disclosed.

28. **B.** Under a firm commitment underwriting, the risk of the unsold shares belongs to the underwriter. The underwriter purchases the securities to be sold by the issuer and resells them to the public; any unsold shares are the underwriter's problem, not the issuer's.

29. **C.** An investment banker is a broker-dealer acting to help an issuer raise money in the capital or money markets. In a firm commitment underwriting, the broker-dealer purchases the securities for resale. An investment banker is not a commercial bank and does not make loans.

30. **B.** A primary offering involves the sale of previously unissued securities. When the securities are sold for the first time (primary offering), the company receives the proceeds from the sale. Of course once the securities are sold, there will be more securities outstanding and in the hands of the public.

31. **D.** The broker-dealer can buy and sell securities as either an agent, charging a commission on a transaction and in which the broker-dealer is not at risk, or in the capacity of dealer, where the broker-dealer is at risk and compensation in the form of a markup or markdown is charged.

32. **A.** An exchange is an auction market in which securities listed on that exchange are traded. There is no minimum price for securities; rather, the highest price bid and the lowest price offered prevail. Trading activity on the exchanges as well as the OTC market is regulated by the Securities Exchange Act of 1934.

33. **D.** The New York Stock Exchange is an auction market, the OTC market is a negotiated market, the third market is the trading of exchange-listed securities over the counter, and all primary offerings are conducted OTC.

34. **C.** The OTC market is a negotiated market.

35. **A.** J&P is acting as a dealer and therefore is compensated by a markup on the offering price to the client. A markup and a commission cannot be charged on the same transaction. If the broker-dealer is acting as agent, he may charge a commission as a principal; he may take a markup.

36. **B.** The lowest offer and highest bid price prevail in the marketplace. Therefore, broker B's order would go first as it represents the lowest price at which the security can be purchased.

37. **C.** The purchaser of a stock buys at the offering price. The price quoted is 97 7/8, or $97.875.

38. **A.** Generally the narrower the spread between bid and ask in an over-the-counter security, the greater the marketability of the issue. Issues with a high degree of marketability are typically more active.

39. **D.** A secondary transaction is the redistribution of *outstanding* securities; the company does not receive the proceeds of the sale. The sale of authorized stock or a new issue is a primary offering.

40. **C.** A third market transaction is the sale of exchange-listed securities in the over-the-counter market.

41. **C.** With an all-or-none underwriting, no sales are final until the entire issue is sold. All-or-none is a form of best-efforts underwriting.

42. **C.** A customer confirmation must contain information on price, quantity, identity and commission or markup charged and must be sent by settlement. Broker-to-broker confirmations must be sent within 24 hours (the day of or the next day after the trade).

43. **A.** NASDAQ is available on three levels of service, but is primarily a method for obtaining information on prices (bid and ask) and inventories of OTC-traded securities.

44. **A.** A broker-dealer participating in a best-efforts underwriting is acting as an agent for the issuer. The issuer, not the broker-dealer, is at risk for unsold shares.

45. **C.** When an individual buys stock, that person owns it and has a long position; an individual selling stock owes it and has a short position.

46. **B.** Under federal law, Regulation T requires settlement on purchases within seven business days of the trade date. Industry practice is five business days from the trade date, allowing a broker-dealer two days to clear up settlement problems before federal law takes precedence.

47. **B.** A primary offering is the first time a security is sold; the issuer receives the money. A secondary transaction is the subsequent sale of previously outstanding securities; the seller receives the proceeds from the sale.

48. **A.** Under a best-efforts underwriting agreement, the underwriter is paid for only those shares it sells. The underwriter is acting as an agent for the issuer.

49. **B.** An underwriter standing by to sell unsold shares after a rights offering is participating in a standby underwriting. The underwriter receives payment for each right subscribed.

50. **B.** A fiduciary places the interest of a client before himself or herself.

51. **B.** The client is selling. The price paid is the bid price, or 32 1/4. The trade was completed, and the terms as of the trade date are locked in regardless of the price movements before settlement.

52. **C.** Market risk is a measure of how much the price of any given security will change when general interest rates change. The longer the security's maturity, the greater the change in its price will be for a given change in interest rates. Treasury bills have the shortest maturity of those securities listed (stocks, although they do not have an actual maturity date, are highly responsive to interest rate fluctuations).

53. **D.** Regular way settlement of government securities occurs the next business day.

54. **C.** The customer has 100 shares of stock purchased for a total of $2,500. After the 5% dividend he has 105 shares of stock with the same total cost basis of $2,500. Each share is now worth $2,500 divided by 105, for a basis of $23.81 per

share. The Internal Revenue Code requires that with stock splits or dividends the basis (or cost) of the stock has to be adjusted to reflect the new value of the shares.

55. **A.** When the term *broker* is used, it means that the firm is acting as an agent and is bringing a buyer and a seller together. Answers B and C describe a dealer.

56. **D.** SIPC insurance is figured by account ownership. George is covered for his $300,000 in securities, and his wife is covered for her $300,000 in securities. The joint account would be treated separately and would be covered for the $400,000 in securities. The total securities coverage for the two of them and their three accounts is $1,000,000. Insurance coverage per account is $500,000, no more than $100,000 of which can be in cash.

57. **B.** The growth fund will give the investor some protection from inflation, and we must assume that the specialty fund is a growth fund (historically, common stock is a better inflation hedge than fixed-income instruments). The other three answers are income-oriented funds.

58. **C.** Whenever the Federal Reserve changes a national policy or requirement (such as reserve requirements, margin requirements or the discount rate), the effect tends to be multiplied throughout the economy. If the reserve requirement is raised, money will be tightened because banks have to hold more in reserve, thus causing interest rates to rise; in turn, companies that borrow will have to raise prices.

59. **A.** When the economy is bad for six months (or two consecutive quarters), we are in a recession; if it continues, we would go into a depression.

60. **C.** The federal funds rate is what banks charge each other for overnight loans. It can fluctuate hourly.

61. **B.** *Matched orders* refers to orders of the same size being executed on the floor of the exchange (instead of a partial fill). The underwriter must exercise diligence in ensuring that the information in the prospectus is correct. The issue must be registered in the state (blue-skyed) to be sold within a state. Stabilization is the process of supporting the price of a new issue in the secondary market to insure a normal and systematic issue of the securities in the primary market.

62. **B.** Be careful to distinguish between a cash account and a cash transaction. Regular way settlement for a government bond is next business day. Most other securities settle regular way on the fifth business day.

63. **D.** The SEC says that broker-dealers must reconcile any dispute as it relates to settlements within 30 calendar days. This is part of SEC Rule 15c3-3 of the Securities Exchange Act of 1934.

64. **D.** The trader has responded to a quote for a specific size.

65. **B.** If the cost of borrowing funds is increasing, members will need to keep more of their own funds available.

66. **B.** If inventories are going up, it is generally taken as an indication that sales are going down.

67. **D.** The gain would be $50 for the bonds (1/2 point for one bond is $5 times 10 bonds) and $100 for the common stock (1/2 point is $.50 times 200 shares).

4 Mutual Funds

1. Which of the following statements about open-end investment companies are true?

   I. They may constantly issue new shares.
   II. They redeem shares at any time.
   III. They may leverage common shares by issuing bonds.

   A. I and II only
   B. I and III only
   C. II and III only
   D. I, II and III

2. Mutual fund shares represent an undivided interest in the fund. This means that

   A. investors can purchase only full shares
   B. the fund can hold securities of certain companies only
   C. the number of shares outstanding is limited to a predetermined maximum
   D. each investor owns a proportional part of every portfolio security

3. Mary Bjorkman owns 150 shares of Cosmo Mutual Fund. Which of the following statements are true?

   I. When a dividend is declared by the fund, she will receive a cash dividend for each share owned.
   II. She will have difficulty liquidating her shares.
   III. The amount of her dividend will reflect her proportional interest in the value of the fund portfolio on the record date.
   IV. She will receive dividends from only 150 shares of stock held in the fund portfolio.

   A. I and III
   B. I, II and IV
   C. II and III
   D. II, III and IV

4. After doing some research, Doug Newton concluded that the electronics industry will probably be very successful in the next ten years. He wants to invest in the industry, but does not want to limit his investments to a few companies. Doug should invest in a

   A. bond fund
   B. money market fund
   C. hedge fund
   D. specialized fund

5. Last year the bond market was very profitable, and Cosmo Fund had 70% of its assets in bonds. Next year the fund's managers expect the stock market to do well, and they adjust the fund's portfolio so that 60% will be invested in stock. Cosmo is probably a(n)

   A. balanced fund
   B. hedge fund
   C. specialized fund
   D. aggressive growth fund

6. Allied Fund pays regular dividends, offers a high degree of safety of principal and especially appeals to investors seeking tax advantages. Allied is a(n)

   A. corporate bond fund
   B. money market fund
   C. aggressive growth fund
   D. municipal bond fund

7. According to the Investment Company Act of 1940, what is the maximum percentage of a corporation's voting securities that a mutual fund may hold?

   A. 5%
   B. 10%
   C. 50%
   D. 75%

8. According to the Investment Company Act of 1940, what is the minimum amount of net assets a fund must have before it can sell shares to the public?

   A. $10,000
   B. $100,000
   C. $500,000
   D. $1,000,000

9. Mutual funds are like other types of corporations in that

   I. they may issue equity and debt
   II. the board of directors makes policy decisions
   III. shareholders have ownership rights

   A. I and III only
   B. II only
   C. II and III only
   D. I, II and III

10. LFS Investment Services charges a fee for its services in managing several mutual funds. Which of the following would be included in the services LFS supplies?

   I. Ensuring that the fund portfolio meets diversification requirements
   II. Attempting to meet the investment objectives of the fund
   III. Analyzing the market and deciding when securities in the portfolio should be bought or sold
   IV. Changing investment objectives in order to maximize potential gain for the shareholders

   A. I, II and III only
   B. II only
   C. II and III only
   D. I, II, III and IV

11. Jennifer King is explaining mutual funds to a prospective investor. Which of the following statements could she use in her conversation with the client?

   I. Mutual fund shares are liquid, so an investor can use them as either short-term or long-term investments.

   II. The fund will always redeem shares at NAV, so there is very little chance of a financial loss.

   III. The redemption value of the shares fluctuates according to the value of the fund's portfolio.

   IV. Because mutual funds are required to make payment within seven days of redemption, you will always be able to receive a return of your original investment.

   A. I, II and IV
   B. I and III
   C. III
   D. III and IV

12. A client comes to you for advice regarding the investment companies in which he should invest. You might tell him to check the

   I. investment company's investment policy
   II. investment company's track record
   III. investment company's portfolio
   IV. sales load

   A. I, II and III only
   B. I and III only
   C. I and IV only
   D. I, II, III and IV

13. Sales literature for a mutual fund must

   A. promise delivery of a prospectus when the shares are delivered to the purchaser
   B. contain a warning that the SEC supervision of the company does not guarantee against a decrease in the market value of the shares
   C. be preceded or accompanied by a prospectus
   D. contain the statement "A prospectus relating to these securities is available upon request"

14. An issuer who sells mutual funds that have been registered under the Securities Act of 1933 is allowed to make which of the following statements?

   A. The securities have been approved by the SEC.
   B. The SEC has passed on the accuracy of the information contained in the prospectus.
   C. The SEC has passed on the adequacy of the information contained in the prospectus.
   D. The securities offered are registered with the SEC.

15. Sales literature and advertising material that have been prepared by the firm's principal underwriter and are to be used by a member firm in connection with the offering of investment company shares must be reviewed by the

   I. firm's advertising manager
   II. NASD
   III. SEC

   A. I
   B. I and II
   C. II
   D. II and III

16. To register new securities, an investment company must

    I. supply detailed information about itself to the SEC
    II. supply detailed information about the securities to be offered to the SEC
    III. obtain the SEC's approval of the issue

    A. I and II only
    B. I and III only
    C. II and III only
    D. I, II and III

17. An open-end investment company may do all of the following EXCEPT

    A. continuously offer shares
    B. borrow money
    C. lend money
    D. issue bonds

18. The Investment Company Act of 1940 allows closed-end investment companies which of the following privileges not allowed open-end investment companies?

    A. Issuing preferred stock
    B. Issuing only voting stock
    C. Borrowing money from a bank
    D. All of the above

19. An open-end investment company wishes to change its investment objective. It may do so only with a

    A. majority vote of the outstanding shares
    B. majority vote of the outstanding shareholders
    C. two-thirds vote of the outstanding shareholders
    D. unanimous vote of the board of directors

20. An open-end investment company must maintain what percentage of net assets to debt?

    A. 33 1/3%
    B. 50%
    C. 100%
    D. 300%

21. The Deluxe Fund, a diversified investment company, has a net asset value of $225 million. Deluxe wishes to invest in the Putman Company. Putman stock is selling at $30 a share, and there are 100,000 shares outstanding. The maximum number of Putman shares Deluxe Fund could buy and still be diversified is

    A. 5,000
    B. 10,000
    C. $12,500 worth
    D. $11,250,000 worth

22. The Investment Company Act of 1940 requires

    A. a statement of investment policy
    B. $100,000 minimum capitalization
    C. that 40% of the directors must be persons who are neither officers nor investment advisors of the company
    D. all of the above

23. Which of the following would probably be found in the portfolio of a money market fund?

    I. T bills
    II. T bonds with a short time to maturity
    III. Bank certificates of deposit
    IV. Common stock

    A. I only
    B. I and II only
    C. I, II and III only
    D. I, II, III and IV

24. A regulated, diversified investment company cannot own more than what percentage of the outstanding shares of any one company (the target company)?

    A. 2%
    B. 5%
    C. 8%
    D. 10%

25. An investment company share that is purchased at its net asset value and can be later
redeemed at the then current net asset value
is a share from a company known as a(n)

    A. open-end investment company
    B. closed-end investment company
    C. front-end load company
    D. no-load open-end investment company

26. Under what circumstances could a mutual
fund temporarily suspend the redemption
provision?

    I. If the New York Stock Exchange is
       closed other than customary weekends
       and holidays
    II. If permitted by the SEC
    III. If an emergency condition exists and
       then only with SEC approval
    IV. At the discretion of the investment com-
       pany management

    A. I, II and III only
    B. II and III only
    C. II, III and IV only
    D. I, II, III and IV

27. To be considered a diversified investment
company, the company must be invested as
follows (SEC definition).

    A. At least 25% of the fund's assets must be
       invested in one industry.
    B. The fund must be invested in at least 20
       different industries.
    C. 75% of the assets must be invested with
       no more than 5% in any one company
       representing not more than 10% of that
       company's stock.
    D. The fund must be invested in both
       stocks and bonds.

28. An announcement of a new issue of a
security that gives the name of the issuer, the
price and the name of the underwriter is
called a(n)

    A. prospectus
    B. offering memorandum
    C. red herring
    D. tombstone advertisement

29. Which of the following would be classified
as an investment company?

    I. Closed-end company
    II. Open-end company
    III. Qualified plan company
    IV. Nonqualified plan company
    V. Fixed annuity company

    A. I and II
    B. I, II and V
    C. II
    D. III, IV and V

30. Where can closed-end investment company
shares be purchased and sold?

    A. In the secondary marketplace
    B. From the closed-end company
    C. In the primary market
    D. All of the above

31. In a mutual fund, the amount of increases
and/or decreases in the NAV over the past
years can be reviewed in the

    A. official statement
    B. customer account form
    C. prospectus
    D. tombstone

32. How does a no-load fund sell its shares to
the public?

    A. Through a network of underwriters and
       dealers
    B. Through a dealer and its sales repre-
       sentatives
    C. By underwriter only
    D. By a direct sale from the fund to the
       investor

33. An investor who owns shares of a mutual fund actually owns

    A. an undivided interest in the fund's debt capitalization
    B. specific shares of stock in the fund's portfolio
    C. an undivided interest in the fund's portfolio
    D. certain unspecified securities among those owned by the fund

34. Which of the following statements describe(s) an open-end investment company?

    A. It can sell new shares in any quantity at any time.
    B. It must redeem shares in any quantity within seven days of request.
    C. It provides for mutual ownership of portfolio assets by shareholders.
    D. All of the above describe an open-end company.

35. When examining the portfolio of a diversified common stock fund, you would most likely find

    A. all growth stocks within one particular industry
    B. stocks of many companies, within many industries
    C. mostly convertible bonds and other debt instruments
    D. There is no telling what you would find.

36. All of the following statements concerning investment companies are true EXCEPT

    A. a nondiversified company is any management company not classified as a diversified company
    B. to be considered a diversified investment company, the company must invest at least 75% of its total assets in cash and/or securities
    C. an investment company that invests the majority of its assets in one company or industry is considered a nondiversified company
    D. a diversified company can be only an open-end investment company

37. Which of the following statements best describes a balanced fund

    A. It has some portion of its portfolio invested in both debt and equity instruments at all times.
    B. It has equal amounts of common stock and corporate bonds at all times.
    C. It normally has equal amounts of common and preferred stock at all times.
    D. None of the above describes a balanced fund.

38. All the following are advantages of mutual fund investment EXCEPT

    A. the investor retains personal control of his or her investment in the mutual fund portfolio
    B. exchange privileges within a family of funds managed by the same management company
    C. the ability to invest almost any amount at any time
    D. the ability to qualify for reduced sales loads based on accumulation of investment within the fund

39. According to the Investment Company Act of 1940

    I. a company must have $1,000,000 in assets before it may begin operations
    II. at least 40% of the board of directors may not be affiliated or hold a position with the fund
    III. the fund must have at least 100 shareholders
    IV. the fund may not borrow more than 33 1/3% of its asset value

    A. I and III only
    B. II, III and IV only
    C. II and IV only
    D. I, II, III and IV

40. Which of the following investments would provide high appreciation potential together with high risk?

    A. Balanced fund
    B. Bond fund
    C. Income fund
    D. Sector fund

41. Which of the following is(are) characteristics of money market funds?

    I.   Portfolio of short-term debt instruments
    II. High beta
    III. Offered without a sales load
    IV. Fixed NAV

    A. I only
    B. I, II and IV only
    C. I, III and IV only
    D. I, II, III and IV

◆ Answers & Rationale

1. A. An open-end company must stand ready to redeem shares within seven days of receiving a customer's request and may continuously offer its shares for sale. Although an open-end company may invest in just about any security, it may issue only one class of voting stock. The company cannot issue any type of debt.

2. D. A mutual fund shareholder owns an undivided interest in the portfolio of the investment company. Because each share represents one class of voting stock, the investor's interest in the fund reflects the number of shares owned.

3. A. A mutual fund share represents an undivided interest in the fund's portfolio. If a dividend is declared, the shareholder receives a dividend for each mutual fund share held. Dividends are paid in cash unless the investor elects to reinvest the cash distribution for the purchase of more fund shares.

4. D. A specialized fund will invest all its assets in a particular type of security or a specific industry.

5. A. This fund is invested in both stock and bonds; it is likely to be a balanced fund. The percentage invested in the two types of securities will be adjusted to maximize the yield that can be obtained. The percentages are seldom fixed.

6. D. Municipal bonds (general obligation) offer safety considered second only to U.S. government securities. Additionally the interest received from the bonds is exempt from federal income tax. The tax-exempt nature of the distributions is a big advantage for the investor in a high tax bracket.

7. B. To be considered a diversified investment company, a mutual fund can own no more than 10% of the voting securities of a target company. Additionally no investment company may have more than 5% of its portfolio invested in the securities of a company, regardless of its classification.

8. B. Before operations can begin, an investment company must have a net capital of at least $100,000. Thereafter the net capital can fluctuate.

9. C. Mutual funds may issue only one class of voting stock. Like corporate stockholders, mutual fund shareholders do have various rights, one of which is the right to elect the board of directors, which sets policies for the fund.

10. A. The objective of the mutual fund may be changed only by a majority vote of the outstanding shares. The fund manager is assigned the day-to-day management responsibilities of the fund. Duties would include attempting to meet the objective as set out by the fund and buying and selling securities to be held in the portfolio.

11. C. Mutual funds are very marketable, but because of the sales charge, they are recommended for long-term investments. Shares are redeemed at NAV. However, the NAV will fluctuate, and upon redemption the investor may have more or less money than originally invested.

12. D. All of these elements listed should be disclosed when comparing funds.

13. C. All sales literature or advertising used in connection with the solicitation of mutual fund shares must be accompanied or preceded by the prospectus.

14. D. The SEC only releases a security for sale; it neither approves nor disapproves of the use, nor does it pass on the accuracy or adequacy of the information contained in the prospectus. A disclaimer regarding this fact must be on the front page of the prospectus.

15. C. All sales literature used in connection with a new offering must be filed for review with the NASD. A principal of the firm must approve its use and is responsible for corrections required by the NASD.

16. A. The SEC does not approve anything. The registration statement and prospectus filed with the SEC must disclose all material facts of the issuer and the security being issued.

17. **D.** A mutual fund is prohibited from issuing any senior securities, although it may purchase just about any type of security as an investment. All shares of a mutual fund must be of the same class.

18. **A.** A closed-end company may issue different classes of securities: common stock, preferred stock and bonds. An open-end company may issue only one class of stock.

19. **A.** The Investment Company Act of 1940 requires the fund to have a clearly defined investment objective. The only action that can be taken to change the investment objective is a majority vote of the outstanding shares (shares vote, not shareholders).

20. **D.** The Investment Company Act of 1940 prohibits a mutual fund from borrowing more than one-third of its net asset value. In other words, the fund must maintain at least 300% assets to debt.

21. **B.** A diversified investment company has at least 75% of its assets invested so that no more than 5% of its assets own more than 10% of a company's stock. In this question, 5% of the Deluxe Fund's assets could purchase the entire Putman Company. Therefore, the Deluxe Fund is limited to only 10% of the Putman Company's stock, or 10,000 shares.

22. **D.** The Investment Company Act of 1940 requires a mutual fund to have an initial capitalization of $100,000, at least 100 shareholders and a clearly defined investment objective. Additionally, the interlocking directorate rules state that at least 40% of the fund's directors must be independent from the operations of the fund.

23. **C.** Money market instruments are considered short-term, very liquid debt instruments. Because common stock is equity, it would not be in a money market fund.

24. **D.** To be considered a diversified investment company, the fund's portfolio must be invested to at least 75% so that no more than 5% of the *assets* own no more than 10% of a company's outstanding *stock*. Remember: 75% invested, 5% assets, 10% stock.

25. **D.** A share purchased at its NAV and sold at its NAV is a no-load fund. NAV plus the sales charge equals the POP; if there is no sales charge, the NAV equals the POP.

26. **A.** The seven-day redemption guideline is law and may be suspended only with SEC permission or if the NYSE is closed on a day other than customary holidays or weekends.

27. **C.** A diversified investment company is a company whose assets are invested 75% so that 5% of its assets own no more than 10% of a target company's outstanding stock. Another way to look at this is that the fund must be invested in at least 15 different companies.

28. **D.** The announcement that a new issue is being offered that includes the name of the issuer, the price of the security and the name of the underwriter from whom it can be purchased is a tombstone advertisement.

29. **A.** Open and closed end funds are classified as investment companies. Plan companies offer plans in which an investment company may be selected as an investment vehicle, but are not investment companies themselves. Fixed annuities are offered by insurance companies only.

30. **A.** A closed-end company share is bought *and sold* in the secondary marketplace.

31. **C.** Changes in NAV (history) will be found in the prospectus for at least ten years if the fund has existed that long.

32. **D.** Because there is no load, there is no underwriter. The fund makes sales directly to the public.

33. **C.** Each shareholder owns an undivided (mutual) interest in the portfolio of the mutual fund.

34. **D.** An open-end investment company can sell any quantity of new shares, redeem shares within seven days and provide for mutual ownership of portfolio assets by shareholders.

35. **B.** A diversified common stock fund will have stocks from many companies and many industries.

36. **D.** A diversified company could be either a closed-end company or an open-end company.

37. **A.** Balanced funds carry both equity and debt issues. It is not necessary to maintain an equal amount of these issues.

38. **A.** The control of the investment is given over to the investment manager. All of the other items mentioned are considered advantages.

39. **B.** A company must have commitments for at least $100,000 in assets before it begins. All of the other items listed are true.

40. **D.** A sector fund offers a higher appreciation potential (coupled with higher risk) than an income-oriented fund.

41. **C.** Money-market mutual funds invest in a portfolio of short-term debt instruments such as T bills, commercial paper and repos. They are offered without a sales load or charge. The principal objective of the fund is to generate current interest income, and generally the NAV does not appreciate.

5   Mutual Funds—Management

1. Usually the fee received by the management company from an investment company depends on the

   A. net assets of the fund
   B. profit of the fund
   C. volume of new shares sold
   D. type of securities in the fund portfolio

2. The money holder of a mutual fund's account would generally be a

   A. commercial bank
   B. investment banker
   C. savings and loan association
   D. stock exchange member

3. The investment advisor's contract must be approved by the

   A. board of governors of the NASD
   B. SEC
   C. NASD district committee
   D. board of directors of the fund and the shareholders

4. The investment advisor in a regulated, diversified open-end investment company will perform which of the following functions?

   I. Make sure the fund invests in such a manner as to retain its diversified status
   II. Attempt to fulfill the fund's investment objective through careful investing
   III. Change investment objectives as he or she believes is in the best interest of the investors
   IV. Investigate the tax status of potential investments

   A. I, II and III
   B. I, II and IV
   C. II and IV
   D. III and IV

5. The price for shares purchased from an underwriter by a dealer is the

   A. public offering price
   B. offering price less the underwriter's concession
   C. NAV plus the underwriter's concession
   D. NAV plus the dealer's allowance

6. When can an investment advisor of a mutual fund liquidate shares held in the portfolio of the mutual fund?

   A. Only with the consent of a majority vote of the mutual fund shareholders
   B. Only with the consent of the investment company board of directors
   C. At any time as long as the liquidation is within the guidelines set forth by the investment company objective
   D. Both A and B

7. June Kaslov wants to buy $1,000 worth of an open-end investment company. She may buy shares through

    I.   the sponsor of the fund
   II.   a brokerage firm
  III.   the custodian of the fund
  IV.   a bank acting as dealer

    A. I and II
    B. I, II and IV
    C. II
    D. III and IV

8. The principal underwriter of an open-end investment company is also known as the

    A. sponsor
    B. dealer
    C. trustee
    D. registrar

9. Which of the following has the authority to approve an investment advisor's contract with the investment company?

    A. NASD District Business Conduct Committee
    B. Board of directors of the fund
    C. Board of governors of the NASD
    D. SEC

10. The management fee for investment companies is usually

    A. .25% of the average gross assets
    B. .5% of the average net assets
    C. based solely on the amount of profit the portfolio generates
    D. none of the above

11. The investment policy of a mutual fund can be changed by a majority vote of the

    A. board of directors
    B. fund's managers
    C. SEC investment committee
    D. outstanding shares

12. One of the members of the board of directors of the Ace open-end diversified investment company owns 3% of all the outstanding voting stock of the XYZ Company. Ace investment company

    A. can invest in XYZ as long as it purchases no more than 3% of the company's voting stock
    B. can invest in XYZ if the director sells off two-thirds of his or her holdings
    C. can invest as long as XYZ purchases an equal amount of Ace investment company shares
    D. cannot invest in the XYZ Company

◆ Answers & Rationale

1. A. The management company usually receives a fee based on the average annual net assets of the fund managed.

2. A. The money holder of a mutual fund is its custodian. In most instances, the custodian will be a commercial bank.

3. D. The investment advisor's contract is approved annually by the board of directors and/or a majority vote of the outstanding shares (shareholders).

4. B. The investment advisor is responsible for making investments according to the objective stipulated by the fund. The fund's objective may be changed only with a majority vote of the outstanding shares.

5. C. A dealer purchasing shares from a fund underwriter would pay the current NAV plus the underwriter's concession.

6. C. The investment advisor is given authority to select and make investments in the mutual fund portfolio. The fund must follow the advisor's advice.

7. A. The custodian does not sell the shares, but holds them for safekeeping. A bank cannot be a member of the NASD and therefore cannot act as a dealer (although subsidiaries independent of the bank may be set up as broker-dealers).

8. A. The term *sponsor* is synonymous with the term *underwriter*.

9. B. The investment advisor's contract is approved by the board of directors of the fund and often a majority vote of the outstanding fund shares. An investment advisor must be registered with, not approved by, the SEC.

10. B. The management fee for an investment company is usually around 1/2 of 1% of the average net assets of the fund.

11. D. Any changes in a mutual fund's investment policies must be made by a majority vote of the fund's outstanding shares.

12. D. Because the director owns more than 1/2 of 1% of stock in XYZ Company, the investment company cannot invest in XYZ stock. Selling two-thirds of the director's holdings will not get him down to this amount. XYZ Company could buy Ace if it decided to.

6 Mutual Funds—Pricing and Valuation

1. If an investor is redeeming 200 shares in the Cosmo Fund and the current POP is $12.50 and the NAV is $11.50, the investor would receive

   A. $2,200
   B. $2,300
   C. $2,400
   D. $2,500

2. If the value of securities held in a fund's portfolio increases and the amount of liabilities stays the same, what will happen to the net assets of the fund?

   A. They will increase.
   B. They will decrease.
   C. They will stay the same.
   D. Appreciation of assets has no effect on the net asset value of a fund.

3. The Consolidated Fund experienced an unrealized loss last month. This loss will

   I. result in a lower NAV per share
   II. mean lower dividend payments to shareholders
   III. reduce the proceeds payable to shareholders who liquidate their shares

   A. I and II only
   B. I and III only
   C. II and III only
   D. I, II and III

4. The public offering price of a mutual fund share equals

   A. bid price minus dividends
   B. bid price plus sales charge
   C. portfolio assets minus liabilities
   D. NAV minus sales charge

5. DEF Mutual Fund has an NAV of $8, a sales charge of $.50 and an underwriter's concession of $.30. An investor with $3,000 could purchase how many DEF shares?

   A. 340
   B. 353
   C. 375
   D. 400

6. Dave Fisher owns 200 shares of Acme Growth Fund, which has a POP of $12 and an NAV of $11. He wants to convert these shares to Acme Balanced Fund, which has a POP of $14.77 and an NAV of $13.66. Acme offers a conversion privilege. How many shares will Dave receive?

   A. 148
   B. 161
   C. 162
   D. 176

7. The price of closed-end investment company shares is determined by the

   A. board of directors
   B. going price in the marketplace
   C. net asset value plus the sales charge
   D. majority vote of the shareholders

8. An investor selling shares of a closed-end investment company will receive

A. the net asset value next calculated after receipt of the investor's redemption request
B. whatever the fund can get by selling the shares in the secondary market
C. the lowest ask price on the market
D. the highest bid price on the market

9. John Jones has been looking in the paper at several investment company quotes. He notices that the XYZ Fund has an NAV of $12 and a POP of $12.50. He also notices that the ABC Fund has an NAV of $11.50 and a POP of $10.98. John can conclude that

A. both funds are probably open-end funds, whereas
B. ABC is probably an open-end fund, whereas XYZ is likely to be a closed-end fund
C. XYZ is probably an open-end fund, whereas ABC is likely to be a closed-end fund
D. ABC and XYZ are both unit investment trusts

10. The price paid by the investor for open-end investment company shares is the

A. bid price
B. net asset value plus the sales load
C. net asset value plus the investment advertising fee
D. price in the financial section of the newspaper

11. Although alternatives are available to a mutual fund issuer regarding the details of redemption procedures, the issuer must, by law

A. make payment for shares within seven days of tender
B. inform the investor of his loss or profit
C. redeem shares at the net asset value
D. redeem shares at the net asset value minus the sales charge

12. The XYZ Fund has a net asset value per share of $8.10. XYZ pays its underwriter a concession of $.10 per share. It has a $.70 per-share sales load and an administrative fee of $.20 per share. How much per share will the investor pay?

A. $8.80
B. $8.90
C. $9.00
D. $9.10

13. The payment to a mutual fund investor redeeming shares is based on which of the following?

A. The previous NAV price on the day the shares are received for redemption
B. The previous public offering price on the day the shares are received for redemption
C. The next computed NAV price after the shares are received for redemption
D. The next computed public offering price on the day the shares are received for redemption

14. Which of the following will increase the per-share net asset value of a mutual fund?

A. Dividend income paid out to investors
B. Realized long-term capital gains, which the investor decides to invest in the purchase of more shares of the fund
C. Unrealized appreciation
D. None of the above

15. The net asset value of the Trivia Fund is $14.17. The public offering price is $15.32. To calculate the sales charge based on the cost of the fund shares, you would perform which of the following calculations?

A. Divide $1.15 by $14.17
B. Divide $1.15 by $15.32
C. Divide $14.17 by $15.32
D. Divide $15.32 by $14.17

16. A mutual fund shareholder purchased some shares at the beginning of an investment period and at the end of the investment period sold the shares for a gain. Which of the following is true?

    A. The NAV per share was lower at the beginning.
    B. The NAV per share was higher at the beginning.
    C. The total assets of the fund could have been higher or lower at the beginning, depending on the securities held in the portfolio.
    D. The expenses of the fund were lower at the end than at the beginning.

17. When an individual orders mutual fund shares, the price she will pay is

    A. determined by supply and demand
    B. calculated within seven business days
    C. the last offering price of the investment company
    D. the next offering price of the investment company

18. While deciding which investment company you should invest in, you notice one that had a net asset value on January 1st, 1991, of $16 a share, and on January 1st, 1992, of $17.50 a share. You also notice that during that year, the asking price declined by over $1 per share. The investment company must be a(n)

    A. closed-end investment company
    B. open-end investment company
    C. specialized company
    D. It is not possible to tell from the information given.

19. An open-end investment company called the Superb Fund closed March 9th at $20 NAV and $21.40 offering price. The prospectus shows the cost of buying the fund for quantities of $25,000 through $49,999 to be 4%. How many full shares can a customer buy for $35,000?

    A. 1,600
    B. 1,635
    C. 1,680
    D. 1,750

20. A financial writer writing comments about a company's stock notes that the offering price is a 22% discount from the NAV. From this information, you would most likely conclude that the company the writer is referring to must be a(n)

    A. open-end investment company
    B. closed-end investment company
    C. contractual plan of a mutual fund
    D. It's not a company at all. The writer is probably referring to Series EE savings bonds.

21. When selling shares of a mutual fund, the broker-dealer may sell shares

    A. at the offering price shown in the current prospectus
    B. at or above the current offering price as shown in the prospectus
    C. at or below the offering price shown in the current prospectus
    D. at a price the broker-dealer can negotiate according to the supply and demand for the shares

22. When referring to the *spread* in a mutual fund, you are referring to

    A. the difference between the bid and the ask
    B. the difference between the net asset value and the public offering price
    C. the salesperson's commission only
    D. a no-load fund

23. You notice that the total assets of Wondra, a regulated open-end investment company, went down 28% last year. You also notice that the stock in which Wondra deposited its capital did very well. Lastly, you notice that Wondra holds a large number of bonds. Which two of the following most likely occurred?

    I. Wondra was holding too much cash.
    II. Interest rates went up.
    III. Wondra paid huge commissions to agents for their extra sales effort.
    IV. A large number of Wondra shares were redeemed.

    A. I and II
    B. I and III
    C. II and III
    D. II and IV

24. Under which of the following circumstances are mutual funds prohibited from charging the full 8.5% sales load?

    A. The fund does permit automatic reinvestment of dividend distributions at the NAV per share.
    B. The fund does not permit automatic reinvestment of dividend distributions at the NAV per share.
    C. The fund requires minimum investments of $1,000,000 at a time.
    D. Mutual funds are permitted to charge 8.5% under any circumstances.

25. On the repurchase of shares, the shares are redeemed at

    A. a price stipulated by the broker-dealer
    B. a price stipulated by the registered representative
    C. the price next calculated by the fund after receipt of the order
    D. the current price of the fund

26. The NAV of mutual fund shares is priced

    A. daily
    B. monthly
    C. annually
    D. whenever the number of shares outstanding increases

27. Which of the following statements about sales charges is(are) true?

    I. Under NASD rules, mutual fund sales charges may not exceed 8.5% of the offering price.
    II. Under NASD rules, mutual fund sales charges may not exceed 8.5% of the share's net asset value.
    III. An investment company must offer rights of accumulation, breakpoints and reinvestment of dividends at NAV in order to charge an 8.5% sales charge.
    IV. Under the Investment Company Act of 1940, the maximum sales charge for purchases of mutual fund shares is 9%.

    A. I
    B. I and III
    C. I, III and IV
    D. II, III and IV

28. If a customer submits a repurchase order to his broker-dealer after the close of the New York Stock Exchange, the customer will receive a price based on the net asset value computed

    A. the previous business day
    B. the same day regardless of when the order is received
    C. the next time the firm computes it
    D. within the next two business days

29. A customer decides to buy shares of an open-end investment company. When is the price of the shares determined?

    A. At the next calculation of net asset value the day the fund custodian receives proper notification from the client
    B. At the next calculation of net asset value the day the broker-dealer wires the custodian on behalf of the client
    C. Both A and B
    D. Neither A nor B

30. You have decided to buy 100 shares of the BMK Mutual Fund, which prices its shares at 5:00 pm every business day. You turn in your order at 3:00 pm when the shares are priced at $10 NAV, $10.86 POP. The sales load is 7.9%. What will your 100 shares cost?

    A. $1,000
    B. $1,079
    C. $1,086
    D. 100 times the offering price, which will be calculated at 5:00 pm

31. When comparing definitions in the stock market and mutual funds, the bid price is similar to the NAV and the ask price is similar to the

    A. net asset value
    B. sales load
    C. public offering price
    D. current market value

32. John Jones is redeeming 1,000 shares of the HCW Mutual Fund. John has submitted his request for redemption, which HCW receives at noon. HCW prices its shares at the close of the NYSE each day, at which time the shares are priced at $12.50 NAV, $13.50 ask. HCW also charges a 1% redemption fee. John will receive what amount for his shares?

    A. $12,375
    B. $12,500
    C. $13,365
    D. $13,500

33. The price of closed-end investment company shares is determined by

    A. supply and demand
    B. the New York Stock Exchange
    C. the board of directors
    D. the net asset value plus the sales charge

34. The offering price of the HQ Fund is $9, and its net asset value is $9.40. The offering price of the Shieko Fund is $23.80, and its net asset value is $19.45. From these quotes you know that

    I. HQ is an open-end fund
    II. HQ is a closed-end fund
    III. Shieko is an open-end fund
    IV. Shieko is a closed-end fund

    A. I and III
    B. I and IV
    C. II and III
    D. II and IV

35. Customers would pay a commission, rather than a sales charge, for which of the following?

    A. Shares of a no-load fund
    B. Shares of an open-end investment company
    C. Shares of a mutual fund
    D. Shares of a closed-end investment company

36. John Jameson has $800 to invest in the XYZ Mutual Fund. If the shares are currently priced at $21.22 each, John will be able to purchase

    A. 37 shares and $14.85 in change
    B. 37.7 shares
    C. 38 shares
    D. no shares because the minimum trading unit is 100 shares

37. The NAV of an open-end investment company

    I.   is calculated seven days a week
   II. is calculated as stipulated in the prospectus
 III. takes into account cash held by the fund but not invested
 IV. when divided by the number of shares outstanding equals the net asset value per share

 A. I and IV
 B. II, III and IV
 C. II and IV
 D. IV

38. The net asset value per share of a mutual fund will fluctuate in value relative to the

 A. value of the fund's portfolio
 B. law of supply and demand
 C. number of shareholders
 D. S&P 500 market index

39. Which of the following characteristics describe the net asset value per share?

    I.   Increases if the assets of the fund appreciate in value
   II. Decreases if the fund distributes a dividend to shareholders
 III. Decreases when shares are redeemed
 IV. Increases if shareholders reinvest dividend and capital gains distributions

 A. I and II
 B. I and III
 C. II and III
 D. II and IV

40. Typically, a no-load mutual fund company sells to the public in which of the following manners?

 A. The fund sells directly to the investor.
 B. The fund sells to a plan company, which in turn sells to the investor.
 C. The fund sells to a dealer who in turn sells to the investor.
 D. The public may only purchase no-load mutual fund shares through a federal bank.

41. Tim Marcus has $15,000 that he wants to invest in a mutual fund. The Hathaway Fund has an NAV of $15 per share and a sales charge of $1.20 per share. There is an underwriter's concession of $.08 per share and a management fee of .5%. How many full shares can Tim buy of the Hathaway Fund?

 A. 880
 B. 921
 C. 925
 D. 1,000

42. The net asset value of a mutual fund is $9.30. If its sales charge is 7%, then its offering price is

 A. $9.95
 B. $9.97
 C. $10
 D. $10.70

43. If a mutual fund charges an 8 1/2% sales charge, all of the following must be offered by the fund EXCEPT

 A. exchange privileges
 B. breakpoints
 C. rights of accumulation
 D. dividend reinvestment at net asset value

44. A mutual fund's expense ratio is its

 A. expenses divided by average net assets
 B. expenses divided by public offering price
 C. expenses divided by income
 D. expenses divided by dividends

45. A mutual fund has an NAV of $13.37. An investor was charged a 4% sales charge on a lump-sum purchase of $50,000. How many shares were purchased?

 A. 3,422
 B. 3,564
 C. 3,589
 D. 3,595

◆ Answers & Rationale

1. B. Shares are redeemed at NAV. If an investor is redeeming 200 shares at an NAV of $11.50, the investor would receive $2,300 (200 × $11.50).

2. A. Appreciation in value of fund assets without an attendant increase in liabilities would lead to an increase in the fund's net asset value (Assets – Liabilities = NAV).

3. B. An unrealized loss is the same as a depreciation in asset value, which results in a lower NAV per share. An investor would receive less at redemption than he would have received if redemption took place prior to the depreciation of the asset.

4. B. The public offering price is the bid price or NAV plus the sales charge added.

5. B. An investor purchasing shares buys at the POP. POP is NAV plus the sales charge. The underwriter's concession is part of the sales charge of $.50. Therefore, the POP is equal to $8.50 ($8.00 + $.50). By dividing $3,000 by $8.50, we get 353 shares.

6. B. Acme apparently offers conversion privileges. Therefore, conversion occurs at net asset value. Dave's value in the growth fund is equal to $2,200 (200 × $11) divided by the NAV of the income fund ($13.66), which gives him 161 shares.

7. B. The price for closed-end companies is determined by supply and demand in the marketplace.

8. D. Again, the price for closed-end companies is determined by supply and demand. The price an investor would receive for redeeming shares would be the highest bid available.

9. C. The price for open-end funds is determined by adding the sales charge to the NAV. An open-end fund can never have a POP less than its NAV. ABC cannot be an open-end fund. Most closed-end funds sell at a discount to their net asset value because the only way the NAV can be received is by liquidating the fund. Unit trusts are not quoted in the press.

10. B. The price paid for mutual fund shares is the public offering price, which is calculated by adding the sales charge to the NAV.

11. A. The Investment Company Act of 1940 requires an open-end investment company to redeem shares upon request within seven days from receipt of the request.

12. A. The public offering price is equal to the net asset value plus the sales charge. In this case: $8.10 + $.70 = $8.80. The other fees are already part of either the sales charge or the NAV.

13. C. Redemption of mutual fund shares is based on the net asset value of the shares calculated at the price next determined after receipt of the mutual fund shares (forward pricing).

14. C. The net asset value of a mutual fund is increased by appreciation of securities held in the portfolio. For example, if IBM held by the fund increases from $100 a share to $110 a share, this increase will be reflected in the NAV of the fund. Dividends paid out or dividend and gains distributions reinvested (the money purchases more shares, diluting the per-share value) result in a lower NAV per-share value.

15. B. To calculate the percentage of sales charge, the difference between the NAV and the public offering price is divided by the POP. Sales charges are a percentage of the POP.

16. A. For an investor to have realized a gain on the sale of the mutual fund shares, the net asset value of the shares would have been lower at the initial purchase compared to the NAV at the sale of the fund shares.

17. **D.** The price for mutual fund shares for redemption or purchase is always the price *next* computed after receipt of the order. Mutual funds use *forward pricing*.

18. **A.** Because the asking price for the company has declined at the same time the NAV per share has increased, the asking price is influenced by supply and demand for the shares in the marketplace. The company must be a closed-end investment company. Because the calculation for the asking price of an open-end company is NAV plus the sales charge, if the company in question had been an open-end company, the asking price would have increased.

19. **C.** Subtract the sales charge from the amount invested and invest at net asset value:

$35,000 × .04 = $1,400 Sales charge
$35,000 − $1,400 = $33,600 (Net to invest)
$33,600 = 1,680 Shares at $20 a share

20. **B.** If the asking price of a fund is less than the NAV, the fund must be a closed-end investment company.

21. **A.** Mutual fund shares may be sold only at the current public offering price by adding the sales charge as shown in the prospectus to the NAV as calculated.

22. **B.** Although answer A is correct, answer B is the better response because the question refers to a mutual fund.

23. **D.** Because Wondra has a portfolio composed of bonds, if interest rates increase, the value of the bonds will decline. If shares are redeemed, the value of the portfolio will decline as the money is paid out. Commissions are paid from sales charges collected; they are not an expense of the fund.

24. **B.** If a fund does not permit dividend reinvestment at NAV, the maximum sales charge is reduced to 7 1/4%. If the fund does not offer rights of accumulation or breakpoints, the maximum sales charge is further reduced to 6 1/2%.

25. **C.** Regardless of when or how an order is received by a mutual fund, the price received is based on the next price (valuation) calculated by the fund. Repurchase allows an investor to redeem the shares by wire order, which will generally enable the investor to redeem at the price calculated on the same day as the wire order.

26. **A.** The NAV of a mutual fund is calculated according to a formula described in the prospectus, but under no circumstances may calculation occur less frequently than once per business day.

27. **C.** The NASD limits sales charges to 8.5% of the POP as a maximum. If the fund does not allow for breakpoints, reinvestment of dividends at net, or rights of accumulation, the maximum is less than 8.5%. Under the Investment Company Act of 1940, the maximum sales charge on mutual funds is deferred to the NASD rules, while a contractual plan specifically may charge 9% over the life of the plan.

28. **C.** Orders to redeem shares will be executed at the next computed price.

29. **C.** The price for mutual fund shares is the next price calculated by the fund after receipt of the request. Answer B describes a repurchase transaction.

30. **D.** Mutual funds use forward pricing. The investor will pay the offering price calculated at 5:00 pm.

31. **C.** Bid and NAV are similar in that they are both the price at which the customer sells shares. The ask price is similar to the public offering price as this is the price the customer pays for the purchase of shares.

32. **A.** John will receive $12.50 per share less a redemption fee of 1%. $12.50 times 100 shares is $12,500. A 1% redemption fee is $125 for a total of $12,375.

33. **A.** Closed-end investment company shares trade in the secondary market; hence, price is determined by supply and demand.

34. **D.** The HQ fund is selling below its net asset value, so it must be a closed-end fund. Shieko is selling above its NAV by more than the 8 1/2% sales load allowed, so it also must be a closed-end fund.

35. **D.** Sales charges could be paid on all types of open-end funds, while commissions are paid on securities traded in the secondary market such as a closed-end company.

36. **B.** John will be able to purchase 37.7 shares. Mutual fund shares may be sold in full or fractional amounts and do not trade in round lots of 100 shares.

37. **B.** NAV must be calculated at least every business day but not on weekends or holidays. It takes into account all of the fund's assets and is arrived at by totaling the assets and dividing that amount by the number of shares outstanding.

38. **A.** Share prices fluctuate in relation to the assets held in the fund's portfolio.

39. **A.** Share prices will increase when assets in the portfolio increase in value. Share prices decrease when the fund distributes a dividend as the shareholder will receive either cash or additional shares. Redeeming or purchasing shares does not affect share prices, only total assets. Reinvesting dividends or capital gains has no effect on share prices either.

40. **A.** No-load fund companies sell directly to the investor through their own sales force.

41. **C.** Tim Marcus can purchase 925 shares. He will pay $16.20 per share. The underwriter's concession is part of the sales fee, while the management fee is a direct expense of the fund and does not affect the price of the shares.

42. **C.** To determine the selling price of the shares, when given the NAV you must divide the NAV by 100% less the sales load, or:

$$\frac{NAV}{100\% - S.L.} = \text{Offering price}$$

$$\frac{\$9.35}{100\% - 7\%} = \$10$$

43. **A.** Funds charging the full 8 1/2% sales load must offer breakpoints, rights of accumulation and dividend reinvestment at NAV. Exchange privileges are the exception.

44. **A.** By dividing a mutual fund's expenses by its average net assets, you can calculate the fund's expense ratio.

45. **C.** The first step is to determine the complement of the sales charge percentage (100% − 4% = 96%); then divide the NAV by the complement ($13.37 ÷ 96% = $13.93). The final step is to divide the invested amount by the purchase price ($50,000 ÷ $13.93 = 3,589) to determine the number of shares purchased.

7 Mutual Funds—Distributions and Taxation

1. What is the source of dividend distributions to mutual fund shareholders?

   A. Capital gains from portfolio transactions
   B. Gross income of the fund
   C. Net income of the fund
   D. None of the above

2. Unrealized gain in the mutual fund portfolio

   I. affects the value of mutual fund shares
   II. is the growth in market value of securities held in the portfolio
   III. is realized by shareholders only when they redeem their shares

   A. I and II only
   B. I and III only
   C. II and III only
   D. I, II and III

3. An investor purchased 200 shares of the Cosmo Fund when the POP was $11.60 and the NAV was $10.60. The current price of the Cosmo Fund is POP $12.50, NAV $11.50. If the investor liquidates her 200 shares now, she will have a

   A. loss of $200
   B. loss of $20
   C. gain of $20
   D. gain of $200

4. An investor has received dividends and capital gains distributions on shares she has held for four months. The investor will pay

   A. long-term rates on the capital gains distributions and ordinary income rates on the dividends
   B. ordinary income tax rates on capital gains and dividends
   C. long-term or short-term capital gains rates, depending on the length of time the fund has held the securities
   D. no tax until she liquidates the shares

5. The conduit theory of taxation means that

   I. the fund is not taxed on earnings it distributes
   II. retained earnings are taxed as regular corporate income
   III. the earnings distributed by a regulated mutual fund are taxed twice

   A. I and II only
   B. I and III only
   C. II and III only
   D. I, II and III

6. ABC Fund invests all of its assets in municipal bonds. This means that

 I. shareholders do not pay federal taxes on dividend distributions
 II. the fund is not subject to federal tax on any interest earnings it retains
 III. shareholders pay all taxes at the preferential capital gains rate

 A. I and II only
 B. I and III only
 C. II and III only
 D. I, II and III

7. Lynn Scoggins's Form 1099 from a mutual fund investment listed her earnings for last year as follows:

Reinvested capital gains	$5,000
Undistributed capital gains	3,000
Reinvested dividends	7,000

 If she filed a separate return and had no other dividend income, what would be Lynn's taxable income from this investment?

 A. $10,100
 B. $10,200
 C. $14,900
 D. $15,000

8. John and Doris Engel file a joint return. What amount of dividend income can they exclude each year?

 A. $0
 B. $100
 C. $200
 D. $400

9. The ABC fund in which John and Doris Engel have invested paid $62 in taxes on their share of retained capital gains. How would John and Doris report this?

 A. They could claim the $62 paid by ABC as a credit against taxes they owe.
 B. They would exclude an additional $62 from dividend income.
 C. They would pay an additional $62 in taxes and have to refund the $62 paid by the fund.
 D. Their tax liability is not affected by the $62.

10. Three years ago, Joyce Gilly purchased 300 shares of ABC Fund. She sold the shares on August 15th for a loss of $400. On September 4th of the same year she repurchased the shares. How would she record the loss for tax purposes?

 A. Forty percent of the loss is deductible.
 B. Fifty percent of the loss is deductible.
 C. Sixty percent of the loss is deductible.
 D. The loss is not deductible.

11. According to the Internal Revenue Code, open-end investment companies may not distribute capital gains more frequently than

 A. monthly
 B. quarterly
 C. semiannually
 D. annually

12. If you invest in a regulated investment company, any dividend you receive from that investment will be taxed

 A. as long-term capital gains
 B. as long-term or short-term capital gains, depending on how long you were an investor
 C. to you as ordinary income but will not be taxed at the fund's level
 D. More information is needed to answer this question.

13. For the year 1981, the ABC Mutual Fund showed the following information:

Average net value for the
year $28,000,000
Dividend income received
for the year   2,100,000
Interest income received
for the year   800,000
Long-term capital gains
for the year   2,000,000
Operating expenses for the
year   300,000

If ABC wishes to retain its designation as a regulated investment company under the Internal Revenue Code Subchapter M, it must distribute to its clients an amount closest to which of the following?

   A. $1,890,000
   B. $2,340,000
   C. $5,940,000
   D. $8,550,000

14. Which of the following costs cannot be deducted as an expense from the investment income of an open-end investment company?

   A. Custodial fees
   B. Auditing fees
   C. Advertising fees
   D. Accounting fees

15. A client wants to purchase mutual fund shares just before the ex-dividend date. You should tell him that this is

   A. not advisable under any circumstances
   B. not advisable because of the tax consequences.
   C. advisable because the client will receive a dividend.
   D. advisable because it will allow the client to pay more per share, thus increasing his chance of getting to the breakpoint and receiving a lower sales charge

16. As the owner of mutual fund shares you will pay no tax on

   A. dividends that are reinvested in the fund
   B. unrealized capital gains
   C. capital gains that are issued as additional shares
   D. dividends that do not qualify for the $100 dividend exclusion

17. When an investor in a growth mutual fund redeems those shares and uses the proceeds to purchase shares of an income fund that is not in the same family of funds, all of the following are true EXCEPT the investor will

   A. have to pay a broker's fee
   B. incur taxes on any gains
   C. realize increased dividend income
   D. have more diversification

18. The ex-dividend date of a mutual fund would be

   A. the fourth business day prior to the record date
   B. whenever the board of directors stipulates the ex-dividend date to be
   C. seven calendar days after the declaration date
   D. seven business days after the declaration date

19. An investment company share normally goes ex-dividend

   A. on the record date
   B. the day after the record date
   C. five days after the record date
   D. seven days after the record date

20. On February 14th an investor purchases 1,000 shares of the ABC bond fund, which has an objective of providing the highest possible level of income on a monthly basis. On February 15th the investor informs his agent that he has changed his mind and wishes to exchange his bond fund shares for shares of a common stock growth fund with an objective of capital appreciation within the same family of funds. The investor's bond fund shares increased in value prior to the exchange. How will this increase in value be taxed?

A. As income because the bond fund's objective was to provide for current income on a monthly basis
B. As a short-term gain because the bond fund was held for less than six months
C. As a long-term gain because the exchange of the bond fund shares was made into a common stock fund with an objective of long-term appreciation
D. Because the shares were exchanged within a family of funds, the increase in value of the bond fund shares is not taxed, but increases the cost base in the common stock fund investment.

21. ABC, an open-end investment company, has the following financial information:

Dividend income	$2,000
Interest income	900
Short-term gains	1,000
Long-term gains	1,000
Expenses	900

In order to qualify as a regulated investment company, ABC must distribute what amount to its investors?

A. $1,800
B. $2,700
C. $3,510
D. $3,600

22. Which of the following statements is true of the calculation of the expense ratio of an open-end investment company?

A. The expense ratio is computed exclusive of the management fee.
B. The expense ratio is computed inclusive of the management fee.
C. The expense ratio is computed taking into account the management fee only.
D. The expense ratio shows the extent of leverage in the fund.

23. A mutual fund paid $.30 in dividends and $.75 in capital gains during the year. The offering price at the end of the year is $6.50. The fund's current yield for the year is

A. 4.6%
B. 6.9%
C. 11.5%
D. 16.2%

24. An investment company's expense ratio is determined by dividing

A. net assets by the number of shares outstanding
B. dividend income by current price, adjusted for capital gains distributions
C. operating expenses by the amount of average net assets
D. operating income plus the underwriter's concession by the net assets at year end

25. Bernard Kalman uses the FIFO method to determine his capital gains. What does this mean?

A. The IRS will assume a liquidation of the first shares that were acquired.
B. Bernard will indicate the specific shares that were redeemed without regard as to when they were purchased.
C. The last shares purchased are the first shares to be redeemed.
D. It does not mean any of the above.

26. Stan Armitrage originally invested $20,000 in the NCA Fund and has reinvested dividends and gains of $8,000. His shares in NCA are now worth $40,000. He converts his investment in NCA to the DQ Fund, which is under the same management as NCA. Which of the following statements is true?

    A. He retains his cost basis of $28,000 in the DQ Fund.
    B. He must declare $12,000 as a taxable gain upon conversion into the DQ Fund.
    C. He retains a $20,000 cost basis in the DQ Fund because of the conversion privilege.
    D. He is not liable for taxes in the current year because he did not have constructive receipt of the money at conversion.

27. When would an investor be liable for tax on reinvested distributions from an open-end investment company?

    A. When the shares purchased from the distribution are sold
    B. When the shares purchased with the distribution have been held for twelve months
    C. At the time the distribution is made
    D. None of the above

28. The Investment Company Act of 1940 requires that mutual funds pay dividends from their

    A. capital gains
    B. net income
    C. gross income
    D. portfolio earnings

29. The ex-dividend date for a mutual fund is

    A. four business days prior to the record date
    B. seven days prior to the record date
    C. the same day as the record date
    D. whenever the board of directors decides the ex-dividend date to be

30. Thomas Grumman buys shares of the Power Investment Company shortly before the ex-dividend date. Before he buys the shares, Thomas Grumman should understand that

    A. the price of the shares will decline on the ex-dividend date by the amount of the distribution
    B. if he reinvests the dividend he will not be liable for taxes on the dividend received
    C. there is a great advantage to him purchasing the shares immediately so that he can receive the dividend
    D. all of the above apply

31. Which of the following makes up the net investment income of an open-end investment company?

    A. Net gains on sales of securities
    B. Dividends, interest and unrealized gains
    C. Income from dividends and interest paid by securities held by the fund minus the operating expenses
    D. Ninety percent of the net asset value of the fund.

32. Which of the following statements are true of mutual fund dividend distributions?

    I. The fund pays dividends from net income.
    II. A single taxpayer may exclude $100 worth of dividend income from taxes annually.
    III. An investor is liable for taxes on distributions whether the dividend is a cash distribution or reinvested in the fund.
    IV. An investor is liable for taxes only if the distribution is received in cash.

    A. I and II
    B. I, II and III
    C. I and III
    D. II and IV

33. Mary Blackburn redeemed 200 of her 500 mutual fund shares. She has not designated which shares were redeemed. Which of the following methods does the IRS use to determine which shares have been redeemed?

    A. Identified shares
    B. Wash sale rules
    C. LIFO
    D. FIFO

34. ACE, an open-end investment company, operates under the conduit or pipeline tax theory. Last year it distributed 91% of all net investment income as a dividend to shareholders. Therefore ACE paid

    A. taxes on 9% of its net investment income last year
    B. taxes on 9% of its net investment income and capital gains last year
    C. taxes on 91% of its net investment income last year
    D. no taxes last year because it qualified as a regulated investment company under IRC Subchapter M

35. Your client has a $21,000 net capital loss this year. He plans to apply the maximum deduction towards his ordinary income for the year. After the year he may

    A. carry $3,000 of the loss forward
    B. carry the loss forward for six years and deduct $3,000 per year
    C. carry the loss forward for seven years and deduct $3,000 per year
    D. not carry the loss forward

36. On January 10th, 1991, John Jones purchased 1,000 shares of the Delta open-end investment company. On January 22nd, 1991, Delta sells 25,000 shares of IBM at a profit. Delta originally purchased the IBM on June 24th, 1988. On February 15th, 1991, Delta distributes the gain from the sale of IBM to shareholders. How will John be taxed on this distribution?

    A. John will be taxed on the long-term gain at ordinary income rates.
    B. The long-term gain qualifies for the 60% exclusion.
    C. If John is using automatic reinvestment, he will not be taxed at all.
    D. John will not be taxed because he did not sell the IBM. Delta is liable for all taxes.

37. Which of the following is the usual source of a mutual fund's capital gains distribution?

    A. Net long-term gains resulting from the sale of the company's mutual fund shares
    B. Net short-term gains resulting from the sale of the company's mutual fund shares
    C. Net long-term gains resulting from the sale of securities in the fund's investment portfolio
    D. Net short-term gains resulting from the sale of securities in the fund's investment portfolio

38. Your open-end investment company client has decided not to take automatic reinvestment of dividend and capital gains distributions. This will

    A. not change the tax status of these distributions
    B. lower her proportionate ownership in the fund each time a distribution is made
    C. be the way individuals requiring income payments will often invest
    D. All of the above apply.

39. Two unrelated customers combining their capital would NOT qualify for which of the following?

   A. Avoiding the odd-lot differential
   B. Opening a JTIC account
   C. Breakpoints on a mutual fund purchase
   D. Joint registration on stock certificates

◆ Answers & Rationale

1. C. Dividend distributions are made from the fund's net investment income. Net investment income is gross income (dividends, interest and, if identified, short-term gains) minus fund expenses.

2. D. Unrealized gains in portfolio securities are the result of the asset's appreciation in value. This appreciation in value will be reflected in an appreciation of the mutual fund shares themselves. An investor wanting to cash in on this appreciation can do so only by selling the shares (realizing the gain).

3. B. The investor's cost base in the shares is $11.60. If the shareholder liquidates, she would receive the net asset value of $11.50, resulting in a loss of $.10 cents per share. Liquidating 200 shares results in a total loss of $20 (200 × $.10).

4. B. Capital gains distributions and income distributions received from a mutual fund are taxed at the investor's ordinary income tax bracket (TRA 1986).

5. D. By qualifying as a regulated investment company (the conduit, or pipeline, tax theory), the fund is liable for taxes only on the income retained. The investor benefits because the income is taxed only twice (at the corporate level and at the individual level) and not three times by adding taxation at the fund level.

6. A. A municipal bond fund would derive its income from interest paid from the municipal bonds held, which is exempt from federal income tax.

7. D. Under the Tax Reform Act of 1986, income and gains distributions are taxable at ordinary income tax rates. The capital gains exclusion has been repealed as has the dividend exclusion. Undistributed gains are still taxable to the shareholder. The taxes paid by the fund on the retained gain are credited to the investor.

8. A. The Tax Reform Act of 1986 repealed the dividend exclusion for individual investors.

9. A. If a fund realizes a gain but declines to distribute it to shareholders, the gain is still taxable to the investor. The fund will pay taxes on the gain on behalf of the shareholders (similar to a withholding tax) and will issue as part of the 1099 a statement showing their share of taxes paid. In this question, that share equalled $62. The Engels can elect to use that share as a credit against their tax liability or can elect to have it refunded. The basis of the shares is increased by the amount of the undistributed gain included in income, less the taxes paid by the fund.

10. D. Joyce repurchased the shares within 30 days of the loss transaction, and the loss is disallowed (wash sale).

11. D. Capital gains distributions cannot occur more frequently than annually. Distribution of net investment income can be distributed as often as the fund wishes.

12. C. A mutual fund qualifying as a regulated investment company distributes at least 90% of its net investment income as a dividend to shareholders. Because the company has qualified, the fund pays no tax on the income distributed. However, the shareholders are taxed at their ordinary income tax rate on the distribution.

13. B. To qualify as a regulated investment company, the fund must distribute at least 90% of its net investment income. Net investment income for the purposes of IRC Subchapter M is income, without regard to gains, minus expenses. In this question then, dividend income ($2,100,000) plus interest income ($800,000) minus expenses ($300,000) equals a net investment income of $2,600,000. Ninety percent of $2,600,000 is $2,340,000.

14. C. Advertising costs are an expense of the underwriter and are paid from the sales charge collected on the sale of investment company shares.

15. **B.** The value of shares will drop by the amount of the dividend on the ex-dividend date. This loss will not be made up by the dividend as the dividend is subject to ordinary income tax. A person in the 28% tax bracket stands to lose 28% of the value of the dividend.

16. **B.** A gain is not taxable until it is realized, or sold.

17. **D.** The exchange of shares from one fund to another, even within a family of funds, is still a taxable event. Just because the objectives have changed does not necessarily mean the income fund will be less diversified than the growth fund.

18. **B.** The ex-dividend date for payment of dividends from a mutual fund is determined by the fund's board of directors. Normally for funds with regular dividend payment schedules, the ex-dividend date is set as the record date.

19. **B.** An investor purchasing shares on the record date becomes a shareholder of record and is entitled to the dividend declared. Orders received after the pricing of shares or the record date would be processed the next day and would purchase shares ex-dividend.

20. **B.** Because the bond fund shares were held for less than six months, the gain is short term. An exchange privilege does not exempt the transfer of funds from taxation. The exchange is a taxable event.

21. **A.** To qualify as a regulated investment company, at least 90% of net investment income (without regard to gains) must be distributed. Net investment income would be dividend income ($2,000) plus interest income ($900) minus expenses ($900) which equals $2,000. Ninety percent of $2,000 is $1,800.

22. **B.** The expense ratio includes the costs of operating the fund compared to fund assets. Expenses included in the ratio are management fees, administrative fees, brokerage fees and taxes.

23. **A.** Current yield of a mutual fund is current income ($.30 dividend) divided by the net asset value ($6.50). Gains are not included in calculation of current yield; they are accounted for separately.

24. **C.** The expense ratio is operating expenses divided by net assets. Answer A is net asset value per share. Answer B is current yield, although gains cannot be included in current yield quotes.

25. **A.** FIFO means *first in, first out.* Answer C describes LIFO, and answer B describes share identification.

26. **B.** The exchange privilege offers exchange without an additional sales charge, but the exchange is still taxable. Stan is taxed on the gain of $12,000 ($40,000 – $28,000).

27. **C.** Reinvested income and gains distributions are taxable in the year they are received.

28. **B.** Dividends are paid from net income (interest plus dividends plus short-term gains when identified minus expenses).

29. **D.** Mutual fund ex-dividend dates are dates set by the board of directors. Corporate stocks in the secondary market have the ex-dividend date four business days before the record date.

30. **A.** Share prices decline on the ex-dividend date. Dividend distributions cause a tax liability, and the purchase of shares right before an ex-dividend date is not a good idea because of the tax liability.

31. **C.** Dividends and interest paid on the securities held in the portfolio make up investment income. From this the fund's expenses are paid before it becomes net investment income.

32. **C.** Funds pay dividends from net income, and the investor is liable for taxes on all distributions. The $100 exclusion annually was eliminated with the new tax code.

33. **D.** When a customer does not choose a method, the IRS uses FIFO.

34. **A.** ACE would pay taxes on any portion of income it does not distribute as long as it distributes at least 90%. ACE paid taxes on 9%.

35. **B.** Capital losses can be used to offset capital gains. A client can use $3,000 in capital losses per year to offset ordinary income. In this case after using $3,000 this year, the client will have $18,000 to carry forward.

36. **A.** John owned shares of the mutual fund when it distributes the gain and is liable for the taxes. This is considered a long-term gain, which is currently taxed as ordinary income.

37. **C.** Capital gains come from the sale of securities held in the company's portfolio. Most of these gains will be the sale of securities held for long periods of time.

38. **D.** Reinvestment does not change the tax status, while taking distributions will lower proportionate ownership. An investment of this type will allow an investor to take distributions without touching the principal.

39. **C.** In order to qualify for a breakpoint, the investor must be a separate legal individual. Two customers pooling their money just to qualify for the benefits of breakpoints do not constitute a separate individual.

8   Mutual Funds—Accounts

1. Under the Uniform Gifts to Minors Act, which of the following gifts is allowable?

   A. A gift with both parents as custodian given to one child
   B. A gift from both parents to more than one child
   C. A gift from one parent to several child
   D. A gift with one custodian and one child

2. Acme Fund allows rights of accumulation. Mary Rulli has invested $8,000 and has signed a letter of intent for a total investment of $10,000. Her reinvested dividends during the 13 months amounted to $900. She must add how much to fulfill the letter of intent?

   A. $1,100
   B. $2,000
   C. $8,000
   D. $10,000

3. Linda Rodriguez invests $35,000 in a fund with breakpoints as follows:

Less than $10,000	8.50%
$10,000 to $49,999	7.00%
$50,000 to $99,999	6.25%

   Linda has also signed a letter of intent for a total of $50,000. What sales charge will Linda pay now on the $35,000 initial investment?

   A. 6.25%
   B. 7.00%
   C. 8.50%
   D. This cannot be determined until 13 months have elapsed.

4. Tim Larsen invested $20,000 in the Alex Growth Fund. He also invested $30,000 in the Alex Leveraged Fund and qualified for the $50,000 breakpoint. This is an example of

   A. the conversion privilege
   B. the combination privilege
   C. a breakpoint sale
   D. the exchange privilege

5. One risk of a withdrawal plan is that

   A. there is a high sales charge for the service
   B. the cost basis of shares will be high
   C. the plan is illegal in many states
   D. the principal value will fluctuate

6. Joan Mitchell has signed up for a mutual fund contractual plan with a 50% front-end load and $300 monthly payments. She has decided to cancel the plan after her second payment but within 45 days. If her current NAV is $340, how much will she get back from the plan?

   A. $340
   B. $550
   C. $600
   D. $640

7. A contractual plan investor in a spread-load plan wants to withdraw after investing $150 a month for eight months. The plan took $240 in sales charges. If the NAV has not changed, how much refund will the investor receive?

   A. $600
   B. $960
   C. $1,020
   D. $1,200

8. Glenda Thatcher has just invested a lump sum in the Cosmo Fund. She has set up a plan to purchase additional shares by reinvesting all dividends and capital gains. These additional shares will be purchased by means of a(n)

   A. accumulation plan
   B. regular plan
   C. dollar cost averaging plan
   D. lump-sum plan

9. Mary Larson and Bob McDonald each have open accounts in the ABC Mutual Fund. Mary has decided to receive all distributions in cash, while Bob is automatically reinvesting all distributions. How do their decisions affect their investments?

   I. Cash distributions may reduce Mary's proportional interest in the fund.
   II. Mary may use the cash distributions to purchase shares later at NAV.
   III. Bob's reinvestments purchase additional shares at NAV rather than at the offering price.

   A. I and II only
   B. I and III only
   C. II and III only
   D. I, II and III

10. Susan James has opened a voluntary accumulation plan to invest $500 per month. What sales charge will she pay on each additional investment if the fund's breakpoints are as follows?

    | Less than $8,000 | 8.50% |
    | $8,000 to $14,999 | 7.75% |
    | $15,000 to $49,999 | 7.25% |

    A. 7.75% up to $15,000
    B. 8.50% up to $8,000
    C. It depends on whether she reinvests distributions from the fund.
    D. It depends on the NAV of the fund.

11. Which of the following characteristics describe a contractual planholder?

    I. Receives a plan certificate
    II. Owns a specific share of underlying mutual fund shares
    III. Owns specific shares of securities in the portfolio of the underlying mutual fund
    IV. Must complete the contractual plan

    A. I and II
    B. I and III
    C. II and IV
    D. III and IV

12. Greg Matthews has decided to terminate his contractual plan one month after opening it. At the time he opened the account, the NAV was $11.50, and it is now $11.80. He has acquired 212 shares and has paid sales charges of $930. What will Greg's refund be?

    A. The total NAV for his shares at the time of their purchase plus 50% of the sales charges
    B. The current NAV of his shares and all sales charges
    C. The current NAV of his shares only
    D. The current NAV of his shares and sales charges that exceed 15% of gross payments

13. Which of the following statements describe contractual plans?

    I. They cannot be sold in certain states.
    II. They do not obligate the planholder to complete the contracted number of payments.
    III. They have a predetermined fixed schedule of sales charges.

    A. I and II only
    B. I and III only
    C. II and III only
    D. I, II and III

14. An investor has requested a withdrawal plan from his mutual fund and is currently receiving $600 per month. This is an example of a

    A. contractual plan
    B. fixed-share periodic payment plan
    C. fixed-dollar periodic payment plan
    D. fixed-percentage withdrawal plan

15. If you invest in a mutual fund and you choose to have automatic reinvestment, you would expect that

    I. dividend distributions will be reinvested at net asset value
    II. dividend distributions will be reinvested at public offering price
    III. capital gains distributions will be reinvested at net asset value
    IV. capital gains distributions will be reinvested at public offering price

    A. I and III
    B. I and IV
    C. II and III
    D. II and IV

16. The point at which a mutual fund sales charge is reduced is called the

    A. breakpoint
    B. load point
    C. intent point
    D. balance point

17. The letter of intent covers purchases made within a period of no more than how many months from the date of the letter?

    A. Three
    B. Six
    C. Twelve
    D. Thirteen

18. Under the Uniform Gifts to Minors Act, you can

    I. give an unlimited amount of cash
    II. give securities
    III. give up to $10,000 cash
    IV. revoke a gift

    A. I
    B. I and II
    C. I, II and IV
    D. II and III

19. Flo Jackson owns $24,000 of Regency Fund shares. She chooses to have the money forwarded to her, using a ten-year fixed-time withdrawal. She will receive a

    A. fixed number of dollars for a variable amount of time
    B. variable number of dollars for a fixed amount of time
    C. fixed number of dollars for a fixed amount of time
    D. variable number of dollars for a variable amount of time

20. A client deposits $2,200 in an open-end investment company. After 60 days, he signs a letter of intent for the $10,000 breakpoint. Six months later, he deposits $11,000. He will

    A. receive a reduced load on $1,000 worth of the shares
    B. receive a reduced load on $8,800 worth of the shares
    C. receive the beneficial effect of a reduced load on $13,200 worth of the shares
    D. not receive any break in the sales load

21. The exchange privilege offered by open-end investment companies allows investors to

    A. exchange personally owned securities for shares of the investment company
    B. exchange shares of one open-end fund for those of another fund in the same company on a net asset value basis
    C. purchase new fund shares from dividends
    D. delay payment of taxes

22. Under the act of 1970, provision regarding the first 48 months of contractual plan payments, what is the maximum sales charge that can be deducted on the first twelve-month period?

    A. 9%
    B. 16%
    C. 20%
    D. 50%

23. To qualify for the quantity discount, which of the following could not be joined together under the definition of "any person"?

    I. A father and his 35-year-old son investing in separate accounts
    II. A husband and wife investing in a joint account
    III. A husband and wife investing in a separate account
    IV. A trust officer working on behalf of a single trust account

    A. I
    B. II, III and IV
    C. II and IV
    D. III and IV

24. On June 5th, an investor made his first investment into a 50% front-end load ten-year periodic payment plan. On June 20th, the investor decided to terminate the plan. The investor will receive

    A. $40
    B. $100
    C. the net asset value and all sales charges in excess of 15% of the total payment made
    D. the net asset value and all sales charges

25. Concerning a fixed-time withdrawal plan offered by a mutual fund

    I. the amount received each month by the client may vary
    II. a fixed number of shares will be liquidated each month
    III. not all funds offer this type of withdrawal
    IV. this plan is self-exhausting

    A. I only
    B. I and II only
    C. I, III and IV only
    D. I, II, III and IV

26. Jean Smith has $9,600 invested in a mutual fund that used an 8 1/2% sales load. Jean wants to start a fixed-percentage withdrawal plan immediately. She wants a 6% annual withdrawal rate and wants the check sent monthly. Her first withdrawal check from the fund will be closest to

    A. $43.92
    B. $48
    C. $527.04
    D. $576

27. A letter of intent for a mutual fund does NOT contain which of the following provisions?

   A. The time limit is 13 months.
   B. The letter can be backdated 90 days to include a previous deposit.
   C. The fund can halt redemption during the period of time the letter of intent is in effect.
   D. The fund might keep some of the initially issued shares in an escrow account to ensure full payment of the full spread.

28. Assume an investor put $400 a month into a contractual plan of a mutual fund for twelve months and now wants to terminate the plan. The fund used a 50% load the first year, and the current value of the account is $3,000. How much would the investor receive on termination of the plan?

   A. $0
   B. $3,000
   C. $4,680
   D. $10,920

29. Betty Smith has been investing as follows in the XYZ Mutual Fund.

$ Amt	Price	# Shares
100	$25.00	4
100	16.67	6
100	12.50	8
100	10.00	10
100	12.50	8
$ 500	$76.67	36

   If Betty sold out today, what would the fund's NAV need to be so she could break even?

   A. $1.44
   B. $6.52
   C. $13.89
   D. $15.33

30. Assume an investor put $400 a month into a contractual plan of a mutual fund for twelve months and now wants to terminate the plan. The fund used a 20% spread load the first year, and the current value of the account is $3,000. How much would the investor receive on termination of the plan?

   A. $0
   B. $3,000
   C. $3,690
   D. $4,680

31. A withdrawal plan offered by an open-end investment company

   A. converts fund shares to insurance annuities
   B. withdraws without penalty any funds invested during the first 90 days
   C. distributes (generally monthly or quarterly) payments of an amount that may be more or less than the net investment income for that period
   D. could not do any of the above

32. Which of the following withdrawal plans offered by the XYZ Mutual Fund will pay the client a fixed monthly payment?

   I. Fixed-dollar withdrawal
   II. Fixed-percentage withdrawal
   III. Fixed-share withdrawal
   IV. Liquidation over a fixed period of time

   A. I only
   B. II and III only
   C. II, III and IV only
   D. I, II, III and IV

33. Henry Green opened an account about twelve years ago with the ABC Mutual Fund. Today his NAV is $20,000. The ABC Fund offers rights of accumulation. Its breakpoints are as follows:

$1 to $24,999	8%
$25,000 to $49,999	6%
$50,000 to $99,999	4%

Henry wishes to deposit $6,000 in the account today. Which of the following would represent his sales charge?

A. $1,000 at 8%, and $5,000 at 6%
B. $4,999 at 8%, and $1,001 at 6%
C. The full $6,000 at 6%
D. The full $6,000 at 8%

34. Under the provisions of an UGMA account, when the minor reaches the age of majority

A. the account should be turned over to the donee
B. the account should be turned over to the donor
C. the account remains as an UGMA account
D. none of the above could be done

35. Kathy Jones has invested in a mutual fund and has signed a statement of intention to invest $25,000. Her original investment was for $13,000, and her current account value is $17,000. For her to complete the letter, she would need to deposit

A. $8,000
B. $12,000
C. $13,000
D. $27,000

36. In a contractual plan with plan completion insurance, upon the death of the plan participant, the plan custodian will

A. send the insurance proceeds to the beneficiary and require the beneficiary to complete the contractual plan
B. send the beneficiary the insurance proceeds
C. receive the insurance proceeds and continue to make monthly investments into the contractual plan for the beneficiary
D. receive the insurance proceeds and complete the plan, turning the fund shares over to the beneficiary

37. Which of the following withdrawal plans would an investor select if she wanted to receive a fixed payment monthly from the investment company?

A. Fixed-time
B. Fixed-share
C. Fixed-percentage
D. Fixed-dollar

38. A customer indicates he wishes to invest $50,000 in mutual funds. The investments are to be split in three different funds, each with its own management company. The registered representative should advise the client that

A. this is an excellent idea because it spreads the risk of investing even more
B. the customer will pay greater commissions on the investment when the money is split between three funds than if the investor put the money into only one fund
C. the customer will be able to exchange shares from one fund to another as conditions change without incurring a new sales charge
D. the investor should buy individual stocks because mutual funds are only for smaller investors

39. The result of a client investing the same amount of money into a mutual fund over a long period of time is a lower

    A. price per share than cost per share
    B. cost per share than price per share
    C. dollar amount invested
    D. dollar amount received

40. According to Section 27h of the Investment Company Act, an investor enters into a $100-per-month ten-year periodic payment plan. The maximum that the investor could pay in sales charges over the first four years would be

    A. $432
    B. $768
    C. $960
    D. $3,072

41. A withdrawal plan is available from which of the following investments?

    A. Municipal bonds
    B. Common stock
    C. Convertible bonds
    D. Open-end investment company

42. In a mutual fund, after opening an account, an investor can generally make additional periodic investments in minimum amounts of

    A. $50
    B. $100
    C. $500
    D. It differs from fund to fund.

43. Marjorie and Harry Kellog are tenants in common in a joint account. Which of the following statements is(are) true?

    A. If one of them dies, the survivor will not automatically assume full ownership.
    B. They need not have equal interest in the account.
    C. They have an undivided interest in the property in the account.
    D. All of the above statements are true.

44. Kim Filby is participating in a periodic payment plan. Fifty percent of her first year's payments are taken as a sales charge. What is the maximum the sales charge can average over the life of the plan?

    A. 8.5%
    B. 9%
    C. 16%
    D. 20%

45. In a mutual fund, a shareholder who elected not to receive share certificates can liquidate all or a portion of his holdings and receive payment from the fund if the fund receives which of the following?

    I. A written request from the shareholder
    II. A signed stock power from the shareholder
    III. A signature guarantee from the shareholder

    A. I only
    B. I and II only
    C. I and III only
    D. I, II, and III

46. In order to get cash for an emergency that arose, Michael MacKay redeemed his mutual fund shares. Within how many days of redemption could he reinvest in the same fund without having to pay additional sales charges?

    A. 7
    B. 30
    C. 45
    D. 60

47. Murray Murbles invests $3,000 in open-end investment company shares. After 60 days, he signs a letter of intent for a $10,000 breakpoint and backdates the letter two months. Six months later, he deposits $10,000 into the fund. He will receive a reduced sales charge on

    A. the $3,000 investment only
    B. $7,000 of the investment only
    C. the $10,000 investment only
    D. the entire $13,000 investment

48. Some open-end investment companies offer their investors a conversion privilege, which permits investors to

    A. exchange general securities for shares in the mutual fund's portfolio
    B. delay payment of taxes on investment company shares that have appreciated in value
    C. purchase additional fund shares from dividends paid by the fund
    D. exchange shares of one mutual fund for those of another fund under the same management, at net asset value

49. Which of the following are characteristic of a mutual fund voluntary accumulation plan?

    I. A minimum initial purchase
    II. Minimum optional additional purchases
    III. Declining level sales charges as money accumulates
    IV. An obligatory purchase goal

    A. I and II only
    B. I, II and III only
    C. II and IV only
    D. I, II, III and IV

50. Which of the following characteristics describe(s) a contractual planholder?

    I. Receives unit trust certificates
    II. Owns an undivided interest in the mutual fund shares underlying the plan
    III. Owns an undivided interest in the portfolio of the underlying mutual fund

    A. I and II
    B. I and III
    C. II and III
    D. III

51. Magnus Mutual Fund permits rights of accumulation. Gordon Dykstra has invested $9,000 and has signed a letter of intent for a $15,000 investment. His reinvested dividends during the 13 months total $720. How much money must he contribute to fulfill the letter of intent?

    A. $5,280
    B. $6,000
    C. $9,000
    D. $15,000

52. Jacob Jones has a large investment in the XYZ open-end investment company. He has selected a fixed-time withdrawal plan. The computation for the withdrawal plan will be based on the

    A. NAV each period
    B. NAV at the first payment
    C. POP each period
    D. POP at the first payment

53. A client is receiving funds from an open-end investment company under the provisions of a withdrawal plan. This means

   A. the client must continue to make investments into the fund
   B. the client will generally be discouraged from making further investments into the fund
   C. the client will always exhaust the plan within a predetermined period of time
   D. that if the client withdraws only dividend and gains distributions, the principal amount of the investment will always remain intact

54. A client chooses a voluntary accumulation plan and signs up for automatic checking account deductions of $100 a month. She tells the registered representative that she intends to continue the plan for ten years.

   A. The client's decision to invest is binding, and she must continue to invest for ten years.
   B. The client can terminate the plan at her option.
   C. The client will be charged a late fee on investments not made in a timely fashion.
   D. The client can terminate the plan if she agrees to pay the balance in lump sum.

55. Your client has $22,000 in his contractual plan provided by the XYZ open-end investment company. He wishes to withdraw $10,000 for a business emergency. Your client

   A. must terminate the plan in order to get any money out of the plan
   B. will not be allowed to make additional investments due to his failure to complete the plan
   C. will be able to withdraw the funds if necessary, but will not be allowed to reinvest them
   D. will be able to withdraw the funds if he wishes and will be able to reinvest them for a nominal transaction fee

56. Under the Investment Company Act of 1940, your client begins a front-end load contractual plan by agreeing to invest $100 per month for the next ten years. The maximum sales charge that can be deducted from the first year's investment is

   A. $50
   B. $108
   C. $240
   D. $600

57. John Jones has invested $100 per month into a contractual plan for the past ten months. The company is charging the maximum load allowed under the Investment Company Act of 1940. Currently, the shares are priced at $10 NAV, $10.50 POP, and John has 120 shares in his account. If John were to terminate the plan now, how much would he receive?

   A. $1,000
   B. $1,200
   C. $1,550
   D. $2,200

58. Under the Uniform Gifts to Minors Act, the owner of the securities held in the account is the

   A. custodian
   B. minor
   C. parent of the minor
   D. donor of the securities

59. John and his wife Linda own shares in the XYZ Mutual Fund as joint tenants with rights of survivorship. If John dies, what happens to the shares in the account?

   A. One half of the shares would belong to Linda, and the remaining half would be distributed to John's estate.
   B. Linda would own all the shares.
   C. Ownership of the shares would have to be determined by probate court.
   D. None of the above would occur.

60. Fred Jacobs has been investing $100 a month in the XYZ Mutual Fund over the past five months. His purchases are as follows:

Month	Price/Share	Quantity
1	$10	10
2	20	5
3	25	4
4	5	20
5	10	10

What is the difference between Fred's average cost and the average price he paid for the shares?

A. $3.80
B. $7.14
C. $10.20
D. $14

61. If an investment company offers rights of accumulation and an investor wishes to get a reduced sales charge, the client must deposit the sufficient funds within

A. 45 days
B. 13 months
C. There is no time limit.
D. Each fund has its own requirements.

62. A customer opens a new cash account. Which of the following signatures is(are) required before orders can be executed?

I. Customer
II. Registered representative
III. Registered principal

A. I only
B. I and II only
C. II and III only
D. I, II and III

63. A change in which of the following should be indicated in a customer's file?

I. Name or address
II. Marital status
III. Objectives

A. I only
B. I and II only
C. I and III only
D. I, II and III

◆ Answers & Rationale

1. **D.**   Under UGMA, an unlimited amount of money may be given to *one child* with *one* entity named as *custodian.*

2. **B.**   Appreciation and reinvested dividends do not count towards completion of a letter of intent. If the investor originally deposits $8,000 and signs a letter for $10,000, then $2,000 remains to be deposited in order to complete the letter.

3. **A.**   By signing the letter of intent, the initial investment qualifies for the reduced load of 6.25%. The shares purchased because of the reduced load will be held in escrow until the letter is completed, at which time, if the letter is not completed, the escrowed shares may be cancelled, or the investor may pay the shortfall in sales charge and keep the shares.

4. **B.**   Investing in two or more funds within the same fund group and being able to combine the investments to qualify for breakpoints is an example of a combination privilege.

5. **D.**   Withdrawal plans have no guarantee of payment. An investor's account value is still at the mercy of market fluctuations.

6. **D.**   Under the Investment Company Act of 1940, an investor terminating a plan within 45 days is entitled to a refund of all sales charges plus the current value of the account. Because the investor has made two payments of $300 each, a total of $600 was invested. From that $600, 50% ($300) was deducted as a sales charge. The current value of the account is $340, so the investor will receive $640 as a refund.

7. **B.**   Refunds from a spread-load plan that has been in effect for more than 45 days are limited to a return of net asset value only. The investor would receive the difference between the amount invested (NAV remains the same) and the sales charges deducted. In this case, a total investment of $1,200 minus the sales charge of $240 equals a refund of $960.

8. **A.**   Glenda has elected to voluntarily reinvest fund distributions through an accumulation plan.

9. **B.**   By electing to receive distributions in cash while others are purchasing shares through reinvestment, Mary's proportional interest in the fund will decline. Most funds usually allow reinvestment of dividends at net asset value. Cash invested is considered a new purchase, and the shares will be purchased at the public offering price, not NAV.

10. **B.**   Although Susan's investment plan will probably carry her to the fund's breakpoints, because she has not signed a letter of intent, she must rely on rights of accumulation. Each investment made until she has invested at least $8,000 will be at the sales charge of 8.5%.

11. **A.**   An individual investing in a contractual plan receives a certificate evidencing ownership of shares held in trust by the plan company. Remember, plan companies are unit investment trusts that invest in shares of mutual funds. The plan participant holds units in the trust, not the specific shares of the mutual fund.

12. **B.**   Termination of a contractual plan within 45 days results in a refund of all sales charges plus the current value of the account.

13. **D.**   Contractual plans are not legal in several states; the contract is unilateral (only the company is bound); and the prospectus will detail the specific charges to be deducted from each payment over the life of the plan.

14. **C.**   If the investor is receiving $600 a month, then the dollar amount of the payment is fixed; this can only be a fixed-dollar plan.

15. **A.**   Most mutual funds offer automatic reinvestment of income and gains distributions at net asset value. If income distribution reinvestment

is subject to a sales charge, then the maximum allowable sales charge for any purchases is reduced.

16.   **A.**   The schedule of sales charges showing reductions for certain levels of investment is the fund's breakpoint chart.

17.   **D.**   A letter of intent is a statement of intention to invest a predetermined amount of money over a 13-month period. The time period begins on the date the letter is signed.

18.   **B.**   There is no limit to the size of the gift that may be transferred under a Uniform Gifts to Minors Act account. The $10,000 is the gift tax exclusion and relates only to the amount of the gift that may be subject to tax.

19.   **B.**   Under a fixed-time withdrawal plan, only the time period of the distribution is fixed. The amount of money received each month or the number of shares liquidated will vary.

20.   **C.**   An investor signing a letter of intent has 13 months to contribute funds to reach the reduced load. The investor may also backdate a letter within 90 days to include an amount previously deposited.

21.   **B.**   Exchange privileges allow investors to move from fund to fund within a family of funds without paying an additional sales charge.

22.   **C.**   The maximum sales charge that can be deducted under a spread-load plan under the act of 1970 in any one year is 20% of the amount invested.

23.   **A.**   For the purpose of qualifying for breakpoints, the definition of any person includes family units, but only minor children, not someone 35 years old.

24.   **D.**   Because the client terminated the plan within the 45-day free look period, the client will receive the value of the account plus all sales charges deducted.

25.   **C.**   A fixed-time withdrawal plan is considered to be self-liquidating. The only variable fixed is the time. The number of shares liquidated, the amount of money received and the percentage of the account liquidated will vary from period to period. Funds may or may not offer withdrawal plans. If they do, the prospectus will describe information concerning the plans.

26.   **B.**   Jean has $9,600 invested. She wants 6% withdrawn annually, but sent monthly. The calculation is as follows:

$$\$9,600 \times .06 = \$576 \text{ per year}$$
or,
$$\$576 \div 12 = \$48 \text{ per month}$$

27.   **C.**   A letter of intent is not binding on the client in any way. Should the client decide to liquidate the account prior to completion of the letter, the company may reduce the redemption only by the amount of shares held in escrow.

28.   **C.**   A front-end load contractual plan is operating under the act of 1940. According to the act's refund provisions, the participant who terminates after 45 days but before 18 months would receive his account value (NAV) plus all sales charges in excess of 15% of the cost to date. Therefore, in this case the client would receive $3,000 (the account value) plus all sales charges in excess of 15% of the cost. The client's cost to date has been $4,800. Fifteen percent of $4,800 equals $720. Sales charges deducted have been 50% of $4,800, or $2,400. The excess, $2,400 minus $720, or $1,680, is returned to the client. Thus $3,000 plus $1,680 equals a refund of $4,680. If this had been the act of 1970, the client would have received only a return of his account value, or $3,000.

29.   **C.**   To break even, the fund shares would have to be $13.89 per share because $500 divided by 36 equals $13.89. This is also the dollar cost average.

30.   **B.**   This time the contractual plan has been sold under the provisions of the act of 1970. After 45 days, the client will receive a return of his account value only, or in this case, $3,000.

31. **C.**   Withdrawal plans offered by investment companies allow the shareholder to elect to receive periodic payments based on a fixed period of time, or a stipulated dollar, percentage or share value. The withdrawal is not guaranteed and may run out prematurely if the earnings of the fund are less than the amount withdrawn periodically.

32. **A.**   In a withdrawal plan, if one variable is fixed, such as fixed-dollar, all other aspects of the payment will vary. If an individual is receiving a fixed-dollar payment, the plan must be a fixed-dollar plan.

33. **C.**   Under rights of accumulation, if an additional investment plus the client's current account value (or money invested) puts the client's account value over a breakpoint, the entire additional investment qualifies for the reduced sales charge. In this case, Henry's additional investment of $6,000 plus his account value of $20,000 puts his account value over the $25,000 breakpoint. The entire $6,000 investment qualifies for the 6% sales charge.

34. **A.**   When a minor reaches the age of maturity, proceeds must be handed over to the child (donee) under the terms of the Uniform Gifts to Minors Act.

35. **B.**   Under a letter of intent, the full contribution stated in the letter must be contributed in order for the letter to be completed. Appreciation is not considered.

36. **D.**   Plan completion insurance provides for funds payable to the plan custodian so that the plan may be completed in full.

37. **D.**   A fixed-dollar plan is the only type of plan that fixes a definite dollar payment.

38. **B.**   Because the funds are under separate management, the load charged on each separate investment will likely be at the maximum. If the client invested the entire sum within one fund or a family of funds, a reduced sales charge may have been available.

39. **B.**   By investing a predetermined amount of money periodically for a long period of time, the investor is investing using the concept of dollar cost averaging. The result is to reduce the cost per share compared to the average market price.

40. **B.**   Section 27h of the Investment Company Act of 1940 refers to spread-load plans. The maximum sales charge that can be deducted is equal to an average of 16% of the contributions over a 48-month period. In this question, the answer is $768 ($4,800 × 16%).

41. **D.**   Mutual funds (open-end investment companies) offer withdrawal plans.

42. **D.**   Periodic investments differ from fund to fund, and an RR must refer to the prospectus for each fund.

43. **D.**   Under tenants in common, owners may have a fractional interest in the undivided ownership of an asset. The interest passes to the decedent's estate at death, unlike JTWROS wherein the survivor succeeds to the interest.

44. **B.**   The maximum sales charge on a contractual plan whether front-end load or spread load is 9% over the life of the plan.

45. **D.**   Orders for redemption without a certificate being issued require a written request, signature guarantee and stock power.

46. **B.**   Funds offering the reinstatement privilege allow the investor to redeem and reinvest shares within 30 days without an additional sales charge. The privilege can be used only once, and only the amount withdrawn can be reinstated.

47. **D.**   The entire investment qualifies for the reduced load. A letter of intent covers purchases within a 13-month period and may be backdated 90 days. Murray actually had eleven months in which to make the additional investment.

48. **D.**   The exchange or conversion privilege allows an investor to exchange shares of one fund

for another fund under the same management without paying an additional sales charge (although the exchange is still a taxable event).

49. **B.** A voluntary accumulation plan is voluntary, not binding. The company may require that the initial investment meets a certain minimum dollar amount. It may also specify that any additions meet set minimums (for example, $50). The sales charge is level, and the plan may qualify for breakpoints based on the accumulated value.

50. **A.** A contractual plan buys mutual fund shares to hold in trust. The planholder then owns an undivided interest in the mutual fund shares evidenced by the unit trust certificate(s).

51. **B.** Gordon must put in the full $15,000 or the additional $6,000. Reinvested dividends and changes in the NAV do not affect the amount required.

52. **A.** First, withdrawal of funds will be based on the NAV. Second, it will be determined each time a payment is made.

53. **B.** Taking money out of a fund at the same time a person is putting money into the fund is generally discouraged.

54. **B.** Voluntary accumulation plans allow for just that. The client can terminate at any time if she so chooses, and there is no penalty for doing so.

55. **D.** Contractual plans permit the withdrawal of funds for any reason. There is no penalty for failure to complete the plan, and the planholder will be allowed to invest at any time.

56. **D.** The Investment Company Act of 1940 permits a 50% sales load on the amount invested in the first year. The client plans to invest $100 a month, or $1,200 the first year. Fifty percent of $1,200 is $600.

57. **C.** We can assume the plan in question is a front-end load plan. The investment company is entitled to keep 50% of all deposits made in the first year. If the investor withdraws from the plan in the first year, the investor is entitled to a return of 100% of the account value (120 shares × $10 NAV) plus all sales charges in excess of 15% of the total deposits. John's total deposits were $1,000 (ten months × $100), and the company kept 50% ($500) as sales charges. The plan company can keep 15% of John's total deposits, or $150 (15% × $1,000), but must refund the balance. Because $500 less $150 equals a refund of $350, the investor will receive $350 plus the current NAV of $1,200, or $1,550.

58. **B.** The minor is the owner of the securities in an UGMA account, while the securities are held in the name of the custodian.

59. **B.** In a JTWROS account securities pass on to the surviving owner.

60. **A.** Fred paid a total of $500 for 49 shares of stock, or $10.20 per share. The average price of the shares during this time was the total of the share prices ($70) divided by the number of investment periods (five), or $14. The difference between the two is $3.80.

61. **C.** Rights of accumulation are good forever, while the letter of intent has a 13-month limit.

62. **C.** When a customer opens a new account, the card is signed by the RR introducing the client to the firm and by the principal, who is accepting the client for the firm. The customer is not required to sign the new account card. The customer's signature is required only on a margin account.

63. **D.** All information that affects your recommendations or the financial situation of a customer must be noted immediately in the file.

9   Mutual Funds—Prospectus

The Dummy Fund (the Fund) is an open-end investment company—a mutual fund. The investment objective of the Fund is to seek long-term growth of capital, with current income as a secondary consideration. Shareholders should read and retain the prospectus for future reference.

SUMMARY INFORMATION ABOUT THE FUND

The Dummy Fund (the Fund) is an open-end, diversified investment company—a mutual fund. This prospectus offers shares of beneficial interest ($1 par value) in the Fund.

What is our investment objective?

The primary investment objective of the Fund is to seek long-term growth of capital, with current income as a secondary consideration. In seeking this objective, the Fund will, under most conditions, invest primarily in common stocks, although other types of securities, such as convertible bonds and preferred stocks, may also be used. Investment emphasis will generally be on what are believed to be well-managed, aggressive companies in expanding industries. The manager may, under certain market conditions, place part of the Fund assets in cash or cash equivalents for liquidity or defensive purposes or make defensive investments in fixed-income securities.

What advantages do I, as an investor, receive by investing in the Dummy Investment Company?

The principal advantage is diversification. Due to the size of our investment company, we are able to diversify much better than most investors could on their own. This diversification is expected to greatly reduce the risk of investing to the client.

The Fund may not and will not:
(1)   Purchase any security (except certain government securities) if more than 4% of the value of the Fund's total net assets would be invested in that security.

(2)   Invest in securities of an issuer that, together with any predecessor, has been in operation for less than three years, and in equity services of issuers for which market quotations are not readily available (but excluding restricted securities limited by item 7 below) if, as a result, more than 4% of the Fund's net assets would then be invested in such securities.

(3)   Borrow money in excess of 10% of its net assets (taken at current value) and then only as a temporary measure for extraordinary or emergency reasons and not for investment purposes. The Fund may borrow only from banks, and immediately after any such borrowing there must be an asset coverage (total assets of the Fund including the amount borrowed less liabilities other than such borrowings) of at least 300% of the amount of all borrowings. In the event that, due to market decline or other reasons, such asset coverage should at any time fall below 300%, the Fund is required within three days not including Sundays and holidays to reduce the amount of its borrowings to the extent necessary to cause

the asset coverage of such borrowings to be at least 300%. If this should happen, the Fund may have to sell securities at a time when it would be disadvantageous to do so.

(4)   Invest in any company in which the combined holdings of the board of directors beneficially are more than 1/2 of 1% of the outstanding shares or securities.

(5)   Engage in margin transactions or short sales.

(6)   Invest in securities of another investment trust.

(7)   Purchase securities the disposition of which is restricted under federal securities laws if as a result such investments would exceed 4% of the value of the Fund's net assets. (As of December 31, 1985, less than 0.002% of the Fund's net assets were invested in such securities.)

(8)   Purchase any security if the Fund would then own more than 10% of the outstanding voting securities or 10% of the securities of any class of any one company.

(9)   Voluntarily pledge, mortgage, charge, hypothecate or otherwise encumber its assets.

(10) Invest for the purpose of exercising control or management.

(11) Make loans, except by purchase of securities of corporations or associations and certain government securities, except by entry into repurchase agreements with respect to not more than 25% of its total assets, and except through the lending of its portfolio securities with respect to not more than 25% of its total assets. (As a matter of policy, securities loans are made to broker-dealers pursuant to agreements requiring that loans be continuously secured by collateral in cash or cash equivalents equal at all times to the market value of the securities lent. The borrower pays to the Fund an amount equal to any dividends or interest received on the securities lent. The Fund may invest the cash collateral received in interest-bearing short-term securities or receive a fee from the borrower. Although voting rights, or rights to consent, with respect to the loaned securities pass to the borrower, the Fund retains the right to call the loans at any time on reasonable notice, and it will do so in order that securities may be voted by the Fund if the holders of such securities are asked to vote upon or consent to matters materially affecting the investment. The Fund may call such loans in order to sell the securities involved.)

(12) Concentrate more than 25% of the Fund's assets in any one industry.

(13) Invest in real estate, commodities or commodity futures, land, mortgages or collectibles (coins, stamps, plates, jewelry, old automobiles).

(14) Act as an underwriter except to the extent that, in connection with the disposition of its portfolio securities, it may be deemed to be an underwriter under certain federal securities laws. Investment restrictions 1 through 11 above (except for the policies stated under restriction 11) are incorporated in the Fund's articles of incorporation and consequently cannot be changed without an affirmative vote of the holders of an absolute majority of the outstanding shares of the Fund. The remaining investment restrictions (12 through 14) are fundamental policies of the Fund and cannot be changed without a vote of a majority of the outstanding voting securities of the Fund. As provided in the Investment Company Act of 1940 a vote of the lesser of: (I) more than 50% of the outstanding shares of the Fund, or (II) 67% or more of the shares present at a meeting if more than 50% of the outstanding shares are represented at the meeting in person or by proxy.

The board of directors may not deal with the Fund as principal in the purchase or sale of securities or borrow money or property from the Fund.

HOW AN INVESTOR BUYS SHARES

An investor may buy shares of the Fund from any representative of the Dummy Fund, Hard Rock Life of Dallas or any broker-dealer appointed by the Dummy Fund to sell shares. Minimum initial investment is $500. Additional investments may be made at any time in the minimum amounts of $50. Orders are reviewed for accuracy and processed on the day they are received by the Fund. The client will be charged the asking price as of the next calculation following the receipt of an accurate order. The asking price is calculated at 5:00 pm every business day. Sales charges vary by the amount of the investment as stated below.

	Sales Charge as Net Amount Invested*	Dealer Discount	Offering Price
Less than $10,000	8.70%	6%	8%
$10,000 but less than $25,000	6.38%	4%	6%
$25,000 but less than $100,000	4.17%	2%	4%
$100,000 but less than $500,000	2.04%	1%	2%
$500,000 but less than $1 million	1.01%	1/2%	1%

*Net of sales charge

The Fund receives the entire net asset value. The underwriter's commission is the sales charge shown above less any applicable dealer discount. The dealer discount is the same for all dealers, except that Dummy Distributors retains the entire sales charge on any retail sales made by it. Dummy Distributors will give dealers 10 days' notice of any changes in the dealer discount.

The Fund will accept unconditional orders to be executed at the public offering price based on the net asset value next determined after the order is placed. In the case of orders for purchase of shares placed through dealers, the applicable public offering price will be the net asset value determined as of 5:00 pm EST on the day the order is placed, plus the sales charge, but only if the dealer receives the order prior to 5:00 pm EST and transmits it to Dummy Distributors (the underwriter) prior to its close of business that same day (normally 5:00 pm). The dealer is responsible for transmitting this order by 5:00 pm. If the dealer fails to do so, the customer's entitlement to that day's closing price must be settled between the customer and the dealer. If the dealer receives the order after 5:00 pm EST, the price will be determined as of 5:00 pm EST on the next day it is open. If an investor sends funds for the purchase of additional shares directly to DUMCO, they will be invested at the public offering price based on the net asset value next determined after receipt.

SYSTEMATIC WITHDRAWAL

The Plans described below are fully voluntary and may be terminated at any time without the imposition by the Fund or the shareholder servicing agent of any penalty. All Plans provide for automatic reinvestment of all distributions in additional shares of the Fund at net asset value. The availability of these Plans may be terminated by the Fund or DUMCO at any time.

MONTHLY CASH WITHDRAWAL PLAN

An investor who owns or buys shares of the Fund valued at $10,000 or more at the current offering price may open a Withdrawal Plan and have a designated sum of money paid monthly (or quarterly) to the investor or another person. Shares are deposited in a Plan account, and all distributions are reinvested in additional shares of the Fund at net asset value (except where the Plan is utilized in connection with a charitable remainder trust). Shares in a Plan account are then redeemed at net asset value to make each withdrawal payment. Redemptions for the purpose of withdrawals are made on the last business day of the month preceding payment at the day's closing at net asset value, and checks are mailed on or about the first day of the next month. Payment will be made to any person the investor designates; however, if shares are registered in the name of a trustee or other fiduciary, payment will be made only to the fiduciary, except in the case of a profit-sharing or pension plan where payment will be made to a designee. As withdrawal payments may include a return of principal, they cannot be considered a guaranteed annuity of actual yield of income to the investor. The redemption of shares in connection with a Withdrawal Plan may result in a gain or loss for tax purposes. Continued withdrawals in excess of income will reduce and possibly exhaust invested principal, especially in the event of a market decline. The maintenance of a Withdrawal Plan concurrently with purchases of additional shares of the Fund would be disadvantageous to the investor because of the sales charge payable on such purchases. For this reason, the minimum investment accepted while a Withdrawal Plan is in effect is $1,000, and an investor may not maintain a plan for the accumulation of shares of the Fund (other than through reinvestment of distributions) and a Withdrawal Plan at the same time. The cost of administering these Plans for the benefit of those shareholders participating in them is borne by the Fund as an expense of all shareholders. The Fund or DUMCO may terminate or change the terms of the Withdrawal Plan at any time. Because the Withdrawal Plan involves invasion of capital, investors should consider carefully with their own financial advisors whether the Plan and the specified amounts to be withdrawn are appropriate in their circumstances. The Fund and DUMCO make no recommendations or representations in this regard.

HOW THE FUND RECEIVES ADVICE

Under a Management Contract dated January 1, 1986, subject to such policies as the board of directors of the Fund may determine, the Manager, at its expense, furnishes continuously an investment program for the Fund and makes investment decisions on behalf of the Fund. Subject to the control of the Fund's board of directors, the Manager also manages, supervises and conducts the other affairs and business of the Fund and matters incidental thereto.

The compensation payable to the Manager under the Contract is a quarterly fee based on the average net asset value of the Fund, as determined at the close of each business day during the quarter, at the following annual rates: 50/100 of 1% on the first $100,000,000 of average net asset value; 40/100 of 1% on the next $100,000,000; 35/100 of 1% on the next $300,000,000; and 32.5/100 of 1% of the average net asset value in excess of $500,000,000. The Manager's compensation is subject to reduction to the extent that in any year expenses (exclusive of brokerage, interest and taxes) of the Fund for such year exceed 1 1/2% of the first $30,000,000 of average net assets and 1% of any excess over $30,000,000. The Manager has undertaken to certain state securities authorities that, so long as it serves as investment manager to the Fund and shares of the Fund are registered for sale in such states, any reimbursement pursuant to the expense limitations of such states will not be limited to compensation received by the Manager from the Fund.

HOW INVESTORS' ACCOUNTS ARE MAINTAINED

The open account is the shareholder's account on the Fund's records which shows the number of shares owned and also provides several additional features.

Each time a transaction takes place on an open account, the shareholder will receive a confirmation setting forth the complete details of the transaction and the balance of shares owned. Annually, a shareholder will also receive a statement of the account that includes information for use in preparing tax returns. Shareholders may elect to receive distributions on their shares under any one of the following options:

I. All distributions in cash.

II. All distributions in additional shares of the Fund.

III. Income distributions in cash and capital gains distributions in additional shares of the Fund.

Shareholders who do not elect one of the above distribution options automatically receive all distributions in additional shares of the Fund. A shareholder may change distribution options at any time by written notice to Dummy Distributors.

THE DUMMY FUND, INCORPORATED

STATEMENT OF OPERATIONS

Year Ending December 31st

Investment Income	1983	1984	1985
Income:			
Dividends	$886,238	$691,984	$660,216
Interest	62,057	33,716	41,981
	948,295	795,700	702,197
Expenses:			
Investment management fee	140,667	131,349	137,653
Transfer fee	133,933	115,606	98,117
Printing	15,386	14,313	14,759
Auditing	11,000	12,000	14,000
Directors fee	10,000	10,480	11,850
State taxes	8,734	7,150	10,900
Custodian fee	9,650	9,807	9,119
Legal	6,282	6,298	6,281
Registration and filing fees	4,770	4,520	4,628
Sundry	1,599	2,039	1,976
TOTAL	342,021	313,562	309,283
NET INVESTMENT INCOME	$606,274	$412,138	$392,914

INVESTMENTS

December 31, 1985

Common Stocks

Issuer-Description	Number of Shares	Cost	Market Value
Aerospace (11.42%)			
Boeing Company	19,500	$ 822,463	$ 987,187
Cessna Aircraft Co.	15,750	272,915	370,125
Fairchild Industries	33,750	786,847	1,451,250
McDonnel Douglas Corp.	18,000	481,815	657,000
		$2,364,040	$3,465,562
Broadcasting Communications and Publishing (1.29%)			
Capital City Communication	10,000	299,543	392,500
Cosmetics (11.35%)			
Avon	7,700	$ 661,584	$ 603,488
Breck	9,000	474,202	493,875
Cosmair	16,000	659,059	1,102,000
Noxell	15,000	765,575	1,248,750
		$2,560,420	$3,448,113
Leisure and Recreation (3.35%)			
MF	14,000	$ 945,050	$ 904,750
GM	10,000	606,975	692,500
Spalding	15,000	705,825	757,500
Winnebago	3,000	483,935	186,375
		$2,741,785	$2,541,125
Food, Beverage and Tobacco (2.37%)			
Philip Morris, Inc.	20,000	$ 469,232	$ 720,000

Issuer-Description	Number of Shares	Cost	Market Value
Electronics (19.10%)			
Beckman Instruments, Inc.	36,000	$ 597,753	$1,053,000
Intel Corporation	7,500	195,417	506,000
M/A-Com, Inc.	30,000	641,990	945,000
Motorola, Inc.	18,500	854,908	945,812
Nat'l Semiconductor	18,000	420,640	623,250
Scientific-Atlanta, Inc.	10,000	376,538	361,250
Printronix, Inc.	7,450	89,400	132,238
Tektronix, Inc.	12,000	395,395	718,500
Texas Instrument, Inc.	5,800	595,852	510,400
		$4,167,893	$5,795,700
Health Products and Services (6.39%)			
Allergan Pharmaceuticals	26,000	$ 689,135	$1,482,000
Hospital Corp. of Amer.	10,300	296,055	458,350
		$ 985,190	$1,940,350
Insurance (7.75%)			
American International Group, Inc.	19,275	$ 775,800	$1,146,863
Mission Insur. Group	30,000	389,571	930,000
MGIC Investment Corp.	10,000	187,953	273,750
		$1,353,324	$2,350,613
Lodging and Restaurants (1.98%)			
McDonalds Corporation	13,800	$ 625,928	$ 600,300

PER-SHARE INCOME AND CAPITAL CHANGES

	1982	1983	1984	1985
Investment income	.15	.19	.17	.19
Expenses	(.08)	(.07)	(.07)	(.08)
Net investment income	.07	.12	.10	.11
Dividends from NII	(.06)	(.09)	(.125)	(.0975)
Net realized gain (loss)	.64	(.98)	.71	1.9375
Net increase (decrease)	(.65)	(.95)	.71	1.95
Net asset value				
Beginning of year	5.68	6.33	5.38	6.09
End of year	6.33	5.38	6.09	8.04
Ratio expenses to average net assets	1.15%	1.22%	1.19%	1.12%
Ratio NII to average net assets	1.04%	2.16%	1.57%	1.43%
Portfolio turnover rate	33.53%	38.96%	43.10%	24.51%
Number of shares outstanding				
End of year	5,347,935	4,773,132	4,344,408	3,775,465

Use the information on pages 101 and 102 to answer questions 1 through 3.

1. The investment objective of the Dummy Fund is

   A. capital appreciation
   B. long-term capital growth with current income as a secondary objective
   C. current income
   D. current income with capital appreciation as a secondary objective

2. What percentage of the total assets of the Dummy Fund may be invested in companies that are less than three years old?

   A. 0%
   B. No more than 4%
   C. No more than 33 1/3%
   D. There is no limit.

3. The Dummy Fund will not invest in which of the following?

   I. Real estate
   II. Commodity futures
   III. Preferred stock
   IV. Treasury bonds

   A. I and II
   B. I and III
   C. II
   D. IV

Use the information on page 103 to answer questions 4 through 9.

4. The Dummy Fund prices its shares at

   A. the close of the stock exchange each day
   B. the opening of the stock exchange each day
   C. 5:00 pm EST each day
   D. 5:00 pm EST each business day

5. John Joplin will be investing in the Dummy Fund. He plans to invest $100,000 in a lump sum. Because the Dummy Fund offers breakpoints, how much will John save in sales charges on this investment compared to what he would have paid under the maximum load the Dummy Fund charges?

   A. $2,000
   B. $4,000
   C. $6,000
   D. $8,000

6. Who is the principal underwriter of the Dummy Fund?

   A. Dummy Distributors
   B. Dummy Services Company
   C. DUMCO
   D. Lloyd Thurston

7. Clifford Brown intends to invest $33,000. The net asset value of the Dummy Fund shares (at the calculation after the receipt of his order) is $16 per share. How many shares will he be able to buy? (Select the nearest full number.)

   A. 1,939 shares
   B. 1,980 shares
   C. 1,989 shares
   D. 2,063 shares

8. You purchase shares of the Dummy Fund after the close of the New York Stock Exchange, but before 5:00 pm EST. Your registered representative turns in the order immediately. What price will you pay for the shares?

   A. Current public offering price
   B. Public offering price that will be calculated at 5:00 pm
   C. Public offering price at the close of the New York Stock Exchange on this day
   D. Public offering price after tomorrow's calculation

9. An investor turns in a request to purchase shares of the Dummy Fund in good order at noon. The broker-dealer does not turn in the order until the following morning, and the price per share is now higher. The price the investor will pay is the

   A. closing price prior to the receipt of the order
   B. closing price the next day
   C. opening price the morning of the second day
   D. This must be settled between the customer and the dealer.

Use the information on pages 103 and 104 to answer question 10.

10. How much must a client have in the Dummy Fund before he may begin a systematic withdrawal plan?

    A. $500
    B. $1,000
    C. $10,000
    D. $15,000

Use the information on page 105 to answer questions 11 and 12.

11. According to the Dummy Fund prospectus provided, how much will the fund pay to an investment advisor each quarter of the year if the fund's average net asset value is $60 million for the year?

    A. $75,000
    B. $300,000
    C. $1,000,000
    D. The information provided is insufficient to answer the question.

12. An investor can elect to receive distributions from the Dummy Fund as follows:

    I. All distributions may be taken in cash.
    II. All distributions may be reinvested in additional shares of the fund.
    III. All dividend distributions may be taken in cash, and capital gains distributions may be reinvested in additional shares of the fund.
    IV. All dividend distributions may be reinvested in additional shares of the fund, and capital gains distributions may be taken in cash.

    A. I only
    B. I and II only
    C. I, II and III only
    D. I, II, III and IV

Use the information on pages 105 through 108 to answer questions 13 through 17.

13. The Dummy Fund's net investment income between 1983 and 1985

    A. decreased by $19,224
    B. decreased by $194,136
    C. decreased by $213,360
    D. increased by $213,360

14. Of the following expenses of the Dummy Fund, which two were the greatest in 1984?

    I. Investment management fees
    II. Custodian fees
    III. Legal fees
    IV. Transfer fees

    A. I and II
    B. I and IV
    C. II and III
    D. III and IV

15. Which of the following statements is true concerning the net investment income of the Dummy Fund between 1984 and 1985?

   A. Net investment income for 1985 was greater than net investment income for 1984.

   B. Net investment income remained the same between 1984 and 1985.

   C. Net investment income for 1984 was greater than net investment income for 1985.

   D. Net investment income was greater than gross income.

16. When looking at the prospectus provided, you notice that the Dummy Fund has made investments in several industries. In which industry has it made the largest investment?

   A. Electronics
   B. Oil services and drilling
   C. Aerospace
   D. Lodging and restaurants

17. What was the difference in the NAV per share of the Dummy Growth Fund from 1983 to 1985 using end-of-year figures?

   A. Decrease of $.95
   B. Decrease of $.24
   C. Increase of $.71
   D. Increase of $2.66

◆ Answers & Rationale

1. **B.** The Dummy Fund's objective is long-term capital appreciation with current income as a secondary consideration. This information is typically located on the cover page of a prospectus, as well as under a section entitled "Investment Policies and Goals of the Fund."

2. **B.** The fund states that it will not "invest in companies less than three years old . . . if, as a result, more than 4% of the fund's portfolio would be invested in such companies."

3. **A.** The fund lists those investments it will not make. The fund states it will not invest in real estate or commodity futures.

4. **D.** The Dummy Fund prices its shares at 5:00 pm each business day. This information is found under the section "How an Investor Buys Shares."

5. **C.** The maximum sales charge is 8%. John qualifies for the 2% sales charge and therefore saves 6%, or $6,000. The breakpoint chart is contained under the heading "How an Investor Buys Shares."

6. **A.** The underwriter for the Dummy Fund is Dummy Distributors.

7. **B.** Clifford Brown has $33,000 to invest, qualifying for a 4% sales load. To calculate the number of shares he would purchase, determine the net amount of money he will invest: $4\% \times \$33,000 = \$1,320$. The sales charge is $1,320; the net amount to invest is $33,000 minus $1,320, which equals $31,680. Dividing $31,680 by the NAV of $16 equals the number of shares purchased, or 1,980.

8. **B.** The Dummy Fund calculates its NAV at 5:00 pm each business day. An investor purchasing shares whose order is received by the fund prior to 5:00 pm will purchase at the public offering price calculated at that time.

9. **D.** According to the Dummy Fund, the fund is not responsible for dealers who do not turn in orders promptly. The price of the fund is determined each business day at 5:00 pm. Because the dealer did not turn in the shares until the next day, any price differential must be settled between the dealer and the client.

10. **C.** Under the withdrawal plan section in the prospectus, an investor must have at least $10,000 invested at the current offering price of the Dummy Fund.

11. **A.** The investment advisor of the Dummy Fund receives a fee based on an annual percentage of 1/2 of 1% of the first $100,000,000 of net assets managed. This is an annual fee. The question asks how much the advisor receives on a quarterly basis if the fund's asset value is $60,000,000. One half of 1% of $60,000,000 is $300,000; $300,000 divided by four equals a quarterly fee of $75,000.

12. **C.** The Dummy Fund does not allow all these options, only the first three listed.

13. **C.** Looking at the statement of operations, the net investment income for 1983 was $606,274; for 1985 it was $392,914. The difference was a decrease of $213,360.

14. **B.** The statement of operations details the fund's expenses. The greatest fund expenses in 1984 were investment management and the transfer fee.

15. **C.** The statement of operations also lists the net investment income for the fund. The NII for 1984 was greater than for 1985.

16. **A.** The portfolio of the Dummy Fund lists those industries in which the portfolio has invested. Next to each industry group there is a percentage listed in brackets. This number is the percentage of the portfolio's investment for that industry. For the electronics industry, the fund has invested 19.1% of its assets.

17.   **D.**   The NAV per share of mutual funds is listed in the fund's per-share and capital changes chart. The NAV per share is listed for the years 1982 through 1985. The listing is in two rows: end of year and beginning of year. The end-of-year figure for 1983 was $5.38; for 1985 it was $8.04. The change was an increase of $2.66.

10 Variable Annuities

1. If a variable annuity has an assumed investment rate of 5% and the annualized return of the separate account is 4%, what would be the consequence?

   I. The value of the accumulation unit will rise.
   II. The value of the annuity unit will rise.
   III. The value of the accumulation unit will fall.
   IV. The value of the annuity unit will fall.

   A. I and II
   B. I and IV
   C. II and III
   D. III and IV

2. Maggie Smith is 65. She had payroll deduction contributions into a tax deferred annuity. Her contributions totaled $10,000 and the current value of her account is $16,000. For tax purposes, what is Maggie's cost basis?

   A. $0
   B. $6,000
   C. $10,000
   D. $16,000

3. An investor is in the annuity stage of a variable annuity purchased 15 years ago. During the present month, the annuitant receives a check for an amount that is less than the previous month's payment. Which of the following events would have caused the annuitant to receive the smaller check?

   A. The performance of the account was less than the previous month's performance.
   B. The performance of the account was greater than the previous month's performance.
   C. The performance of the account was less than the assumed interest rate.
   D. The performance of the account was greater than the assumed interest rate.

4. The separate investment account funding a variable annuity that is managed by the insurance company offering the variable contract is considered

   A. a unit investment trust
   B. a face-amount certificate company
   C. a management investment company
   D. none of the above

5. The separate account funding a variable annuity that purchases shares in a mutual fund offered by the life insurance company is considered

   A. a unit investment trust
   B. a face-amount certificate company
   C. a management investment company
   D. none of the above

6. A prospectus for an individual variable annuity contract

   I. must provide full and fair disclosure
   II. is required by the Securities Act of 1933
   III. must be filed with the SEC
   IV. must precede or accompany every sales presentation

   A. I only
   B. I, III and IV
   C. II and III only
   D. I, II, III and IV

7. Kirk Thomas is about to buy a variable annuity contract. He wants to select an annuity that will give him the largest possible monthly payment. Which of the following payout options would do so?

   A. Life annuity with period certain
   B. Unit refund life option
   C. Life annuity with ten-year period certain
   D. Life only annuity

8. Tim Simmons owns a variable annuity contract with an AIR of 5%. In January the realized rate of return in the separate account was 7%, and Tim received a check based on this return for $200. In February the rate of return was 10%, and Tim received a check for $210. To maintain the same payment Tim received in February, what rate of return would the separate account have to earn in March?

   A. 3%
   B. 5%
   C. 7%
   D. 10%

9. Your client tells you he wants a source of retirement income that is stable, but that also could offer some protection against purchasing power risk in times of inflation. You should recommend

   A. a variable annuity
   B. a fixed annuity
   C. a combination annuity
   D. common stocks and municipal bonds

10. Which of the following statements about a straight-life variable annuity is(are) true?

    I. The number of annuity units a client redeems never changes.
    II. The number of accumulation units a client owns will never change.
    III. If the client dies during the annuity period, the remaining funds will be distributed to the beneficiary.
    IV. The monthly payout is fixed to the Consumer Price Index.

    A. I only
    B. I and II only
    C. I, II and III only
    D. I, II, III and IV

11. According to the NASD, the maximum sales charge on a variable annuity contract is

    A. 8.5% of the total amount invested
    B. 8.5% of the net amount invested
    C. 9% of the total amount invested
    D. There is no maximum on variable annuity contracts.

12. The value of a variable annuity separate account fluctuates in relationship to the

    A. general account maintained by the insurance company
    B. value of the separate account portfolio
    C. Consumer Price Index
    D. S&P 500 market index

13. At age 65, Fred Jacobs purchased an immediate variable annuity contract. Fred made a lump-sum $100,000 initial payment and selected a life income with ten-year period certain payment option. Fred lived until age 88. The insurance company made payments to Fred

    A. until his initial payment of $100,000 was exhausted
    B. for ten years
    C. for 23 years
    D. at a fixed rate for ten years and at a variable rate up until his death

14. The difference between a fixed annuity and a variable annuity is that the variable annuity

   I. offers a guaranteed return
  II. offers a payment that may vary in amount
 III. will always pay out more money than a fixed annuity
 IV. attempts to offer protection to the annuitant from inflation

  A. I and III
  B. I and IV
  C. II and III
  D. II and IV

15. The insurance company's separate account is

   I. used for the investment of moneys paid by variable annuity contract holders
  II. separate from the general investments of the insurance company
 III. operated in a manner similar to an investment company
 IV. as much a security as it is an insurance product

  A. I only
  B. I and II only
  C. I, II and III only
  D. I, II, III and IV

16. A mutual fund and a variable annuity's separate account are similar in that

   I. the investment portfolio is professionally managed
  II. the client may vote for the board of directors or board of managers
 III. the client assumes the investment risk
 IV. payout plans guarantee the client income for life

  A. I, II and III only
  B. II and IV only
  C. III and IV only
  D. I, II, III and IV

17. What will happen if a client, age 35, invests $100 a month in a variable annuity for seven years and suddenly dies?

  A. The client's beneficiaries will not receive any money until the year in which the client would have turned 59 1/2.
  B. The insurance company keeps all the contributions made to date because the contract was not annuitized.
  C. The client's beneficiaries will receive only the amount contributed.
  D. The client's beneficiaries would receive the greater of the contributions or current value of the account if the contract were insured.

18. Your client is 68 years old, retired and in good health. She is concerned about budgeting funds. She needs funds for day-to-day living expenses starting now. As her representative, you could suggest that she purchase

  A. as much whole life insurance as she can afford
  B. a periodic-payment deferred variable annuity
  C. a single-payment deferred variable annuity
  D. an immediate annuity

19. An insurance company offering a variable annuity makes payments to annuitants on the 15th of each month. The contract has an assumed interest rate of 3%. In July of this year the contract earned 4%. In August the account earned 6%. If the contract earns 3% in September, the payments to annuitants will be

  A. less than the payments in July
  B. greater than the payments in August
  C. less than the payments in August
  D. the same as the payments in August

20. Which of the following factors may determine the amount of payout from a variable annuity?

    I.   Mortality experience of the company
    II. Age and sex of the annuitant
    III. Insurability of the annuitant
    IV. Rate of return of the separate account

    A. I, II and IV only
    B. II only
    C. II, III and IV only
    D. I, II, III and IV

21. Angus Smith has been investing in a nonqualified deferred annuity through a payroll deduction plan offered at the school system where he works. Angus has invested a total of $10,000. The annuity contract is currently valued at $16,000, and he plans to retire. On what amount will Angus be taxed if he chooses a lump-sum withdrawal?

    A. $6,000
    B. $10,000
    C. $16,000
    D. He will not owe taxes because the annuity was nonqualified.

22. If a client, age 52, chooses to cash in her annuity contract before payout begins, she will

    I.   be taxed at the ordinary income tax rate on earnings in excess of cost base
    II. have to pay a 10% penalty on the amount withdrawn that exceeds cost base
    III. have to pay a 5% penalty on the amount withdrawn that exceeds cost base
    IV. be taxed at ordinary rates on the amount withdrawn that represents cost base, and will be taxed at capital gains rates on the amount withdrawn that exceeds cost base

    A. I
    B. I and II
    C. I and III
    D. III and IV

23. An annuity may be purchased under which of the following methods?

    I.   Single payment, deferred annuity
    II. Single payment, immediate annuity
    III. Periodic payment, deferred annuity
    IV. Periodic payment, immediate annuity

    A. I and II only
    B. I, II and III only
    C. III and IV only
    D. I, II, III and IV

24. Mildred Rossi purchased a variable annuity with an immediate payout plan. In the first month, she received a payment of $328. Which of the following statements about Mildred's investment is(are) true?

    I.   Her next payment is guaranteed to be $328.
    II. She made a lump-sum investment.
    III. She purchased the variable annuity from a registered representative.

    A. II only
    B. II and III only
    C. III only
    D. I, II and III

25. Mildred Rossi assumes the risk involved with her variable annuity. What does this mean?

    I.   She is not assured of the return of her invested principal.
    II. The underlying portfolio is primarily common stocks, which have no guaranteed return.
    III. As an investor, she can be held liable for the debts incurred by the insurance company.

    A. I and II only
    B. II and III only
    C. III only
    D. I, II and III

26. Cosmo Insurance Company is facing a poor business year and a period of steep economic decline in general. Cosmo's income payments to its fixed annuity contract holders will likely

   A. increase
   B. decrease
   C. stay the same
   D. cease

27. The portfolio of a general account of a life insurance company is normally used to fund

   A. variable annuities
   B. fixed annuities
   C. either fixed or variable annuities
   D. none of the above

28. Gary Zins has just purchased an immediate variable annuity. Which of the following are characteristic of Gary's investment?

   I. Lump-sum purchase
   II. Distribution of dividends will occur during the accumulation period.
   III. Accumulation and payment of dividends will occur during the payout period.

   A. I and II only
   B. I and III only
   C. II and III only
   D. I, II and III

29. Which of the following statements about deferred variable annuities are true?

   I. Purchase payments can be either lump sum or periodic.
   II. Contract holders are guaranteed a rate of return.
   III. Earnings accumulate in the contract owner's account during the prepayment period.

   A. I and II only
   B. I and III only
   C. II and III only
   D. I, II and III

30. Doris Ack is planning for retirement. She wants to be assured of a minimum income per month, and she wants some protection from inflation. Doris should consider a plan with

   A. installments for a designated amount
   B. period certain
   C. a combination fixed and variable payout
   D. installments for a designated period

31. A variable annuity contract guarantees a

   I. rate of return
   II. fixed mortality expense
   III. fixed administrative expense

   A. I and II only
   B. I and III only
   C. II and III only
   D. I, II and III

32. Bob Barrett, a registered representative, is discussing variable annuities with a client. He explains that under the contract the annuitant receives payments for life. Bob is describing a(n)

   A. payment guarantee
   B. insurance protection
   C. expense guarantee
   D. mortality guarantee

33. Separate accounts are similar to mutual funds in that both

   I. may have diversified portfolios of common stock
   II. are managed by full-time professionals
   III. give investors voting rights

   A. I and II only
   B. I and III only
   C. II and III only
   D. I, II and III

34. If units of a separate account represent indirect ownership of mutual fund shares, the separate account must be registered as

    A. a management investment company
    B. a unit investment trust
    C. an operating investment company
    D. both A and B.

35. Harvey Kent has purchased a deferred variable annuity with monthly payments of $150. What do his monthly payments purchase?

    A. Accumulation units
    B. Annuity units
    C. Unit investment trust certificates
    D. Individual shares of stock held in the separate account portfolio

36. At the end of the year, Harvey Kent owns 900 accumulation units, which represent approximately 0.05% of the holdings in the variable annuity separate account. This means that

    A. Harvey will receive approximately 0.05% of the separate account assets during the payout period
    B. Harvey's account will receive about 0.05% of the portfolio's current earnings
    C. Harvey owns 900 shares of the underlying mutual fund
    D. None of the above are true.

37. Harvey Kent's annuity has a portfolio that contains mostly common stocks. What does this mean for Harvey?

    I. In a rising market, the value of Harvey's account may rise.
    II. In a rising market, the value of an accumulation unit may rise.
    III. Harvey is protected from loss.

    A. I and II only
    B. I and III only
    C. II and III only
    D. I, II and III

38. The value of an individual's variable annuity is directly related to

    A. an amount determined by insurance regulations
    B. the Consumer Price Index
    C. the profits of the insurance company
    D. the performance of the portfolio of the separate account

39. At retirement Herman Miller decides to annuitize his variable annuity contract. After his final purchase payment, he had 1,857 accumulation units. What factors will be considered when determining the amount of payout he will receive?

    I. The value of one annuity unit
    II. The conversion value shown in the company's annuity table
    III. The value of Harvey's share of the separate account

    A. I and II only
    B. I and III only
    C. II and III only
    D. I, II and III

40. Margaret Long has annuitized her variable annuity contract. The contract has an assumed interest rate of 4%. Margaret's first check was for $225. In order for her check to remain at $225, what rate of return will the separate account have to earn?

    A. Less than 4% but greater than 0%
    B. 4%
    C. Greater than %
    D. It doesn't matter; the payment is guaranteed.

41. If a separate account with an assumed interest rate of 4% experiences an actual return of 5% for the year, which of the following would be true?

    A. Accumulation units would increase in value.
    B. Annuity units would increase in value.
    C. An investor who annuitized her contract would expect the monthly payments to increase.
    D. All of the above would occur.

42. John Jackson has been making periodic payments into a deferred variable annuity. John's annuity value is $1,200, and the current value of an accumulation unit is $3. How many accumulation units does John have?

    A. 0
    B. 400
    C. 1,200
    D. 3,600

43. Annuity payments made to contract owners are

    A. tax exempt
    B. taxed only on the cost basis
    C. taxed only on the portion that represents investment earnings
    D. taxed as capital gains

44. Barry Sims is paying into his variable annuity plan. Last month he received a statement from his insurance company stating that his account had been credited with $127 in net investment income and realized capital gains. How should Barry handle these earnings?

    A. Report them as ordinary income on this year's tax return.
    B. Report them as long-term gains on this year's tax return.
    C. Report them as an early withdrawal subject to the 5% penalty.
    D. Defer them from current taxation.

45. Susan Swanson has paid $14,000 into her variable annuity. Currently, her account is valued at $20,000. If she were to terminate her contract and take the proceeds in a lump sum, she would need to know her cost basis. What is Susan's cost base?

    A. $6,000
    B. $14,000
    C. $20,000
    D. $34,000

46. Susan Swanson has paid $14,000 into her variable annuity. Currently, her account is valued at $20,000. If Susan surrendered her contract, how much would she report as taxable income received?

    A. $6,000
    B. $14,000
    C. $20,000
    D. $34,000

47. If Susan Swanson annuitized her contract and her first payment was for $350, $200 of which was considered return of investment, how much of this payment must be reported for income tax purposes?

    A. $150
    B. $200
    C. $350
    D. $550

48. A variable annuity contract is designed primarily as a

    A. guaranteed hedge against inflation
    B. retirement device
    C. means of rapidly accumulating money
    D. Variable annuities are designed for all of the above reasons.

49. The securities held in the separate account of a variable annuity will consist primarily of common stock because

   A. the yield on stocks is usually higher than the yield on bonds
   B. prices of common stock tend to reflect increases or decreases in the cost of living
   C. the value of common stock is easy to calculate
   D. common stock ownership provides limited liability to shareholders

50. A variable annuity has an AIR of 3.5%. This past year, the separate account grew at a rate of 10.5%. What effect will this have?

   A. This extra appreciation will have no effect on the investors.
   B. This extra appreciation should now be used to help make projections into the future.
   C. If the client is in the annuity period (receiving funds), this extra appreciation will increase his monthly checks.
   D. This will be taxed to the investor during the accumulation period as ordinary income.

51. A variable annuity contract holder commences the payout period, receiving an initial benefit of $100 based on an assumed interest rate of 4%. In the second month, the contract holder receives $125 based on an annualized investment rate of 10% earned by the separate account. If the separate account experiences an annualized net investment rate of 8% during the third month, the payout to the contract holder would be

   A. less than $100
   B. less than $125, but greater than $100
   C. $125
   D. greater than $125

52. An owner of a variable annuity is guaranteed that the annuity company will make payments for a minimum of 20 years. From this information, you know that the annuity is a

   A. variable life annuity
   B. 20-year endowment policy
   C. 20-year fixed-payment policy
   D. variable annuity contract with period certain

53. An annuitant receives payment under a variable annuity for a number of years. At his death, his widow receives a lump-sum payment. The annuity was a

   A. variable life annuity
   B. variable unit refund annuity
   C. variable joint and survivor annuity
   D. 20-year endowment annuity

54. Which of the following is not guaranteed in a variable annuity contract?

   A. Expense assumptions
   B. Interest assumptions
   C. Mortality assumptions
   D. Sales load

55. A variable annuity contract is similar to a life insurance policy because it could contain all of the following EXCEPT

   A. death benefits
   B. beneficiary designation
   C. loan provisions
   D. guaranteed cash values

56. Your client could purchase each of the following types of annuity contracts EXCEPT a

   A. periodic payment deferred annuity contract
   B. periodic payment immediate life annuity contract
   C. lump-sum payment immediate life annuity contract
   D. lump-sum payment deferred annuity contract

57. Variable annuities and mutual funds are similar in that they both must register

   A. under the Investment Advisers Act of 1940

   B. under the Securities Exchange Act of 1934

   C. under the Investment Company Act of 1940

   D. with the State Insurance Commission

58. An individual takes out a fixed annuity. All else being equal, which one of the following settlement options will pay him more per month than will the others?

   A. Life income with ten-year certain

   B. Straight life annuity

   C. Joint annuity

   D. Last survivor annuity

59. Which of the following risks does a client assume when he purchases a variable annuity contract?

   A. Mortality risks

   B. Investment risks

   C. Risk of an increased cost of operation of a separate account

   D. All of the above risks

60. A retired school teacher, age 65, has had $10,000 placed into a nonqualified annuity, the current value of which is $16,000. He wishes to take a lump-sum distribution. To calculate his taxes, he will need to know his cost base. What is his cost base?

   A. $0

   B. $10,000

   C. $10,000 ordinary, plus $6,000 capital gains

   D. $16,000

61. What is the penalty for withdrawing money from a nonqualified variable annuity before age 59 1/2?

   A. 5%

   B. 6%

   C. 10%

   D. 50%

62. What is the maximum allowable sales charge on the total amount invested in the first twelve months of a ten-year periodic payment deferred variable annuity program?

   A. 8 1/2%

   B. 9%

   C. 15%

   D. 50%

63. A client has a variable annuity that has an assumed interest rate of 4%. The client received a first benefit check of $110. The separate account rate of return between the first and the second month was 10%. The client received a second check for $125. What was the actual rate of return of the separate account between the second and third month if the client's third benefit check was also for $125?

   A. Less than 4%

   B. 4%

   C. More than 4%, but less than 10%

   D. 10%

64. An investor owning which of the following variable annuity contracts would hold accumulation units?

   I. Periodic payment deferred annuity

   II. Single payment deferred annuity

   III. Immediate life annuity

   IV. Immediate life annuity with ten-year certain

   A. I and II only

   B. I, III and IV only

   C. I and IV only

   D. I, II, III and IV

65. A retired school teacher, age 65, has periodically deposited a total of $10,000 in a nonqualified variable annuity. She was employed by a public school system. The current value of her account is $16,000. She wishes to take a lump-sum withdrawal of the full amount. On how much of this will she be taxed at the ordinary income tax rate?

   A. $0
   B. $6,000
   C. $10,000
   D. $16,000

66. The annuity unit of a variable annuity changes in value in a manner that corresponds most closely to changes in which of the following?

   I.   Dow Jones index
   II. Cost of living index
   III. Value of securities held by the insurance company
   IV. Value of the securities kept in a separate account

   A. I and III only
   B. I, III and IV only
   C. IV only
   D. I, II, III and IV

67. In a nonqualified variable annuity, which of the following best describes the risks borne by the annuitant?

   A. The annuitant must pay taxes on the earnings in the current period.
   B. Mortality risks
   C. Interest rate risks
   D. Operating expense risks

68. When recommending a variable annuity to a prospective purchaser, which of the following should you take into account?

   A. Purchaser's savings account
   B. Amount of purchaser's insurance
   C. Purchaser's employer's pension plan
   D. All of the above

69. In calculating the investment performance of a separate account, you would take into account

   A. realized capital gains
   B. unrealized capital gains
   C. dividend income
   D. all of the above

70. The capital gains tax rate that an individual pays on appreciation in the reserves held for his variable annuity in a separate account while the contract is in the accumulation period is

   A. 0%
   B. 10%
   C. 25%
   D. 50%

71. A client, age 42, has been depositing money in a variable annuity for five years. He plans to stop investing, but has no intention of withdrawing any funds for at least 20 years. He most likely is holding

   A. accumulation units
   B. annuity units
   C. accumulation shares
   D. mutual fund units

72. During the accumulation period of a periodic payment deferred variable annuity, the number of accumulation units

   A. varies and the value per unit is fixed.
   B. is fixed and the value per unit is fixed.
   C. is fixed and the value per unit varies.
   D. varies and the value per unit varies.

◆ Answers & Rationale

1. B. The accumulation unit will increase in value as the portfolio earned 4%; however, the annuity unit value will decrease because actual return of the portfolio (4%) was less than the assumed interest rate of 5% necessary to maintain payments.

2. C. Contributions to a nonqualified annuity are made aftertax. The growth of the annuity is deferred representing ordinary income when withdrawn. Cost base is $10,000.

3. C. In the annuity stage of a variable annuity, the amount received will depend on the performance of the account compared to the assumed interest rate. If actual performance is less than the AIR, the value of the check will decline.

4. C. A separate account that is managed by an insurance company and is used to fund variable contracts is defined by the Investment Company Act of 1940 as a management investment company.

5. A. A separate account purchasing shares of mutual funds to fund variable contracts does not actively manage the securities held; instead, the account holds the shares in trust for the contract holders. This account is classified as a unit investment trust under the act of 1940.

6. D. A variable annuity is a security and therefore must be registered with the SEC. As part of the registration requirements, a prospectus must be filed and distributed to prospective investors prior to or during any solicitation for sale.

7. D. Generally a life only contract will pay the most per month because payments cease at the death of the annuitant.

8. B. If the actual rate of return equals the assumed interest rate, the check will stay the same. Recall that the payout is based on an accumulated value to be distributed over the life of the annuitant (like compounding). Therefore, for Tim to receive the $210 in March the account must earn 5%.

9. C. Because the investor wants the objectives provided by both a fixed and variable annuity, a combination annuity would be suitable.

10. A. Annuity units are fixed; their current value when cashed in determines the payout amount. A life only annuity ceases payments at the death of the annuitant. The company keeps any undistributed payments. Accumulation units will fluctuate in value and number during the accumulation period.

11. A. NASD rules allow a maximum sales charge on a variable annuity contract of 8 1/2%.

12. B. The value of the separate account fluctuates in relation to the securities held in the account.

13. C. An annuity with life and ten-year certain will pay for the greater of ten years or the life of the annuitant. Fred lived for 23 more years, which is more than the ten certain.

14. D. Variable annuities are different from fixed because the payments vary and they were designed to offer the annuitant protection against inflation.

15. D. The separate account is used for the monies invested in variable annuities. It is kept separate from the general account and operated very much like an investment company. It is considered both an insurance product and an investment product.

16. A. Both a mutual fund and a variable annuity offer professional management and a board of managers or directors, and the client assumes the investment risk. Only variable annuities have payout plans that guarantee the client income for life.

17. D. The client's beneficiaries would receive the current market value, but if the contract were insured they would receive the greater of the amount invested or the current market value.

18. **D.**   Your client needs immediate income. Of the choices listed only the immediate annuity will offer this to the client.

19. **D.**   The contract in question earned 3% in September. The assumed interest rate for the contract is 3%. Payment size will not change from the payment made the previous month.

20. **A.**   Mortality experience, age, sex and rate of return all have a bearing on the size of payout. The insurability of the annuitant has no bearing.

21. **A.**   Payments into a nonqualified deferred annuity go in after taxes. Taxes must be paid on the earnings of $6,000.

22. **B.**   Cashing in an annuity will cause the annuitant taxation at the ordinary income tax rate on all earnings in excess of the cost base. Any withdrawal at age 52 is subject to a 10% penalty unless it is for death or disability.

23. **B.**   A periodic payment immediate annuity would be rather difficult to provide. As the annuitant is contributing, he would also be receiving.

24. **B.**   A variable annuity does not guarantee the amount of monthly payments. Mildred's next monthly payment may be more, less or the same as her initial payment. Because Mildred's payments began immediately, she must have made a single lump-sum investment to the company. Finally, because a variable annuity is a security, the salesperson must be a registered representative.

25. **A.**   The annuitant bears the investment risk in a variable annuity. The portfolio is not guaranteed to return a specified rate, and the principal invested will also fluctuate in value according to the securities held in the separate account portfolio.

26. **C.**   Payments from a fixed annuity are guaranteed. The company, not the annuitant, assumes the investment risk.

27. **B.**   The general account is used to fund the guaranteed contracts issued by the insurer, including fixed annuities.

28. **B.**   There is no accumulation period with an immediate annuity. A single lump-sum investment is made, and payments begin immediately. During payout, the principal and earnings are distributed as the payout.

29. **B.**   A variable annuity has no guaranteed earnings rate. A deferred annuity can be purchased with either a lump-sum investment or with periodic payments. During the accumulation period, earnings (losses) of the separate account are credited (or subtracted from) the value of the annuitant's account.

30. **C.**   Doris wants a fixed payment and protection from inflation. She wants to combine the objectives of a fixed and variable annuity.

31. **C.**   A variable annuity does not guarantee an earnings rate; however, it does guarantee to make payments for life (mortality) and normally guarantees that expenses will not increase above a specified level.

32. **D.**   The company assumes the mortality risk by guaranteeing payments for life.

33. **D.**   Separate accounts as well as mutual funds may contain a diversified portfolio of securities and be managed by a professional investment advisor. Voting rights for policy and management elections are available.

34. **B.**   Ownership is considered indirect if the separate account purchases mutual fund shares and holds them in trust for the benefit of the account owner. The separate account does not actively manage the portfolio, but relies on the mutual fund management for appreciation of the fund shares.

35. **A.**   During the accumulation stage of an annuity, the contract owner's investments purchase accumulation units. Annuity units are purchased

only when the annuitant decides to annuitize the contract.

36. B. Like mutual fund distributions, separate account earnings are distributed according to the contract owner's interest in the portfolio.

37. A. Harvey assumes the investment risk of the contract, including both upward and downward movements. If the market is rising, the value of the separate account is increasing, which is reflected in an increase in accumulation unit value and ultimately Harvey's account value.

38. D. The variable annuity account value is proportionate to the performance of the separate account.

39. C. In order to calculate the value of the first payment, when annuitizing a contract, the company will multiply Herman's account value by a factor summarizing age, sex, option and the AIR. This value is then used to purchase annuity units, the current value of which will determine subsequent payments.

40. B. The assumed interest rate is a base for projection. For benefit checks to remain stable, the account must earn the AIR. If actual return is greater than the AIR, the check will increase; if it is less, the check will decrease in comparison to the previous month's check only.

41. D. The separate account is earning 5%, so both accumulation and annuity units increase in value. Because the AIR is 4% and actual earnings are 5%, the amount of the annuitant's benefit check will also increase.

42. B. The number of accumulation units is equal to the account value divided by the current value of an accumulation unit ($1,200 ÷ $3 = 400).

43. C. Annuity payments received by the annuitant are taxable only on the portion received that exceeds cost base (cost base divided by life expectancy).

44. D. During the accumulation period, all income and gains received are tax deferred and reinvested in the separate account.

45. B. Susan's cost base is the amount of money she has contributed, or $14,000. The amount that is taxable is the difference between cost base and amount distributed—in this case, $6,000 ($20,000 − $14,000).

46. A. The difference between cost base and amount distributed—in this case, $6,000 ($20,000 − $14,000).

47. A. The amount of annuity payment considered return of cost base is not taxed ($200); the difference ($150) is taxable at ordinary rates ($350 − $200 = $150).

48. B. A variable annuity is a contract that guarantees payment for as long as the annuitant lives. However, a variable contract does not guarantee the amount of payment. The investor assumes the investment risk.

49. B. Historically, the value of common stock has kept pace with inflation.

50. C. If the separate account of the variable annuity is performing at a rate that is greater than the interest rate assumed by the investor, then the value of the annuitant's payment will increase.

51. D. The assumed interest rate (4%) serves as a base of projection for calculating periodic payments. If the actual return is greater than the AIR, then the benefit checks will increase in value. Since the account actually earned 8%, which is higher than the AIR, the value of the check would increase again (greater than $125). Remember to compare the actual return to the AIR and not to the previous month's performance.

52. D. Payments guaranteed for a period of time or until death, whichever is greater, is a period certain contract.

53. **B.** An annuity option that allows for a lump-sum payment of the contract's undistributed principal and interest is a unit refund contract.

54. **B.** A variable annuity assumes an interest rate for projection. The performance of the account is not guaranteed.

55. **D.** A variable annuity does not guarantee the value of the contract.

56. **B.** An immediate annuity contract begins payment to the annuitant within a short period of time. The contract does not allow for installment payments; payment is a single lump-sum investment.

57. **C.** Because the separate account is considered an investment company, the separate account must be registered as either an open-end investment company or a unit investment trust under the Investment Company Act of 1940.

58. **B.** With all other variables (such as money deposited, age, and sex) the same, the life only option will pay the most per month to the annuitant upon payout.

59. **B.** An investor assumes the risk of investment in a variable annuity contract. The contract does offer an expense guarantee and accepts the mortality risk.

60. **B.** Contributions to a nonqualified annuity are made aftertax (cost base); the growth of the contract is tax deferred and subject to ordinary income tax upon distribution ($10,000 is cost base).

61. **C.** Except in cases of death or disability, any distribution from an annuity in excess of cost base is subject to ordinary income tax and a 10% penalty.

62. **D.** A periodic payment deferred variable annuity program is an annuity sold under the contractual plan rules. Because the act the plan is operating under was not defined, the maximum

sales charge that could be deducted in the first twelve months would be 50% as specified under the act of 1940.

63. **B.** For the payout to remain the same from a variable annuity, the performance of the separate account must have earned the interest rate assumed. If the account earns more than the AIR, the benefit check would increase. If the account earns less than the assumed interest rate, the benefit check would decline compared to the previous month's check.

64. **A.** Accumulation units represent units of ownership in a life insurance company's separate account while the contract is in the deferral stage. Annuity units are the units of ownership while the contract is in the payout stage (annuitized). Immediate annuities purchase annuity units directly.

65. **B.** Contributions to a *nonqualified* annuity represent cost base dollars. When the contributions are paid out, they represent a return of capital and are not subject to tax. The growth in an annuity is tax deferred and is taxable upon receipt. In this question, of the total distribution of $16,000, $10,000 was a return of contributions, leaving $6,000 taxable as ordinary income.

66. **C.** The value of an annuity unit will reflect changes in the assets held in the life insurance company's separate account.

67. **C.** In a variable annuity, performance of the account is not guaranteed; the investor accepts the risk the account will not perform at the assumed interest rate.

68. **D.** When recommending any investment to a prospective client, suitability of the investment must first be determined.

69. **D.** Performance of a separate account will depend on increases and decreases of the securities held in the portfolio. Whether gains are realized or unrealized, the account will reflect the gain or loss.

70. **A.** Gains in a separate account are tax deferred. The annuitant will pay ordinary income tax on the distribution upon receipt.

71. **A.** The client is in the deferral stage of the annuity and would be holding accumulation units. The value of the client's account would be converted into annuity units when and if the client decides to annuitize the contract.

72. **D.** The value of an accumulation unit varies according to the value of the insurance company's separate account. During the accumulation stage of a variable annuity, the number of units will also vary as the income distributions and additional contributions will be purchasing more units. At the conversion of accumulation units into annuity units, only then is the number of units fixed, but the value still fluctuates according to the value of the separate account.

11 Variable Life Contracts

1. A variable life insurance policy is defined as any policy that provides for a death benefit that varies according to the

    A. investment experience of the life insurance company's general account
    B. amount of the premium invested into the insurance company's general account
    C. investment experience of the life insurance company's separate account
    D. investment experience of the variable annuity set up to provide for retirement benefits

2. Which of the following statements can an agent use to describe the scheduled premium VLI product offered by his life insurance company?

    A. The variable life policy is a life insurance policy providing for variable death benefit, cash values and premium payments depending on the performance of investments held in an insurance company's separate account.
    B. The variable life policy is a fixed-premium life insurance policy providing for variable death benefit and cash values depending on the performance of investments held in an insurance company's separate account.
    C. The variable life policy is a fixed-premium life insurance policy providing for a fixed death benefit and cash values that fluctuate depending on the performance of investments held in the insurance company's separate account.
    D. None of the above can be used.

3. Sales literature and advertising used in connection with the solicitation or sale of variable life products is defined as

    I. circulars and leaflets describing the variable life product
    II. prepared presentations used at a seminar open to the public
    III. newspaper advertising of the benefits of variable life insurance
    IV. a letter that is sent to 50 of the agent's present clients describing variable life insurance

    A. I, II and III only
    B. I and III only
    C. III only
    D. I, II, III and IV

4. The variable death benefit provided by the variable life insurance contract is best described as the amount of the death benefit

   A. other than incidental benefits payable under a variable life insurance policy dependent upon the investment performance of the separate account, which the insurer pays in excess of the minimum benefit
   B. guaranteed by the variable life insurance policy
   C. including incidental benefits payable under a variable life insurance policy dependent upon the investment performance of the separate account, which the insurer pays as a minimum guaranteed death benefit
   D. other than incidental benefits payable under a variable life insurance policy dependent upon the investment performance of the general account, which the insurer pays as a minimum guaranteed death benefit

5. The following securities and investments may be used by the insurance company to fund the variable life separate account EXCEPT

   I. real estate purchased for investment, not for lease
   II. stocks listed and traded on the NYSE
   III. new debt issues that have not yet been listed on an exchange but are expected to be listed
   IV. securities issued by the insurer

   A. I
   B. I, III and IV
   C. I and IV
   D. II and III

6. The separate account established for variable life insurance contracts may be used

   A. to fund any other variable contracts issued by the life insurance company
   B. only to fund the variable life insurance contract
   C. only for variable annuities offered by the insurance company
   D. to fund the variable life contract only if premiums are not enough to fund the insurance company's general account

7. In order for an agent to sell variable life insurance in the state, the

   I. agent must be licensed to sell VLI contracts
   II. agent's life insurance company must be authorized to issue VLI contracts within the state
   III. applicant must be registered to purchase VLI contracts within the state
   IV. agent must be licensed to sell life insurance within the state

   A. I only
   B. I, II and IV only
   C. II and III only
   D. I, II, III and IV

8. Scheduled premium VLI offered for sale within the state must offer

   I. a fixed-level premium
   II. insurance for the lifetime of the insured
   III. a minimum guaranteed death benefit
   IV. a guaranteed schedule of cash values

   A. I only
   B. I and II only
   C. I, II and III only
   D. I, II, III and IV

9. The variable death benefit payable from the variable life insurance contract shall provide for a death benefit that reflects the investment

A. experience of one or more separate accounts

B. performance of one or more general accounts

C. performance of the general and separate accounts

D. performance of the separate account over and above the amount guaranteed by the death benefit provided by the general account

10. The nonforfeiture provisions provided by a variable life insurance contract may be a

I. variable extended term insurance policy
II. fixed extended term insurance policy
III. variable fully paid insurance policy
IV. fixed fully paid insurance policy

A. I and III only
B. II, III and IV only
C. II and IV only
D. I, II, III and IV

11. A statement regarding the purpose of the variable life insurance must appear in the prospectus in bold type relating to the fact that variable life insurance is

A. an investment similar to a systematic investment plan in a mutual fund

B. an investment similar to a systematic investment plan in a variable annuity

C. insurance similar to a systematic investment plan in a mutual fund

D. None of the above are necessary.

12. The amount of cash value available as a policy loan the insurer must allow after the contract has been in force for three years is

A. 75% of cash value
B. 90% of cash value
C. 100% of cash value
D. No policy loan is allowed from a variable life contract.

13. Which of the following individuals could act as investment advisors for the life insurance company's separate account?

I. Person registered as an investment advisor under the Investment Advisers Act of 1940
II. Person convicted of fraud within the past ten years
III. Person convicted of fraudulent conversion 20 years ago with the commissioner's permission
IV. Person registered as a financial planner as long as the insurance company does not interfere with the individual's management conduct

A. I only
B. I and III only
C. I, III and IV only
D. I, II, III and IV

14. The exchange period for converting a variable life policy into a whole life policy must be for a period of not less than how many months?

A. 6
B. 12
C. 18
D. 24

15. Which of the following fees and expenses may be deducted from the gross premium paid in a variable life insurance contract?

I. Mortality risk fee
II. Expense fees
III. Amount to provide for insurance
IV. Sales expenses including commissions paid to agents

A. I and II only
B. III only
C. IV only
D. I, II, III and IV

16. The maximum amount that may be deducted for mortality and expense fees is equal to

    A. 0.5%
    B. 0.75%
    C. the maximum stated in the contract
    D. The fee depends on the mortality experience of the insurance company.

17. If the assumed interest rate of a scheduled premium VLI contract is 4%, and if the separate account earned at a rate of 10%, the contract owner would expect that the premium necessary to fund the contract would

    A. increase
    B. decrease
    C. remain the same
    D. decrease only when the death benefit is revised

18. John Jones purchased a variable life insurance contract on July 3rd, 1982. On July 29th, 1985, John decides to exchange his contract for a fixed benefit policy offered by the same insurance company. As his agent, you can tell John that

    A. his new policy will have the same contract date and age as his VLI policy
    B. his new policy will include the same riders as his VLI policy
    C. he will not require a new evidence of insurability
    D. None of the above

19. Nonforfeiture options provided by variable life insurance must provide

    I.   that at least one option is on a fixed basis
    II. that all options are offered on both a fixed and variable basis
    III. a variable extended term option
    IV. a fixed extended term option

    A. I and III
    B. I, III and IV
    C. I and IV
    D. II

20. The separate account of a variable life insurance contract has an assumed interest rate of 4%. Its performance in the past six months has been 3%. The account is now earning 8%. Which of the following statements is true?

    A. The death benefit increases immediately.
    B. The death benefit will increase at the next valuation.
    C. The death benefit will increase only if the earnings are enough to offset the negative performance of the previous months.
    D. The death benefit is fixed at the guaranteed rate.

21. Which of the following statements concerning a policy loan from a variable life insurance policy is FALSE?

    A. The interest charged on the policy loan cannot exceed the interest rate stated in the contract.
    B. The interest due will be added to the contract loan if it is not paid on the due date.
    C. The policy loan can be for an amount not more than 50% of the cash value of the contract in the first year.
    D. If the loan amount exceeds net cash value, the insurer may cancel the contract in 31 days following notice to the policyholder if enough of the loan is not paid to equal a positive cash value.

22. If the assumed interest rate of the variable life insurance policy is 4% and the separate account earns 6%, the policyholder would expect the

    I.   cash value to increase
    II. cash value to decrease
    III. death benefit to increase
    IV. death benefit to decrease

    A. I
    B. I and III
    C. II and IV
    D. IV

23. If the assumed interest rate of the variable life insurance policy is 4%, in order for death benefit to increase, the separate account must earn a rate of at least

    A. less than 4%
    B. 4%
    C. greater than 4%
    D. Because the 4% is guaranteed, any earnings increase the cash value and death benefit.

24. The information required to be included in the prospectus furnished to persons offered variable life insurance includes a

    I. summary explanation in nontechnical terms of the principal features of the policy
    II. statement of investment policy of the separate account
    III. statement of the separate account's net investment return for the past ten years
    IV. statement of the deductions and charges against the gross premium including all commissions paid to agents for each policy year the commissions are to be paid

    A. I and II only
    B. I, II and III only
    C. I, II and IV only
    D. I, II, III and IV

25. A distinguishing characteristic of scheduled premium VLI is that an increase or decrease in the value of the separate account used to fund the VLI contract will lead to an increase or decrease in the

    I. annual premium payable
    II. death benefit payable exclusive of the minimum guaranteed in the contract
    III. amount of cash value
    IV. number of individuals the insured can name as beneficiaries of the contract

    A. I, II and III only
    B. I and IV only
    C. II and III only
    D. I, II, III and IV

26. An applicant for variable life insurance must receive a prospectus

    A. prior to or during the solicitation for sale
    B. before the policy is delivered
    C. before the first premium payment is due
    D. Variable life insurance policies do not require a prospectus for sale.

27. The net premium paid by the contract owner will increase

    A. the death benefit of the contract
    B. the cash value of the contract
    C. both A and B
    D. neither A nor B

28. All the following are limitations on investments of the insurance company's separate account EXCEPT a separate account may not purchase

    A. the voting securities of any issuer if the ownership represents more than 10% of the outstanding voting securities of the issuer
    D. securities of any one issuer, except for U.S. government securities, if as a result more than 10% of the separate account's assets are invested in that particular issuer
    C. shares of a mutual fund registered under the Investment Company Act of 1940
    D. securities issued by itself or an affiliate to be used in the separate account of a variable life insurance contract

29. If illustrations of benefits payable are provided, such illustrations shall

    A. be prepared by the insurer and shall not include future projections based on past investment performance
    B. be prepared by the insurer and include future projections based on past investment performance
    C. state that the projection is hypothetical and is for the purpose of illustration only
    D. comply with both A and C

30. Deductions and charges against the variable life insurance separate account may include

    I. expense and mortality risk fees
    II. sales load
    III. state premium taxes
    IV. cost of insurance

    A. I and III
    B. I and IV
    C. II and III
    D. II and IV

31. The maximum interest rate that may be charged on a policy loan is

    A. 6%
    B. 8%
    C. 10%
    D. none of the above

32. The maximum rate of interest that may be charged on premiums in default for the purpose of reinstating a policy is limited to

    A. 4%
    B. 6%
    C. 8%
    D. 10%

33. Premiums for a scheduled payment variable life policy are

    I. fixed as to the premium amount
    II. variable as to the premium amount, depending on the face amount of the policy
    III. fixed as to time of payment
    IV. variable as to time of payment

    A. I and III
    B. I and IV
    C. II and III
    D. II and IV

34. An individual has purchased a flexible premium variable life insurance policy. The separate account selected to fund the contract is a money market portfolio. During the past year short-term interest rates have risen dramatically. Which of the following will most likely occur?

    A. The policy's cash value will likely appreciate reflecting the increased earnings of the separate account.
    B. The policy's cash value will likely depreciate reflecting the decrease in asset value due to the increase in interest rates over the year.
    C. The policy's cash value will not be affected by earnings in the separate account.
    D. Only the policy's face amount, not its cash value, will be affected by the increase in interest rates.

35. An individual is deciding between the purchase of a flexible premium variable life contract and a scheduled premium variable life contract. If the individual is concerned about maintaining a minimum death benefit for estate liquidity needs, you would recommend the

    A. flexible premium policy because earnings of the contract directly affect the face value of the policy, and earnings can never be negative
    B. scheduled premium policy because earnings do not affect the contract's face amount
    C. flexible premium policy because the contract's face amount cannot be less than a predetermined percentage of cash value
    D. scheduled premium policy because the contract is issued with a minimum guaranteed face amount

36. Cash value of a variable life contract fluctuates depending on the performance of the separate account. Depending on whether the contract is a flexible or scheduled premium policy, cash value is

    I. directly affected by separate account performance in a flexible premium policy
    II. directly affected by separate account performance in a scheduled premium policy
    III. affected by account performance compared to an assumed interest rate in a flexible premium policy
    IV. affected by account performance compared to an assumed interest rate in a scheduled premium policy

    A. I and II
    B. I and IV
    C. II and III
    D. III and IV

37. Fees such as mortality and risk expenses are deducted from the

    I. premium payment for flexible premium policies
    II. premium payment for fixed premium policies
    III. benefit base for flexible premium policies
    IV. benefit base for fixed premium policies

    A. I and II
    B. I and IV
    C. II and III
    D. III and IV

38. An individual purchasing a flexible premium variable life contract should know that

    I. premiums are discretionary as to timing and amount
    II. death benefit may be equal to the contract's face amount
    III. death benefit may be equal to the contract's face amount plus cash value
    IV. cash value and duration of the policy are directly affected by the performance of the separate account

    A. I, II and IV only
    B. I, III and IV only
    C. I and IV only
    D. I, II, III and IV

39. A benefit offered by a flexible premium variable life policy not offered by a fixed premium variable life policy is

    A. the policy is funded by a separate account selected by the insured
    B. positive separate account performance may increase the contract's cash value
    C. the policyholder may adjust death benefits and premium levels to suit current insurance needs
    D. none of the above

40. An individual purchased a fixed premium variable life contract with an assumed interest rate of 4%. During the year, the separate account funding the VLI contract returned an annualized yield of 3%. The contract's cash value will

    A. increase
    B. decrease
    C. stay the same
    D. not be affected by separate account performance

41. If the individual in the above question had purchased a flexible premium policy instead of a fixed premium policy and the separate account earned 3%, the contract's cash value would

A. increase
B. decrease
C. stay the same
D. Separate account performance does not affect the value of flexible premium policies.

42. Which of the following statements are true concerning flexible premium contracts?

I. The contract holder determines premium amounts.
II. The contract holder determines death benefit.
III. Cash value is affected by separate account performance.
IV. Investment experience affects duration of the policy.
V. The contract may lapse due to insufficient cash value.

A. I and II only
B. I, II and III only
C. I, II, III and IV only
D. I, II, III, IV and V

43. An investor purchases a fixed premium variable life contract on July 1st. Four days after receiving notification of his free-look right, the individual cancels the policy. The investor would receive

A. a full refund of all monies paid to date
B. all money invested in the separate account and 30% of the sales charge
C. 30% of the money invested in the separate account plus all sales charges
D. no refund of the premium paid

44. Which of the following parties is responsible for preparing the hypothetical projections of account performance?

A. Insurer (issuer)
B. Agent
C. Insurance commissioner
D. SEC

45. The maximum sales charge that can be deducted on a variable life contract is limited to 9% of

A. the first year's premium
B. each premium collected
C. the payments to be made over the life of the contract
D. the policyholder's life expectancy

46. In determining the sales charge for a variable life contract, certain expenses are deducted from the premium. Those expenses deducted include

I. amount of premium increasing cash value
II. administrative and policy fees
III. risk fees
IV. premium taxes

A. I only
C. I and II only
B. I, II and III only
D. I, II, III and IV

47. Clayton Jones purchased a variable life contract last year. Of the initial premium of $1,000, $300 was deducted as a sales charge. Of the second year's premium of $1,000, $100 was deducted as a sales charge. Currently, the cash value of the contract is $1,000. If Clayton terminates the contract today, he would receive

A. $0
B. $400, the sales charges only
C. $1,000, the cash value
D. $1,400, the cash value plus all sales charges

48. According to federal law, the insurance company must allow a variable life policyholder the option to convert the policy into a whole life contract for a period of

A. 45 days
B. 12 months
C. 18 months
D. 24 months

49. If within a two-year period, a variable life contract holder terminates the policy, the contract holder must receive as a refund the

A. current cash value of the contract
B. current cash value of the contract plus 30% of the sales charges deducted
C. current cash value of the contract plus 10% of the sales charges deducted
D. current cash value of the contract plus all sales charges deducted in excess of 30% of the premium in the first year and 10% of the premium in the second year

50. Cash value does not have to be determined if

A. changes in the value of the separate account do not affect the contract's cash value
B. no request for redemption or payment is made to the separate account
C. the day is a regularly scheduled holiday
D. all of the above

◆ Answers & Rationale

1. **C.** Variable life is any policy that provides for insurance protection that varies according to the investment performance of one or more separate accounts.

2. **B.** Scheduled premium VLI is a fixed premium contract providing for a minimum guaranteed death benefit. Cash values and death benefit may increase or decrease depending on the investment performance of the separate account. Cash values may decline to zero, but the death benefit may never decline below the minimum guaranteed.

3. **D.** All of the materials listed are considered as either literature or advertising when used in connection with the solicitation of variable life insurance.

4. **A.** The variable death benefit is that amount of insurance above the minimum guaranteed which may increase or decrease depending on the performance of the separate account.

5. **C.** Real estate, if not to be leased, and investment in the insurer's own stock are prohibited investments.

6. **B.** Separate accounts established for the variable life insurance contract may be used only for the variable life contract.

7. **B.** The agent must be licensed to sell life insurance and variable life insurance, and the insurance company must also be authorized to offer VLI within the state.

8. **C.** Scheduled premium VLI must have a fixed premium, and the insurance coverage must be for the life of the insured (assuming no premium in default). Also the contract must provide for a minimum death benefit at least equal to the face amount of the policy at issue.

9. **A.** The variable death benefit reflects the investment performance of the separate account funding the VLI contract.

10. **B.** Nonforfeiture provisions offered in a variable life contract may be variable or fixed; however, extended term insurance may be on a fixed basis only.

11. **D.** The statement regarding variable life is as follows: "The purpose of this variable life insurance contract is to provide insurance protection. No claim is made that the contract is in any way similar or comparable to a systematic investment plan of a mutual fund."

12. **A.** 75% of cash value is the minimum that must be available in a VLI contract.

13. **B.** A person registered as an investment advisor could manage the separate account. If the person managing the account is not an RIA, then the company must report to the commissioner and set up specific guidelines for the individual to follow. A person convicted of a felony involving securities or securities-related transactions within the past ten years cannot manage the account unless the commissioner approves the individual to act as manager.

14. **D.** The allowable exchange period must be for a minimum of 24 months from the contract date.

15. **C.** Sales load is deducted from the gross premium; the other fees are deducted from the separate account (benefit base).

16. **C.** The maximum that may be charged for expense and mortality fees is the maximum stated in the contract.

17. **C.** Investment performance of the separate account does not affect the premium due. The premium is fixed and remains level throughout the premium paying period.

18. **D.** John has had the VLI contract for more than 18 months; the exchange privilege option has expired.

19. **C.** Nonforfeiture options may be offered on a fixed or variable basis; however, extended term can be offered on a fixed basis only. This meets the requirement that at least one option be offered on a fixed basis.

20. **C.** The account must earn enough to offset previous negative earnings before an increase in death benefit can occur.

21. **C.** The policy loan allowed is 75% of the contract's cash value.

22. **B.** If the separate account earns at a rate that is greater than the rate assumed, the extra earnings may lead to an increase in death benefits and cash value.

23. **C.** The account must have an actual return greater than rate assumed in order for the death benefit to increase.

24. **D.** All of the information listed here must be presented in the prospectus distributed to clients.

25. **C.** The separate account performance will affect cash value or death benefit only. Premiums are fixed and level.

26. **A.** A prospectus must be given to an applicant prior to or during a solicitation for sale.

27. **B.** The net premium will increase the cash value in the contract but does not affect the death benefit. Death benefit is affected by increases and decreases in the earnings of the separate account only.

28. **C.** A separate account may purchase shares of a mutual fund registered as an investment company under the Investment Company Act of 1940.

29. **D.** Illustrations must state that they are hypothetical and may not project future performance based on past performance.

30. **B.** Cost of insurance and mortality and expense risk fees are deducted from the separate account. Sales loads and premium taxes are deducted from the premium.

31. **D.** The maximum interest rate for variable contracts is the published monthly average for the contract ending two months before the date on which the rate may be determined. This rate may exceed 10% and fluctuates.

32. **B.** The maximum for reinstatement is 6%.

33. **A.** Scheduled payment VLI contracts have fixed premiums and payment periods.

34. **A.** Because most money market portfolios experience a 30- to 90-day turnover in assets, the portfolio will have likely acquired the higher yielding assets during the year. If the portfolio is returning a higher yield, the cash value of the flexible premium policy will reflect the higher return and increase in value.

35. **D.** A scheduled premium VLI contract is issued with a guaranteed minimum death benefit. If the client is concerned about having the minimum guarantee, then the scheduled contract should be offered.

36. **A.** Cash value is affected by separate account performance directly in both a flexible and a scheduled premium variable life policy.

37. **D.** Expenses are deducted from benefit base (cash value) for both scheduled and flexible premium VLI contracts.

38. **D.** Flexible premium policies allow for the insured to determine the amount and timing of premium payments. Depending on the policy, death benefits may equal the face value of the contract, a percentage of cash value or a combination of the two. If performance of the separate

account is such that cash value drops below an amount necessary to maintain the policy in force, the policy will lapse.

39. **C.** The policyholder determines the insurance and payment periods in a flexible premium VLI contract.

40. **A.** With a fixed-premium policy, cash value reflects actual performance of the separate account. Even though the AIR is 4% and actual performance is 3%, the account still earned 3% and cash value will likely increase.

41. **A.** With a flexible premium policy, account performance affects the contract directly. If the account earned 3%, cash value will increase (although by very little).

42. **D.** All of the statements listed are true.

43. **A.** According to the act of 1940, if the policyholder cancels the plan within the free-look period, the client will receive all monies paid.

44. **A.** The insurer (issuer) of the variable life contract is responsible for preparing hypothetical representations of cash value and death benefit performance.

45. **C.** The maximum sales charge is limited to 9% of the contract's life (actual life expectancy or 20 years, whichever is greater).

46. **D.** All of the fees and charges listed would be deducted from the premium to arrive at the amount considered sales charge.

47. **C.** Under the act of 1940, an insurance company must refund the cash value of a VLI contract plus all sales charges deducted in *excess* of 30% of the first year's premium and 10% of the second year's premium. Because in this question sales charges did not exceed these amounts, only the cash value will be refunded.

48. **D.** Although state law may allow for periods other than 24 months, federal law requires a two-year conversion privilege.

49. **D.** The law requires a full refund of cash value plus a return of sales charges in excess of 30% in year 1 and 10% in year 2. After two years, only cash value need be refunded.

50. **D.** The separate account must be valued at least daily (NYSE is open for business). The cash value of a contract must also be valued during regular business days unless activity in the separate account is such that cash value is not affected.

12 ◇ Retirement Plans

1. A school teacher has placed money into a tax-qualified variable annuity over the past twelve years. The teacher has contributed $26,000, and the value of the annuity today is $36,000. If the teacher withdraws $15,000 today, what would be the tax consequences if the teacher is in the 15% tax bracket?

   A. $1,500
   B. $2,250
   C. $4,500
   D. There are no taxes due on this withdrawal.

2. In a nonqualified plan, all the following are true EXCEPT

   A. the plan is a trust
   B. contributions are made aftertax
   C. the plan must be in writing
   D. the plan can be discriminatory

3. When establishing a Keogh plan, the plan must include

   A. all full-time employees with at least one year of service
   B. all full-time employees with two years of service or more
   C. all employees
   D. the proprietor only because employees can start their own IRAs

4. Distributions to an employee from a profit-sharing plan after retirement are made from

   A. interest on the profits of assets held by the plan
   B. profits on the assets held by the plan only
   C. the amount allocated to the individual's account during the employee's participation in the plan
   D. the amount allocated to the individual's account plus accumulated earnings during the employee's participation in the plan

5. Diane Smith had payroll deductions totaling $10,000 placed into a tax-qualified deferred annuity, and her current value in the account is $16,000. For tax purposes her cost base would be

   A. $0
   B. $6,000
   C. $10,000
   D. $16,000

6. Cusper Earl is the sole owner of a business. He earns $160,000 a year and makes the maximum contribution to a defined benefit Keogh plan. How much money may be contributed to his IRA?

   A. $0
   B. $2,000
   C. $15,000
   D. $30,000

7. Horace Horowitz is 61 years old. He would like to take a lump-sum distribution from his Keogh. What would be the tax treatment of this lump-sum distribution?

   A. It will be taxed as ordinary income.
   B. It will be taxed at long-term capital gains rates.
   C. There will be a 10% penalty.
   D. There will be a 50% penalty.

8. Which of the following statements describe nonqualified deferred compensation plan?

   I. It requires no approval from the IRS.
   II. It does not allow the employer to deduct the cost of the plan.
   III. It allows the employer to deduct the cost of the plan when the employee has constructive receipt of the benefits.
   IV. It allows the employee to receive the benefit of deferral if he/she signs a contract stating the funds are to be used for retirement and then abides by the contract.

   A. I and III
   B. I, III and IV
   C. II and III
   D. II and IV

9. When a client withdraws money from an IRA after age 59 1/2, the

   A. amount withdrawn is subject to a 10% penalty
   B. amount withdrawn is subject to taxes at the capital gains rate
   C. entire amount in the IRA is subject to taxation at the ordinary rate, regardless of the amount withdrawn, at age 59 1/2
   D. amount withdrawn is subject to taxation at ordinary income tax rates

10. When referring to employee retirement plans, the term *nonqualified* refers to plans

   I. not approved by the IRS
   II. that offer tax-deductible contributions and tax-deferred growth
   III. under which the employer may discriminate as to the inclusion of employees within the plan
   IV. where the employer may deduct contributions made on behalf of the employee as the contributions are made

   A. I and II
   B. I and III
   C. I, III and IV
   D. II and III

11. If an employer installs a Keogh plan, that plan must include all full-time employees, age 21, with how many years of service?

   A. One
   B. Two
   C. Five
   D. None of the above

12. Keogh plans are retirement programs designed for use by nonincorporated businesses. These plans allow the self-employed individual to contribute on a tax-deductible basis

   A. the lesser of 25% of earned income or $30,000
   B. the lesser of 25% of all income or $30,000
   C. the greater of 25% of earned income or $30,000
   D. the greater of 25% of all income or $30,000

13. Linda Mayhew is a retired teacher participating in a qualified tax sheltered annuity. Contributions made on her behalf total $15,000. This year she received a lump-sum payment of $21,000. How would this payment be taxed?

    A. As a capital gains distribution
    B. As ordinary income
    C. $6,000 as capital gains and the remainder as ordinary income
    D. As ordinary income, except for the $15,000, which represents return of her contribution

14. Doug McTaggert has entered into an agreement with his employer stating that if he remains with the company until age 65, the company will pay Doug $75,000 at the rate of $10,000 per year. The payments will commence at age 65 or death, whichever comes first. What type of plan is described here?

    A. Payroll deduction
    B. Fixed annuity
    C. Variable annuity with installments for a designated amount
    D. Deferred compensation

15. Doug McTaggert has begun saving periodically by having a portion of his paycheck invested into a mutual fund he selected from a range of investments offered by his employer. The money invested is automatically deducted from his paycheck. What type of plan is being described here?

    A. Payroll deduction
    B. Fixed annuity
    C. Variable annuity
    D. Deferred compensation

16. If John Jones enters into a deferred compensation plan with Ajax Corporation and before John Jones's retirement Ajax goes bankrupt

    A. Ajax is still required to pay the deferred compensation
    B. Ajax could terminate the deferred compensation plan without penalty
    C. Ajax could terminate the deferred compensation plan but would be liable for penalties
    D. none of the above apply

17. John Jones entered into a deferred compensation plan with his employer. The plan states that John will receive $12,000 per year after retirement (at age 65) from the company. If John terminates his employment with the company before age 65

    A. the company is still obligated to make the $12,000 annual payments after age 65
    B. the company is obligated to make payments as soon as John leaves
    C. John forfeits his right to the deferred compensation
    D. John can roll the deferred accumulations into his IRA

18. Fred Dorsey's deferred compensation plan states that he does not have constructive receipt of the benefits until age 65 or death. This means that

    A. before age 65, he can receive the benefits in any form other than cash
    B. he does not have the right or guarantee of payments and cannot claim them as an asset until he receives them
    C. he cannot specify a beneficiary until age 65
    D. the benefits are held in a trust account in his name, but he cannot claim them until age 65

19. A nonqualified employee retirement plan is different from a qualified employee retirement plan in that a nonqualified plan

   I. is approved by the IRS
   II. may discriminate as to participation
   III. allows the employer to deduct contributions as they are made
   IV. allows the employer to deduct contributions when they are paid to the employee

   A. I and III
   B. I and IV
   C. II and III
   D. II and IV

20. Which of the following investments could not be used as a funding vehicle for an IRA?

   A. Mutual fund shares
   B. Variable annuities
   C. Fixed annuities
   D. Collectibles

21. Which of the following investors would be eligible to establish an IRA?

   I. Independently wealthy individual whose sole source of income is $125,000 per year in dividend and interest income
   II. Law student who earned $1,200 in a part-time job
   III. Woman who earned $3,500 last year selling cosmetics but whose spouse is covered by a company profit-sharing plan

   A. I and II only
   B. I and III only
   C. II and III only
   D. I, II and III

22. Gordon Jacobs earned $34,000 this year, and his wife Cynthia earned $46,000. Which of the following statements is(are) true?

   I. Gordon may contribute $2,250 to his IRA.
   II. Cynthia may contribute $2,250 to her IRA.
   III. Cynthia and Gordon may each contribute $2,000 to separate IRAs.
   IV. Cynthia and Gordon may contribute a total of $4,000 to an IRA.

   A. I and IV only
   B. II and IV only
   C. III only
   D. I, II, III and IV

23. Karen Jacobs earned $26,000 last year and by error contributed $2,300 to her IRA. On what amount of the contribution will Karen be subject to the 6% penalty?

   A. $0
   B. $300
   C. $2,000
   D. $2,300

24. Karen Jacobs earned $26,000 last year and by error contributed $2,300 to her IRA. To avoid paying another penalty, she could

   A. remove $300 from the IRA
   B. contribute only $1,700 next year
   C. contribute her $2,000 as usual
   D. do either A or B

25. Karen Smith decides to take a well-earned vacation to celebrate her 30th birthday. She withdraws $4,000 from her IRA to pay for a cruise. What penalty tax will she be subject to on the amount withdrawn?

   A. $0
   B. $240
   C. $400
   D. $2,500

26. Karen Smith withdraws $4,000 from her IRA to pay for a cruise. How will she treat the withdrawn amount on her income tax return?

    A. She will report $4,000 as ordinary income.
    B. The $4,000 is a return of her contribution and therefore not taxable.
    C. Only that portion considered investment earnings will be reported as a long-term gain.
    D. She will report $3,600 as ordinary income.

27. At age 52, Mike Jones changed jobs and received a lump-sum distribution of $44,000 from his previous employer's pension plan. Mike opened an IRA for $34,000 and invested the remaining $10,000 in a Treasury bill. How will Mike report the distribution on his tax return?

    A. $10,000 as ordinary income
    B. He may income average the $44,000 over four years and report $11,000 in ordinary income for each of the next four years.
    C. $44,000 as ordinary income
    D. The amounts received are tax deferred until age 59 1/2.

28. Which of the following individuals would be eligible to participate in a tax sheltered annuity?

    I.   Maintenance engineer at a state university
    II. Teacher in a public school system
    III. Minister

    A. I and II only
    B. I and III only
    C. II and III only
    D. I, II and III

29. Which of the following statements about tax sheltered annuities is(are) true?

    I.   Employees may make withdrawals without penalty.
    II. Payouts are taxable at capital gains rates.
    III. Taxes on earnings are deferred.

    A. I and II only
    B. II and III only
    C. III only
    D. I, II and III

30. Investors may make early withdrawals from an IRA or a Keogh plan without penalty

    A. if they retire early
    B. if they become disabled
    C. if they file for bankruptcy
    D. under no circumstances

31. Which of the following employees of a self-employed individual would not have to be covered under a Keogh plan?

    I.   Employee who has worked 15 hours per week for the past six years
    II. Employee who has worked during the summer for the past four years
    III. 21-year-old employee who has worked 25 hours per week since the start of the business two years ago

    A. I and II only
    B. II and III only
    C. III only
    D. I, II and III

32. Harriet Flory earned $80,000 from self-employment and made the maximum contribution to a defined contribution Keogh plan. She also wants to make the maximum IRA contribution. Which of the following statements is true?

    A. She may contribute a total of $2,000 to an IRA.
    B. She may not contribute to the Keogh plan if she also contributes to the IRA.
    C. If she contributes the maximum to her Keogh plan, any IRA contribution would not be tax deductible but would grow tax deferred.
    D. She could not contribute to an IRA because she is covered by the Keogh plan.

33. Which of the following persons may set up a Keogh plan?

    A. Accountant who works for a large corporation
    B. Single proprietor who owns a hardware store
    C. Chemical engineer employed by Dow Chemical Co.
    D. Doctor who is employed by Humana Hospital and has no outside practice

34. A distribution of funds from a Keogh plan may be made without penalty if the

    A. investor becomes disabled
    B. IRS is notified within 60 days
    C. investor makes a major purchase, such as a car
    D. investments in the account decrease in value

35. Bob Madden is 67 and has just retired. He has $56,000 in his Keogh plan, to which he has contributed for eight years. None of his payments were voluntary nondeductible contributions. If Bob requests a periodic payment of $1,000 per month, how will the distribution of his payments be taxed?

    A. Part will be taxed as ordinary income, part as long-term gains.
    B. Ordinary income tax will be charged on the amount exceeding cost basis.
    C. Ordinary income taxes will be charged on the entire amount.
    D. No taxes will be paid on the distribution because Bob is older than 59 1/2.

36. Which of the following are advantages of a Keogh plan?

    I. Contributions may be tax deductible.
    II. Taxes on earnings are deferred during the accumulation period.
    III. Taxes are usually deferred until the participant is in a lower tax bracket after retirement.

    A. I and II only
    B. I and III only
    C. II and III only
    D. I, II and III

37. A corporate pension plan differs from a deferred compensation plan in that the

    I. pension plan is qualified and the deferred compensation plan is not
    II. employers are obligated to fulfill the terms of the pension plan but not the deferred compensation plan
    III. tax liability of employees is deferred under the deferred compensation plan but not under the pension plan

    A. I and II only
    B. I and III only
    C. II and III only
    D. I, II and III

38. Under a defined contribution plan

    I. the participant is guaranteed a contribution that is normally based on a percentage of salary
    II. the participant's retirement benefits are based on the balance in his individual account
    III. the employer may discriminate among employees as to participation

    A. I and II only
    B. I and III only
    C. II and III only
    D. I, II and III

39. Lorraine Gilbert has begun a new job with Amalgamated. According to the company's retirement policy, if she stays for 25 years she will receive $1,200 each month at retirement until her death. She is guaranteed this benefit, and all tax liability is deferred until receipt of payments begins. Amalgamated's plan is a

    A. defined benefit pension plan
    B. deferred compensation plan
    C. Keogh plan
    D. defined contribution profit-sharing plan

40. A teacher has a 403(b) tax-qualified deferred annuity. The school system he works for deposits $10,000 for him into the plan over a twelve-year period. Now, at retirement, the teacher withdraws the total value of $16,000. On what amount does he pay tax?

    A. $6,000
    B. $8,000
    C. $10,000
    D. $16,000

41. A lump-sum distribution from a Keogh plan would qualify for

    A. no income averaging
    B. five-year income averaging
    C. ten-year income averaging
    D. fifteen-year income averaging

42. An employee has a nonqualified retirement program at her job. Which of the following statements are true?

    I. The employer receives no deduction for payment until the money is transferred.
    II. Because the plan is nonqualified, the IRS does not care if the agreement is in writing.
    III. The employee must pay income tax upon constructive receipt.
    IV. During the accumulation period, the employer will pay tax on any interest and/or capital gains earned by the account.

    A. I, II and III only
    B. I, III and IV only
    C. II, III and IV only
    D. I, II, III and IV

43. An artist defers taxes on part of the commissions she receives from her artwork through the use of a Keogh plan. She is also a part-time employee of a company without pension or profit-sharing benefits. The artist can

    A. combine the earned salary with her existing Keogh plan
    B. set up a new Keogh plan
    C. set up a new IRA and make nondeductible contributions
    D. do none of the above

44. A customer receives a lump-sum distribution from his pension plan. He will invest it in an IRA. What is the maximum rollover time permitted without a penalty?

    A. 5 full business days
    B. 30 days
    C. 60 days
    D. 90 days

45. Whether you have an IRA, an HR-10 plan, or both, what is the age at which you must begin to withdraw money?

    A. 59 1/2
    B. 65
    C. 70 1/2
    D. You never have to withdraw.

46. A client of yours works full time for the XYZ Company. He is covered by a qualified pension plan. He also works for the local hardware store part time to make a few extra dollars. The hardware store offers no retirement plan. Your client can

    A. deposit up to 25% of his income from the hardware store into his own Keogh plan
    B. not start any other plan
    C. ask XYZ to deposit extra money in his plan because of his other income
    D. start his own IRA

47. Which of the following statements is(are) true regarding qualified pension funds?

    I. They must not discriminate.
    II. They must have a vesting schedule.
    III. They must be in writing.
    IV. Every month the employer must update the current status of all accounts.

    A. I, II and III only
    B. I and III only
    C. III only
    D. I, II, III and IV

48. A man earns $45,000 per year, and his wife does not work in an outside-the-home job. He is covered by a retirement plan at work. The maximum contribution to an IRA the couple can make this year is

    A. $250 into a spousal IRA because the wife is not covered by another retirement plan
    B. a total deductible contribution of $2,250 with no more than $2,000 in any one account
    C. a total contribution of $2,250 with no more than $2,000 in any one account of which only 50% is deductible
    D. $0 because they cannot have an IRA while the husband is covered by a company-sponsored retirement plan

49. The contributions made to a qualified pension plan may be based on

    I. years of service
    II. compensation received
    III. the employer's profit

    A. I only
    B. I and II only
    C. II only
    D. I, II and III

50. A company starts a pension plan for an employee who already has an IRA. This employee now

    A. must roll over his IRA into the company pension plan
    B. must stop contributing to the IRA, which will continue to accumulate on a tax-deferred basis
    C. may continue to contribute to his IRA but the contributions may not be 100% deductible depending on his level of compensation
    D. may continue to make deductible contributions up to $2,000 per year to his IRA

51. A husband and wife are both employed, and each qualifies to open an IRA. To make their maximum allowable contributions, they should open

    A. a joint IRA and deposit $2,000
    B. a joint IRA and deposit $4,000
    C. two separate IRAs and deposit $2,000 each
    D. two separate IRAs and deposit $2,250

52. Which of the following would be eligible under the Keogh plan?

    I. Self-employed doctor
    II. Engineer receiving extra compensation as an outside consultant
    III. Advertising executive who made $5,000 during the year free-lancing
    IV. Executive employed by a corporation who received $5,000 in stock options

    A. I, II and III only
    B. I, III and IV only
    C. II, III and IV only
    D. I, II, III and IV

53. Which of the following statements are true regarding the withdrawal of funds from a qualified retirement plan?

    I. The employee will be taxed at the ordinary income tax rate on his cost base.
    II. Funds may be withdrawn after retirement (as defined) with no tax on the withdrawn amount.
    III. Funds may be withdrawn early by the beneficiary if the covered person dies.
    IV. All qualified plans must be in written form.

    A. I and II only
    B. II, III and IV only
    C. III and IV only
    D. I, II, III and IV

54. Which of the following statements describes a disadvantage of a nonqualified deferred compensation plan?

    A. The funds accumulate under the plan on a tax-deferred basis.
    B. Funds are designed to aid the employees at retirement time.
    C. Deferred compensation plans are of value only to the highest paid employees of the corporation.
    D. In the case of business bankruptcy, it might occur that there are no funds available to pay the deferred compensation to retired employees.

55. All of the following statements concerning IRA contributions are true EXCEPT

    A. between January 1st and April 15th, contributions may be made for the current year, the past year or both
    B. contributions for the past year may be made after April 15th, provided an extension has been filed on a timely basis
    C. if you pay your tax on January 15th, you can still deduct your IRA contribution even if not made until April 15th
    D. contributions can be paid into this year's IRA from January 1st of this year until April 15th of next year.

56. A doctor has compensation of $160,000. What is the maximum he may contribute to his Keogh plan?

    A. $5,000
    B. $22,000
    C. $28,000
    D. $30,000

◆ Answers & Rationale

1. **B.** Contributions to a tax-qualified annuity are taxable when withdrawn at ordinary income tax rates. Because the teacher described here is withdrawing $15,000, that amount is subject to tax. Fifteen percent of $15,000 equals a tax liability of $2,250.

2. **A.** Qualified plans are a trust, not nonqualified plans.

3. **A.** Keogh plans and corporate retirement plans generally allow for eligibility requirements of one year of service and age 21. However, if a Keogh plan offers 100% vesting immediately, the plan may require eligibility after two years of full-time service.

4. **D.** Distributions from a profit-sharing plan are made from the individual's account reflecting the accrued amount of contributions and earnings on the contributions. Contributions to the plan are normally based on a predetermined percentage of profits.

5. **A.** If contributions are made into a tax-qualified annuity, the contributions are made before tax. The growth is deferred. Diane has no cost base in this question. The entire $16,000 will be taxed as ordinary income.

6. **B.** The question asks what Cusper's IRA contribution may be; the maximum is the lesser of 100% earned income or $2,000.

7. **A.** The distribution described here would be taxed as ordinary income. A 10% penalty would apply if Horace were under age 59 1/2; the 50% penalty would apply if he did not take the distribution according to his life expectancy by April 1st of the year following the year he turned 70 1/2.

8. **B.** Nonqualified deferred compensation plans do not require approval from the IRS. The plan does allow the employer to deduct the cost when payment is made to the employee. The employee must sign a contract stating that the funds are for retirement and abide by the contract.

9. **D.** Money withdrawn from an IRA after age 59 1/2 is subject to ordinary taxation on the amount withdrawn. There is no 10% penalty starting at 59 1/2 years of age.

10. **B.** Nonqualified retirement plans do not require IRS approval. Nonqualified plans also allow the employer the right to discriminate as to inclusion in the plan. Contributions are not tax deductible, and the employer can deduct contributions only when they are paid to the employee, not when they are made by the company.

11. **A.** A Keogh plan must allow for the inclusion of all full-time employees, age 21, with one year of service (two years if 100% vesting is offered).

12. **A.** Keogh plans allow contributions for the lesser of 25% of earned income or $30,000.

13. **B.** Contributions to a TSA, as in all qualified plans, are made before taxes. Payments from these plans require the payment of taxes at the ordinary income tax rate.

14. **D.** The plan described here is most likely a deferred compensation plan. There is an agreement between Doug and his employer to pay Doug a sum of money after retirement. If this were a qualified plan, vesting would determine whether Doug would be paid rather than the stipulation that he stay with the company.

15. **A.** A payroll deduction is described here. Contributions are aftertax, and growth is taxed currently.

16. **B.** A deferred compensation plan is nonqualified; Ajax can terminate the plan at will. John becomes just another creditor in line (quite far back in line, too).

17. **C.** The contract between John and his employer states that the payment will be made after retirement. If John leaves the employer prior to retirement, the agreement is no longer valid (that is why deferred compensation plans are often referred to as golden handcuffs).

18. **B.** The money held by the deferred compensation plan is not Fred's until distribution occurs. This is also the reason a funded deferred compensation plan is not taxable to Fred until he receives it.

19. **D.** A nonqualified plan does not qualify for special tax treatment under the Internal Revenue Code; as such it is not approved. Contributions by the employer are deductible only when the contribution is paid (and taxable) to the employee. The plan may be discriminatory.

20. **D.** While almost any investment vehicle may be used to fund an IRA, certain investments are specifically not allowed: life insurance, collectibles and individual pieces of real estate. (REITs and limited partnerships are allowed.)

21. **C.** An individual may contribute the lesser of 100% of earned income up to a maximum of $2,000. Interest and dividend income is passive income, not earned income.

22. **C.** Both Gordon and Cynthia can contribute the maximum of $2,000 to separate IRAs. The $2,250 limitation is for married couples with one nonworking spouse. Still, the $2,250 must be split between two accounts with no more than $2,000 contributed in one account.

23. **B.** The contribution in excess of $2,000 (and the earnings associated with the excess) is subject to a penalty of 6%.

24. **D.** The penalty can be avoided in future years by removing the excess or by reducing the contribution the following year.

25. **C.** Withdrawals from an IRA prior to age 59 1/2 are subject to a 10% penalty (10% of $4,000 is $400).

26. **A.** The $4,000 withdrawn is taxed as ordinary income. The 10% penalty does not reduce the amount reported as income.

27. **A.** A rollover from a qualified plan to an IRA, if made within 60 days, is not taxable. However, any amount not rolled over ($10,000 in this case) is considered a distribution and is subject to tax as ordinary income.

28. **D.** Employees of 501(c)3 and 403(b) organizations, which include charities, religious groups, sports organizations and school systems, qualify for tax sheltered annuities (TSAs).

29. **C.** A TSA allows a tax-deductible contribution (reduction in salary) to be made by the employer, the earnings of which grow tax deferred. There are penalties for early withdrawal or failure to distribute the money. When withdrawn, the money is ordinary income.

30. **B.** Except for death and disability, withdrawals from an IRA or a Keogh plan prior to age 59 1/2 are subject to a 10% penalty.

31. **A.** Eligibility is required for individuals who are at least 21 years old and who are working at least 1,000 hours a year (20 hours per week).

32. **C.** Because Harriet is above the compensation limits and is an active participant in another retirement plan, she could still contribute up to $2,000. Her IRA contribution would not be deductible but would still grow tax deferred.

33. **B.** Keogh plans are for unincorporated businesses (self-employed).

34. **A.** A premature distribution is allowed without penalty if the participant dies or becomes disabled.

35. **C.** Distributions from any qualified plan are taxed as ordinary income.

36. **D.** The benefits of a qualified plan are tax-deductible contributions and deferred growth. Receipt of income normally occurs at retirement when the individual is in a lower tax bracket.

37. **A.** Pension plans are qualified retirement plans allowing tax-deductible contributions and deferral of tax on earnings of the account. Employers must abide by contribution limits, vesting schedules and eligibility requirements. A deferred compensation plan is normally nonqualified, and the employer may discriminate as to who is included. Tax on compensation is deferred to the employee until receipt at retirement.

38. **A.** Under a defined contribution plan, contributions may be based on years of service or, more frequently, salary. Benefits are provided by what the accumulated contributions will provide at retirement. The plan is qualified and may not discriminate.

39. **A.** Because Lorraine is guaranteed the $1,200 and the benefit is defined, the plan must be a defined benefit plan.

40. **D.** A TSA plan is a qualified retirement plan; the contributions to the plan are made before tax and the growth of the contract is tax deferred. Any distribution from a TSA plan would be fully taxable to the participant at the ordinary income tax rate.

41. **B.** Keogh and corporate retirement plans qualify for five-year income averaging.

42. **B.** Nonqualified plans must be in writing. For a deferred compensation plan, the employer cannot deduct any payment until the money is paid to the employee. The employee pays ordinary income tax on the distribution.

43. **C.** An IRA can be set up with any plan or number of plans as long as the individual has the earned income to contribute. However, the contribution may or may not be tax deductible.

44. **C.** Rollovers can be made once a year, with the rollover to be completed within 60 days. If the rollover is not completed within that time, it is considered a distribution from the plan, subject to taxes and penalties.

45. **C.** Distributions from an IRA or a Keogh must begin according to life expectancy by April 1st of the year following the year in which the individual attains age 70 1/2.

46. **D.** An IRA can be opened regardless of an individual's participation in other retirement programs as long as the individual has earned income to contribute. Only self-employed income can be contributed to a Keogh plan.

47. **A.** All qualified plans must be in writing; they must not be discriminatory; and they must allow for 100% vesting in no less than 15 years. Plan participants must be notified of their status in the plan at least *annually* (ERISA).

48. **C.** The maximum IRA contribution for an individual and a nonworking spouse for a year is $2,250. The maximum contribution per account is $2,000. The law does not mandate how the contribution should be split between the individual account and spousal option, although the limit per account is $2,000. Additionally, the TRA of 1986 reduces the deductibility for IRA contributions for those individuals actively participating in other qualified plans. For taxable income between $40,000 and $50,000 (joint), the portion of an IRA contribution is reduced by a prorated amount. Because income in this question is halfway between the amounts, only 50% of the contribution is deductible.

49. **B.** Contributions to a qualified pension plan may be based on salary, years of service or a combination of the two. The contributions to a *pension* plan must be made without regard to the company's profit. Contributions to a profit-sharing plan may be based on profit or a percentage thereof.

50. **C.** Contributions to an IRA are still allowed up to $2,000 per year. However, for participants active in other qualified plans, the contribution may or may not be deductible depending on the individual's adjusted gross income.

51. **C.** Each individual with earned income may open an IRA and deposit 100% of this earned income up to $2,000 per year.

52. **A.** A Keogh plan (HR-10) may be opened only by an individual with self-employment income.

53. **C.** Cost base in a retirement plan is money contributed aftertax; upon receipt there is no tax liability. Money withdrawn from a qualified plan will be taxed as ordinary income upon receipt.

54. **D.** A participant in an unfunded deferred compensation plan is nothing more than an unsecured creditor in the event the company goes bankrupt. There is no guarantee that the participant will receive any money.

55. **B.** Contributions can be made to an IRA only until the first tax filing deadline (April 15th) even though you may have filed an extension. Anyone with earned income can make a contribution to an IRA.

56. **D.** Keogh contributions are limited to 25% of aftertax income (the equivalent of 20% of pretax income) to a maximum of $30,000. In this case the doctor's $160,000 income times 20% equals $32,000, $2,000 more than the maximum contribution.

13 ◇ SEC Regulations

1. Which of the following would be considered an unaffiliated person in a mutual fund?

   A. Member of the board of directors of the mutual fund who also is employed as the investment advisor
   B. Shareholder who owns 10% of the fund's shares
   C. Person who holds a position with the underwriter for the fund
   D. Member of the board of directors who cannot hold another position within the investment company

2. Clyde Baedecker has $350,000 in securities and $201,000 in cash with his brokerage firm. If the brokerage firm were forced to liquidate, how much of the account would be covered by SIPC?

   A. $250,000 of the securities and all of the cash
   B. All of the securities and $100,000 of the cash
   C. All of the securities and $150,000 of the cash
   D. All of the cash and $299,000 of the securities

3. Which of the following statements describe the Securities Exchange Act of 1934?

   I. It requires registration of securities.
   II. It requires registration of broker-dealers with the SEC.
   III. It prohibits inequitable and unfair trade practices.
   IV. It provides for regulation of the over-the-counter market.

   A. I and II only
   B. II and III only
   C. II, III and IV only
   D. I, II, III and IV

4. The Securities Act of 1933 requires that which of the following be offered only by prospectus?

   I. Treasury bonds
   II. Mutual fund shares
   III. Variable annuities
   IV. Unit investment trusts

   A. I and II
   B. II and III
   C. II, III and IV
   D. III and IV

5. Which of the following statements are true of the Securities Act of 1933?

   I.   The act applies only to listed securities traded over the counter.
   II. One chief purpose of the requirements for registration and prospectuses is to provide full disclosure of pertinent information to the public.
   III. The act is designed to prevent fraud in the sale of newly issued securities.

   A. I and II only
   B. I and III only
   C. II and III only
   D. I, II and III

6. The Securities Act of 1933 applies only to new issues. Which of the following situations would be governed by this act?

   I.   Cosmopolitan Securities buys 3,000 shares of Amalgamated stock for its own account from a client.
   II. Hubert Gillian Investment Corporation is underwriting a primary distribution of stock.
   III. Gleason Investment Corporation is the distributor of Gleason Growth Fund shares.

   A. I and II only
   B. I and III only
   C. II and III only
   D. I, II and III

7. An announcement of a new issue of a security that gives the name of the issuer, the price and the name of the underwriter is called a(n)

   A. offering statement
   B. tombstone
   C. red herring
   D. prospectus

8. The Securities Exchange Act of 1934 was designed to

   I.   maintain orderly markets
   II. control the regulation of new issues
   III. provide liquidity for securities holdings
   IV. regulate securities trading

   A. I, II and IV only
   B. I and IV only
   C. II and III only
   D. I, II, III and IV

9. One of the main objectives of the Investment Company Act of 1940 is to

   A. protect an investment company's investors from loss
   B. regulate the over-the-counter market
   C. require registration of investment companies with the SEC
   D. ensure that all investors are fully informed about all types of securities

10. When the Prosperity Fund, an open-end investment company, issues and sells new shares, it must comply with the requirements of the

   I.   Investment Company Act of 1940
   II. Securities Act of 1933
   III. Securities Exchange Act of 1934

   A. I and II only
   B. I and III only
   C. II and III only
   D. I, II and III

11. According to the Investment Company Act of 1940, which of the following are required of investment companies?

   I. Investment company registration statement filed with the SEC
   II. Minimum net worth of $100,000 before the offer of shares to the public
   III. Statement of investment policies and of diversification status

   A. I and II only
   B. I and III only
   C. II and III only
   D. I, II and III

12. Joe Delaney has an account with a broker-dealer, Consolidated Securities. Joe plans to purchase 300 shares of XYZ Mutual Fund. How soon must Joe pay for the securities?

   A. Within five business days
   B. Within seven calendar days
   C. Within seven business days
   D. Whenever Consolidated's policy states that Joe must pay

13. If Joe Delaney fails to make payment for the XYZ Mutual Fund shares within the required amount of time, the broker-dealer could

   I. cancel the order
   II. fine Joe a penalty based on the dollar amount of the sale
   III. freeze Joe's account

   A. I and II only
   B. I and III only
   C. III only
   D. I, II and III

14. The prospectus was first required by the

   A. 1922 Truth in Securities Act
   B. Securities Act of 1933
   C. Investment Company Act of 1940
   D. Prospectuses have always been required.

15. The difference between the Maloney Act of 1938 and the Securities Act of 1933 is that the act of 1933 concerns itself with

   A. the establishment of the NASD
   B. predicting the success of a security issue
   C. Regulation T
   D. full and fair disclosure

16. Which of the following statements describe(s) hypothecation?

   I. It occurs when a broker-dealer pledges a client's securities as collateral for a loan.
   II. It requires the written permission of the client.
   III. It is very rare.
   IV. It is prohibited because it is the same as a wash sale.

   A. I and II
   B. I and III
   C. II and III
   D. IV

17. A client, in a cash account, purchased stock from his broker-dealer. He does not make payment for the shares within seven days. According to Regulation T, the broker-dealer must now

   A. liquidate enough stock to settle the account
   B. grant an automatic 30-day extension
   C. arrange for an outside loan for the client
   D. grant an extension of five business days

18. You plan to obtain a loan at your local bank. You are going to use your 500 shares of General Motors stock as collateral. To determine how much collateral value the bank may assign to the stock, the bank will

   A. check the Federal Reserve Board's Regulation T
   B. check the Federal Reserve Board's Regulation U
   C. check the Federal Reserve Board's Regulation G
   D. not approve your loan; banks do not make loans based on stock as collateral because it fluctuates in value

19. Which of the following persons must register as an investment advisor?

   A. Broker giving investment advice to a client as part of his regular duties
   B. Broker publishing a market letter
   C. Broker acting as financial planner for his clients and charging a fee
   D. Bank trust officer

20. You have an account with your broker. Due to SIPC, your cash and securities are covered up to

   A. $40,000 per account
   B. $500,000 for cash
   C. $500,000 for cash and securities, but no more than $100,000 of cash per separate customer
   D. None of the above explains your coverage accurately.

21. The Investment Company Act of 1940 provides that open-end but not closed-end companies

   A. may alter investment policies with stockholder approval
   B. must give semiannual reports to shareholders
   C. must give annual reports to the SEC
   D. may make continuous offerings

22. The Investment Company Act of 1940 defines all the following as types of management investment companies EXCEPT the

   A. unit investment trust
   B. open-end investment company
   C. closed-end investment company
   D. nondiversified investment company

23. Sales literature, as defined by the SEC, is any

   A. communication by a broker-dealer or his agent
   B. written communication used to induce the purchase or sale of investment company shares
   C. communication delivered in interstate commerce
   D. communication used to induce the purchase or sale of investment company shares

24. The use of a prospectus in selling a security relieves a salesperson of the responsibility to disclose to a customer

   A. negative financial information about the company
   B. poor growth potential of the company
   C. speculative factors about the security
   D. The salesperson must disclose all of the above.

25. The sales representative is relieved from the antifraud rule of the SEC if he

   A. only tells the client that he guarantees the trade, and the client can have his money back at any time
   B. sends the client a prospectus
   C. repeats exactly what his employer told him to say
   D. Nothing relieves the representative from the antifraud rules while he is selling.

26. Which of the following situations might fall into the category of a hot issue?

   A. New issue is offered at $30 and immediately appreciates to $35.

   B. New issue is offered at $30 and immediately decreases to $25.

   C. Market maker buys at $17 and immediately sells with a spread of $2.

   D. Broker-dealer sells inventory at $60 three weeks after buying at $30.

27. Except under limited circumstances, NASD rules on freeriding and withholding prohibit the purchase of a hot issue by which of the following people?

   I. Finder

   II. Bank officer who has a significant relationship with the issuer

   III. Officer of a broker-dealer firm that is a member of the NASD

   IV. Registered representative

   A. I and II only

   B. I, III and IV only

   C. III and IV only

   D. I, II, III and IV

28. Which of the following securities are exempt from the 1933 act?

   I. Federal and state issues

   II. Small business investment companies

   III. Nonprofit organizations

   IV. State-chartered commercial banks

   A. I only

   B. I and II only

   C. I, II and III only

   D. I, II, III and IV

◆ Answers & Rationale

1. **D.** An affiliated person is defined as any person, officer, director, partner or employee directly or indirectly controlling, controlled by or under common control of the fund. Additionally, an affiliated person is defined as a person holding or controlling with the power to vote 5% or more of the outstanding securities of the fund. However, no person is considered an interested person solely by reason of membership as a director or just because the person is an owner of securities.

2. **B.** SIPC covers cash and securities up to $500,000, but only $100,000 in cash.

3. **C.** The Securities Act of 1933 requires registration of securities (paper act). The act of 1934 (people act) requires registration of people and exchanges transacting securities business in order to prevent manipulative and deceptive practices. The NASD is the SRO of the OTC market, but the SEC has final authority.

4. **C.** Treasury securities are exempt from registration requirements as are municipal issues and do not require a prospectus.

5. **C.** The Securities Act of 1933 applies to all newly issued securities and requires a registration statement and prospectus to be filed with the SEC. The purpose of filing and distributing the prospectus is to provide full disclosure of the offering and thus deter the sale of fraudulent securities.

6. **C.** The Securities Act of 1933 requires registration of newly issued securities. The purchase of the Amalgamated stock, in this case, is a secondary transaction and thus regulated by the Securities Exchange Act of 1934. The underwriting of a primary distribution (also the sale of mutual fund shares because they are a continuous primary offering) is subject to the reporting and filing requirements under the Securities Act of 1933.

7. **B.** A tombstone advertisement announces the sale of a primary offering. The advertisement tells the price of the security, where a prospectus may be obtained and where the security may be purchased.

8. **B.** The Securities Exchange Act of 1934 was enacted to regulate the trading of securities and individuals effecting transactions of securities in the secondary market.

9. **C.** Under the Investment Company Act of 1940, companies in the business of investing or reinvesting in securities are required to register with the SEC as a face-amount company, a unit investment trust or a management company.

10. **D.** A mutual fund issuing shares must comply with the Securities Act of 1933 (registration) and the Investment Company Act of 1940 (one class of security, type of investment company). The Securities Exchange Act of 1934 deals with the people who sell the shares and the markets in which the shares are sold, but also details antifraud requirements, which must be observed by the company.

11. **D.** The Investment Company Act of 1940 requires registration of the fund under one of three general classifications: a minimum initial net worth of $100,000, at least 100 shareholders and a specifically defined investment objective.

12. **C.** Under Regulation T, settlement for a purchase must occur within seven business days. Regular way settlement in the OTC market is five business days, allowing a two-day cushion before federal law takes effect.

13. **C.** If Joe fails to pay for the shares within seven business days, the broker must sell the shares to pay for the transaction. Any gain or loss will be settled between the broker and Joe, and Joe's account will be frozen for 90 days. The order has taken place and cannot be canceled.

14. **B.** The Securities Act of 1933 requires the filing of a prospectus with the registration statement prior to the sale of an issue interstate.

15. **D.** The Maloney Act of 1938 amended the Securities Exchange Act of 1934, recognizing the NASD as the SRO for the over-the-counter market. The Securities Act of 1933 requires a prospectus and registration statement to be filed disclosing the relevant facts concerning the issue. The act further requires a prospectus to be distributed prior to or during a solicitation for sale so that a prospective purchaser will be fully informed and fairly treated.

16. **A.** Hypothecation is the pledging of a client's securities for a loan to the broker-dealer. The requirements include written authorization from the client and the securities to be in the name of the broker-dealer (street name).

17. **A.** Regulation T requires settlement within seven business days of the trade. If the client does not settle, the broker must liquidate the account in order to settle.

18. **B.** Regulation U is the regulation governing banks and the amount of collateral they can extend for the purchase of marginable securities.

19. **C.** Any time a specific fee is charged for investment advice, the person giving the advice must be registered as an investment advisor under the Investment Advisers Act of 1940.

20. **C.** The Securities Investor Protection Corporation insures separate accounts for up to $100,000 of cash, or $500,000 of cash and securities.

21. **D.** An open-end investment company is characterized as an investment company that continuously redeems and offers shares. A closed-end company is set up much like a regular corporation; once its shares are sold, the stockholder must redeem shares in the secondary marketplace, not with the closed-end fund.

22. **A.** The Investment Company Act of 1940 classifies investment companies into three main categories: face-amount companies, unit investment trusts and management investment companies. *Management* investment companies are further *sub-classified* as open-end, closed-end, diversified or nondiversified.

23. **D.** Sales literature is defined (by the SEC) as any communication used to induce the purchase of a security.

24. **D.** Distributing the prospectus may satisfy the prospectus delivery requirements of the Securities Act of 1933, but it does not relieve the representative from the antifraud rules or the rules and regulations as set forth under the Securities Exchange Act of 1934.

25. **D.** The representative is always subject to the antifraud provisions of the Securities Exchange Act of 1934.

26. **A.** When a stock goes up in price dramatically upon issue, it is said to be hot. Although there is no mathematical formula, a rise in price of 1/8th point or more upon issue is generally considered an example of a hot issue.

27. **D.** Officers and directors of broker-dealers can never buy a hot issue and neither can the firm for its own inventory. A registered rep never can buy a hot issue. Those persons listed in choices I and II, as well as relatives, cannot buy a hot issue unless the amount they are purchasing is insignificant and they have an underwriter to assist in the solicitation of public interest during the 20-day cooling-off period.

28. **D.** Each of the securities listed is exempt from registration under the act of 1933. Others would include commercial paper, Rule 147, Regulation A and Regulation D issues.

14 NASD Regulations

1. Which of the following would constitute a discretionary account?

   A. Trading account of the registered representative
   B. Trading account of the broker-dealer
   C. Account where the investor gives the broker-dealer the authority to buy or sell securities in the customer's account
   D. Mutual fund account allowing periodic withdrawals

2. Which of the following would come under NASD guidelines concerning sales literature or advertising?

   A. Giving a prepared presentation to the local Kiwanis Club
   B. Distributing a letter to all clients
   C. Distributing copies of an article from a magazine
   D. All of the above

3. A client calls up and orders 100 shares of XYZ Company. The agent sends the order in for 200 shares. The agent may effect

   A. an excessive transaction
   B. a discretionary transaction
   C. an illegal transaction
   D. all of the above

4. A registered representative of a member firm wishes to open an account with another member firm. The executing member shall take all the following actions EXCEPT

   A. notify the employer member in writing prior to the execution of the transaction of the intention to open or maintain the account for the representative
   B. immediately transmit to the employer duplicate copies of confirmations or other statements with respect to the representative's account
   C. transmit to the employer duplicate copies of confirmations or other statements with respect to the representative's account upon request of the employer member
   D. notify the registered representative of the executing member's intent to notify the employer member

5. A registered representative may arrange the purchase of an interest in a privately offered limited partnership only if the representative

   I. informs her broker-dealer after the trade
   II. informs her broker-dealer before the trade
   III. provides all documents and information as required by her broker-dealer
   IV. Because the sale is private, the representative does not have to do anything out of the ordinary.

   A. I and II
   B. II
   C. II and III
   D. IV

6. The NASD's Rules of Fair Practice prohibit members from

    I. lending a client's securities without prior authorization from the client
    II. inducing a client to purchase shares of a mutual fund by implying the client will profit from a pending dividend
    III. receiving discounts in securities transactions from another member

    A. I and II only
    B. II and III only
    C. III only
    D. I, II and III

7. The principal underwriter of an open-end investment company decides to give a $300 bonus to the registered representative from any other member firm who sells the most shares. This arrangement is

    I. unacceptable
    II. acceptable if the SEC approves
    III. acceptable if the underwriter is an NASD member
    IV. acceptable as long as it is not considered compensation

    A. I
    B. I and IV
    C. II
    D. II and III

8. Which of the following would be eligible for membership in the NASD?

    A. Bank organized under state and federal laws
    B. Closed-end investment company
    C. Broker or dealer whose regular course of business consists of transactions in securities or the investment banking business
    D. All of the above

9. Which of the following statements about sales literature for mutual funds is(are) true?

    I. The material used to solicit the sale of mutual fund shares may require approval by a principal of the firm.
    II. All mutual fund sales literature must be approved by the NASD within three days of its first use.
    III. If the sponsor of the mutual fund has had the literature reviewed by the NASD in advance, no further approvals are required by the firm.

    A. I and III only
    B. II and III only
    C. III only
    D. I, II and III

10. According to the NASD Rules of Fair Practice, a member firm may give certain selling concessions to

    A. the general public
    B. other NASD member firms
    C. nonmember broker-dealers
    D. all of the above

11. The Guardian Fund has prepared a piece of sales literature to be distributed to individuals who respond to Guardian's tombstone advertisement. If the fund sends the literature to a prospect, the literature must

    A. contain directions for obtaining a prospectus
    B. include the good points contained in the prospectus
    C. contain the SEC disclaimer
    D. be accompanied by a prospectus

12. The NASD was established to

    I. set and standardize charges and commissions
    II. encourage just and equitable principles of trade
    III. adopt and enforce Rules of Fair Practice among brokers and dealers

    A. I only
    B. II and III only
    C. III only
    D. I, II and III

13. An NASD broker-dealer trading in shares of an open-end investment company is prohibited from buying shares of the fund

    A. to cover existing orders
    B. for the firm's own investment purposes
    C. at a discount
    D. for the purpose of resale at a later date

14. The Norse Company, an NASD member, wants to buy shares in the ABC mutual fund from the fund's sponsor at a discount. This arrangement is possible if the sponsor of the ABC mutual fund

    A. is not an NASD member
    B. is also an NASD member and a sales agreement between the two firms is in effect
    C. has a sales agreement with the Norse Company
    D. None of the above would be possible.

15. Under what conditions does the Investment Company Act of 1940 require a written statement disclosing the source of dividend payments?

    A. Whenever a dividend is paid
    B. Whenever net income is part of the dividend
    C. Whenever all or part of the dividend payment comes from a source other than current income or accumulated undistributed net income
    D. The Investment Company Act does not require disclosure, only the Internal Revenue Code requires disclosure of the amount of the dividend.

16. When using the annual report as sales literature, the

    I. principal of the firm must approve its use as such
    II. prospectus must accompany the report
    III. figures contained in the report must be as of a specific date
    IV. report must contain the complete portfolio list

    A. I, II and III only
    B. I and III only
    C. II, III and IV only
    D. I, II, III and IV

17. In the sale of open-end investment company shares, the prospectus

    A. is not necessary
    B. must be delivered to the client either before or during the sales solicitation
    C. must be delivered before the sales solicitation
    D. must be delivered at or before the delivery of the fund share certificate

18. Which of the following persons would most likely become a member of the NASD?

    I. Person convicted of a crime involving fraudulent conversion in the securities business within the past ten years
    II. Person who transacts business for her own account and for others in the over-the-counter market
    III. Person acting only as a specialist on the New York Stock Exchange

    A. I and III only
    B. II only
    C. II and III only
    D. I, II and III

19. When deciding on the suitability of a particular investment for a client, that client's need for liquidity is

    A. not necessary to be determined
    B. only necessary to be determined if the individual is planning on retirement
    C. an important element to be considered when determining the suitability of an investment
    D. only important if the client has no other liquid investment

20. Which of the following individuals may NOT purchase shares of a hot issue of stock?

    A. General partner of a member firm
    B. Spouse of the person who is the managing underwriter of the issue
    C. Senior officer of a bank
    D. All of the above

21. A sale of securities in a dollar amount just below the point at which an investor could take advantage of a lower sales charge by making a larger purchase

    I. is called a breakpoint sale
    II. would not be a conflict of interest
    III. is contrary to just and equitable principles of trade
    IV. requires the approval of the District Business Conduct Committee

    A. I
    B. I and III
    C. I, II and IV
    D. II

22. NASD rules permit members to

    A. execute an order to sell shares of a customer's securities, knowing that delivery of these shares will be two weeks later
    B. continue to compensate a registered representative for sales that were made while the representative was working for the firm according to a previous contract
    C. arrange for a customer to receive $5,000 worth of credit in order to purchase mutual fund shares
    D. give a selling concession to a nonmember firm because of the large number of shares the nonmember is purchasing

23. While recommending the purchase of a security, a registered representative presented material indicating a possible upward move in the price of the recommended security. This recommendation to buy was probably

    I. fraudulent
    II. in violation of the Rules of Fair Practice
    III. not suitable for all investors
    IV. acceptable if the statements about prices and earnings were clearly labeled as forecasts

    A. I
    B. I and II
    C. III
    D. III and IV

24. An employee who is involved in the management of an NASD member's business, particularly in the supervision of business solicitation or in training, would have to be registered as a

    A. broker
    B. dealer
    C. partner
    D. principal

25. Which Federal Reserve Board regulation prohibits brokers and dealers from extending credit for the purchase of open-end investment company shares?

    A. Regulation A
    B. Regulation G
    C. Regulation U
    D. Regulation T

26. The NASD's Code of Procedure contains guidelines for

    A. handling violations of the NASD's Rules of Fair Practice
    B. reviewing and approving accounts, trades, correspondence and sales literature
    C. resolving disputes between two NASD members
    D. resolving disputes between NASD members and non-NASD firms

27. Which of the following statements would be acceptable in sales literature for the Prosperity Growth Fund?

    I. In a period from January 1st, 1966, to January 1st, 1986, the total value of an initial $10,000 investment increased by an average of 8.4% annually. The results should not be considered as representative of the capital gain or loss that may be realized from an investment in the fund today.
    II. The Prosperity Growth Fund has net assets of almost $2 billion and a proven growth record over a 25-year period. These features and SEC approval help to ensure that your investment dollar is growing at the maximum rate.
    III. The Prosperity Fund's advisor expects to select securities for the portfolio that have the greatest potential for capital appreciation and a high return on equity. An investment in the Prosperity portfolio means that your investment dollar can keep pace with inflation.

    A. I only
    B. I and II only
    C. II and III only
    D. I, II and III

28. Which of the following are eligible for membership in the NASD?

    I. JPP Inc., a broker-dealer that engages in over-the-counter securities transactions
    II. Mutual Exclusion, a life insurance company that sells only traditional insurance products
    III. Cosmo Securities, the broker-dealer division of Cosmo Insurance Corporation
    IV. Registered representative for Cosmo Securities

    A. I and III only
    B. I and IV only
    C. II and III only
    D. I, II, III and IV

29. Which of the following statements about the NASD is(are) true?

   I. The NASD has authority to regulate the OTC market.
   II. All branch offices of a member broker-dealer must register with the NASD.
   III. All broker-dealers must hold NASD membership.

   A. I only
   B. I and II only
   C. II and III only
   D. I, II and III

30. The NASD Rules of Fair Practice define *freeriding and withholding* to mean

   A. accepting and processing transactions for members of the public without charging a commission
   B. distributing new issues to brokers, dealers or others at markups in excess of the cost of the services performed
   C. failing to make a bona fide public offering of a hot issue at the public offering price while participating in the stock's distribution as a member of an underwriting syndicate or a selling group
   D. offering mutual fund shares to the public at a discount from the public offering price

31. OTL Inc., a member broker-dealer, is offering securities to the public. It may offer a discount to

   A. the general public
   B. nonmember broker-dealers
   C. member broker-dealers
   D. no one

32. Which of the following must review sales literature and advertising material for investment company shares that principal underwriters have prepared?

   I. Principal of the underwriting broker-dealer distributing the shares
   II. NASD
   III. SEC

   A. I
   B. I and II
   C. II and III
   D. III

33. Erik Freidrich wants to invest through an NASD member firm. Erik is concerned about the fiscal health of the broker-dealer. Which of the following statements is true?

   A. Erik can ask the NASD for the firm's financial information.
   B. Erik cannot get information about the firm's financial situation.
   C. Erik can obtain the financial statements of the firm from the SEC.
   D. Erik can request financial disclosure from the broker-dealer, and the firm must provide Erik with its most recent balance sheet.

34. According to the NASD Rules of Fair Practice, which of the following statements are true?

   I. Members may never pledge or lend a customer's securities.
   II. Members may deal with nonmembers only on the same terms as with the public.
   III. Members are responsible for review of discretionary accounts.

   A. I and II only
   B. I and III only
   C. II and III only
   D. I, II and III

35. OXY Inc. is an NASD member broker-dealer. It is an underwriter of mutual funds. In its dealings with nonmember firms, OXY may

    I. neither buy nor sell securities at a discount from the public offering price
    II. offer gifts exceeding $50 in value
    III. make special concessions on transactions subject to NASD approval

    A. I
    B. I and II
    C. II and III
    D. III

36. The Rules of Fair Practice allow which of the following activities?

    I. ABC Inc., a member firm, purchases mutual fund shares at a discount from XYZ Inc., a member and the underwriter of the shares.
    II. ABC Inc. believes that the NAV of the PRQ Fund will increase soon. ABC buys a large number of shares from the underwriter to hold until the price goes up. At that time, the firm will sell the shares to the public for a profit.
    III. PQR Inc. is marketing a new technology mutual fund. It holds a promotional meeting at which registered representatives are treated to a football game, dinner and entertainment.

    A. I and II only
    B. I and III only
    C. II and III only
    D. I, II and III

37. The NASD issued a complaint against ABC, an NASD member firm, charging that ABC failed to adequately supervise one of its employees involved in a private placement. Which body of rules would govern this complaint?

    A. Code of Arbitration procedure
    B. Rules of Fair Practice
    C. Federal Reserve Board regulations
    D. Code of Procedure

38. While opening a new account, you find out the customer is 88 years old, retired, living on his savings, sick and has never invested before. As his broker, you

    A. must be careful to recommend suitable investments
    B. accept only cash in full before each order
    C. have each order signed by the customer and his lawyer
    D. get ready to be sued

39. A registered representative of an NASD member wishing to avoid a lawsuit may do so if he

    A. sends a written request for termination of his registration
    B. changes broker-dealers with written permission from both the old company and the new company
    C. obtains a written disclaimer from the client
    D. does none of the above

40. In the distribution of hot issues, selling group members are prohibited from

    A. freeriding and withholding
    B. selling at the public offering price
    C. selling to another broker or dealer so that the other broker or dealer can fill an order
    D. all of the above

41. Excessive activity in a customer's account primarily for the purpose of generating excess commissions to the registered representative is referred to as

    A. twisting
    B. churning
    C. whirling
    D. all of the above

42. Over the years, stockbrokers have been known to get themselves into hot water by overinvesting. Hence, any trade made by an NASD registered representative must be approved by the

    A. NASD
    B. SEC
    C. DBCC
    D. branch manager of his office

43. The NASD rules regarding sales literature apply to which of the following?

    A. NASD registered representative putting on investment seminars that are open to the public
    B. Registered representative appearing on a TV show to discuss investments
    C. Registered representative sending to 300 of his clients a form letter that refers to the purchase of ABC Fund shares
    D. All of the above

44. The District Business Conduct Committee is an arm of

    A. the SEC
    B. the NASD
    C. the New York Stock Exchange
    D. all of the above

45. The NASD Code of Procedure

    A. handles trade practice complaints regarding violations of the Rules of Fair Practice
    B. is the application for and the granting of extensions of time
    C. is the processing of applications for registrations of representatives
    D. handles over-the-counter transactions and new stocks

46. The District Business Conduct Committee can impose a limited set of penalties under a Summary Complaint Procedure. The penalty is a

    A. $1,000 fine and/or censure
    B. $2,500 fine and/or censure
    C. $5,000 fine and/or censure
    D. $15,000 fine and/or censure

47. A breakpoint sale is illegal and is

    A. a payment of compensation to a registered representative after he ceases to be employed by a member
    B. the sale of investment company shares in dollar amounts just below the point at which the sales charge is reduced on quantity transactions to incur the higher sales charge
    C. the sale of investment company shares in anticipation of a distribution soon to be paid
    D. all of the above

48. According to NASD Rules of Fair Practice, an underwriter of an open-end investment company would be providing items of material value in which of the following instances?

    I. Gifts under $50 per person per year
    II. Gifts under $99 per person per year
    III. Wholesale overrides included in the prospectus
    IV. Discounts not in the prospectus

    A. I
    B. I and III
    C. I and IV
    D. II and IV

49. A broker-dealership is fined by the DBCC of the NASD. The firm wishes to appeal. To which of the following bodies should it direct its appeal?

    A. Client
    B. Board of Governors at the DBCC
    C. Board of Governors of the NASD
    D. United States District Court

50. An NASD member that is a fund underwriter must notify the NASD when payment is not received from another member in connection with wire orders within how many days from the date of the transaction?

A. Five business days
B. Seven calendar days
C. Ten business days
D. Fifteen business days

51. When a client opens an account, which of the following pieces of information will need to be noted on the application?

I. Client's name and signature
II. Whether the client is employed by an NASD member firm
III. Signature of the registered rep
IV. Signature of the office manager, partner or other designated principal
V. Statement that the client understands the risks involved

A. I only
B. I, II, III and IV only
C. I, II and IV only
D. I, II, III, IV and V

52. Continuing commissions in connection with the sale of investment company securities

A. are a form of deferred compensation; therefore, when a registered representative resigns from the NASD, he must be paid all commissions to which he is and will be entitled
B. may be paid to a retired employee if a bona fide contract calling for such payment was entered into by the registered representative while employed by a member
C. must be paid by a member whether or not the person receiving the commissions is a registered representative of a member
D. are illegal at any time

53. According to the NASD Code of Arbitration, which of the following may institute arbitration proceedings against a registered representative?

A. Customer
B. Employer
C. Anyone in the investment banking industry
D. Any of the above

54. Which of the following statements concerning the annual report to shareholders of mutual funds are true?

A. It need not comply with the NASD advertising rules.
B. It is required to list the changes in a company's portfolio.
C. It is identical to the current prospectus.
D. It does not need to comply with any of the above.

55. Under the Rules of Fair Practice, all of the following would be violations of the special deals rules EXCEPT a

I. gift of $99 cash
II. gift of $25 in value
III. dinner at a local night club for the agent and his spouse as guests of the wholesaler
IV. pair of tickets to a baseball game
V. pair of season tickets for a professional baseball team

A. I and V
B. II, III and IV
C. II, III and V
D. II and V

56. Commingling of securities being hypothe-
cated is a prohibited act. Commingling is

A. pledging a client's securities as collateral
for a loan with the client's permission
B. holding a client's securities in the name
of the broker-dealership
C. pledging for the same loan a client's
securities held in street name along with
securities of the dealership
D. none of the above

57. As an employee of an NASD member, you
may recommend a security to a customer,
predicting a rise in price

A. if the customer signed a letter relieving
you of your obligation to abide by the
NASD Rules of Fair Practice
B. if you are sure the price will rise
C. if the customer is an experienced trader
D. under no circumstances

58. In general, a registered representative could
have power of attorney for accounts of each
of the following EXCEPT a(n)

A. corporation
B. individual
C. partnership
D. custodian

59. A registered representative of an NYSE
member firm who wishes to work outside
the firm after hours would require permission from the

A. member firm
B. NASD
C. NYSE
D. SEC

60. Which of the following statements is true of
a limited power of attorney that a customer
gives his rep?

A. The rep needs written permission from
the customer for each trade.
B. The customer must renew the power of
attorney every year.
C. The customer can still enter independent
orders.
D. The branch manager must initial each
order before it is entered.

61. General communications by a broker-dealer
firm, such as advertising or research reports,
could not be approved by which of the following?

A. Member
B. Principal of a member
C. Supervisory analyst
D. Certified financial analyst

◆ Answers & Rationale

1. C. A discretionary account is an account where a representative has been given authority to select the amount and type of investment for a client. The authorization must be written.

2. D. Sales literature is any public solicitation concerning securities.

3. A. Sending the order in for 200 shares when the client ordered only 100 shares is an excessive transaction.

4. B. When an employee opens an account with another member, the employee will be notified by the executing member that the employing member will be notified that the account is to be opened, and copies of confirmations and other reports will be available upon request.

5. C. In a private securities transaction the representative must obtain permission for the sale from his broker-dealer prior to the transaction. The transaction must be through the books of the broker-dealer, and any information requested by the broker-dealer must be supplied. The broker-dealer is still responsible for actions of the representative in this private transaction.

6. A. The Rules of Fair Practice prohibit unauthorized borrowing (stealing) and selling dividends. Discounts are allowed to other NASD members if a dealer agreement has been signed.

7. A. Gifts in excess of $50 per person per year are not allowed.

8. C. Broker-dealers in the securities business may become members; banks cannot. A closed-end fund is an investment company and not a broker-dealer.

9. A. Sales literature must be approved by a firm's principal prior to use. If the literature has been reviewed by the NASD, it need not be submitted by every broker-dealer intending to use it.

10. B. Members may give other members concessions, but must deal with the public and nonmembers at the public offering price.

11. D. Any solicitation requires a prospectus to be delivered prior to or during the solicitation. Sales literature is solicitation.

12. B. The commissions charged are not set, but must be fair and reasonable for the service provided as enumerated in the NASD Rules of Fair Practice.

13. D. A broker-dealer may purchase shares only to fulfill existing orders or for its own investment account, not for inventory.

14. B. This arrangement is possible if both are NASD members and there is a sales agreement in effect.

15. C. The Investment Company Act of 1940 requires disclosure when all or part of the dividend payment comes from a source other than current income or accumulated undistributed net income.

16. D. The principal of the firm must approve the use of the annual report as sales literature, and the figures contained must be current and complete. A prospectus is always required.

17. B. The sale of mutual fund shares requires that the client get the prospectus before or during the sales solicitation.

18. B. A person conducting business in the over-the-counter market needs to be a member of the NASD. Transacting business on the exchange requires membership with the NYSE.

19. C. Liquidity is very important when determining suitability for a client.

20. D. None of the people listed may purchase hot issues.

21. **B.** This is called a breakpoint sale and is contrary to just and equitable principles of trade.

22. **B.** Registered reps may continue to be compensated for sales that were made while working for the firm and in accord with the contract.

23. **D.** No investment is suitable for all investors. Statements about future prices and earnings may be used if they are clearly labeled as forecasts.

24. **D.** Supervision of business solicitation or training requires being registered as a principal.

25. **D.** It is Regulation T that regulates the extension of credit by brokers and dealers for investment company shares.

26. **A.** The Code of Procedure contains the guidelines for handling violations of the NASD Rules of Fair Practice.

27. **A.** Advertising cannot be misleading. To say that past performance is indicative of future results or that the SEC approves of the company or product is clearly fraudulent.

28. **A.** Firms effecting transactions in the over-the-counter market are eligible for NASD membership. The representative for the firm becomes registered, but is not an NASD member.

29. **B.** Firms transacting business in the over-the-counter market must register with the SEC and are eligible for membership with the NASD (although it is not required). If a broker-dealer is a member, each branch office of the broker-dealer must be registered with the NASD.

30. **C.** Freeriding and withholding are the sale or retention of a security in order to profit from an increase in selling price soon after the security is made available to the public (hot issue).

31. **C.** Only member firms are entitled to discounts or concessions on the sale of a security. Otherwise, the public offering price is maintained.

32. **B.** Because investment company shares are a continuous primary offering, sales literature and advertising must be filed with the NASD for review. The principal for the firm must approve the sales literature prior to use and is the individual contacted by the NASD if it is determined that the material is misleading.

33. **D.** Under the Rules of Fair Practice, a member must make available its most recent balance sheet to prospective customers for review.

34. **C.** Hypothecation of securities is the pledging of client securities for loans, allowing the extension of credit for margin accounts, and hypothecation is allowed. Members must maintain the public offering price and are responsible for review of discretionary accounts (a principal must endorse each transaction).

35. **A.** As a member, OXY must treat non-members as the general public and can, therefore, offer no discounts or concessions. Gifts or gratuities in excess of $50 per person per year are prohibited.

36. **B.** Orders for mutual fund shares can be accepted only to fill existing orders, not for holding in an account and later resale. Dinner and sporting tickets are not a violation as long as the practice is occasional.

37. **B.** Failure to adequately supervise is a violation of the Rules of Fair Practice. The Code of Procedure is the method prescribed for handling infractions of the Rules of Fair Practice. The Code of Arbitration is for money complaints.

38. **A.** Any investment solicited for sale must be suitable for that particular client. If not, it is considered inconsistent with just and equitable principles of trade.

39. **D.** A registered representative cannot avoid litigation arising from the conduct of business in the securities market. Rescission is allowed under state law.

40. **A.** If an issue turns hot or sells for a premium soon after its offering, a broker-dealer withholding or freeriding would be in violation of the NASD Rules of Fair Practice and SEC regulations.

41. **B.** Excessive activity for the purpose of generating commissions is known as churning.

42. **D.** The securities laws regulate the activities of associated persons. One of those regulations stipulates that the company is responsible for the conduct of its representatives. Hence, all correspondence and sales by the representative must be approved by a branch manager.

43. **D.** Any written communication such as seminar and TV scripts, form letters and so on falls under the NASD guidelines of sales literature or advertising.

44. **B.** The District Business Conduct Committee is an arm of the NASD. The DBCC is the first body to judge and hear complaints.

45. **A.** The Code of Procedure prescribes the method for handling trade practice complaints and sets the standards for fines or other actions.

46. **B.** Under the summary complaint procedure, should the DBCC feel that facts concerning a violation are not in dispute, the DBCC may offer the respondent summary complaint. The maximum penalties are a $2,500 fine and/or censure.

47. **B.** Breakpoint sales are a violation of the NASD Rules of Fair Practice. A breakpoint sale is the sale of fund shares just below the point where a sales charge is reduced in order to maintain the higher commission.

48. **D.** Items of material value are gifts or money paid in excess of $50 per person per year. Additionally, discounts not disclosed in a prospectus would be considered of material value.

49. **C.** The Board of Governors is the body that handles appeals of DBCC decisions.

50. **C.** An NASD member is prohibited from withholding orders from another member (sponsor or investment company) for more than ten business days. To do otherwise is a violation of the NASD Rules of Fair Practice.

51. **D.** When opening an account, the minimum information needed is the name of the client, whether the client is employed with another NASD firm and the client's tax identification number. Additionally, the registered representative must have discussed the risks of the investment with the client and must sign the appropriate forms. All accounts will be reviewed by a supervisor (principal of the firm).

52. **B.** Continuing commissions may be paid to a registered representative as long as there is a contract calling for such payment and the person remains registered.

53. **D.** Anyone can institute arbitration proceedings against a registered representative. In fact, as a condition of registration, the representative agrees to submit to arbitration.

54. **B.** Reports to shareholders will list the changes to the fund's portfolio.

55. **B.** Items of material value are gifts in excess of $50 per person per year. Occasional tickets to entertainment or sporting events are OK. Season tickets, however, are considered to be of material value.

56. **C.** Commingling is the mixing of securities held and is a violation of the Rules of Fair Practice. Answer A defines *hypothecation*. Answer B defines *street name*.

57. **D.** Predictions are a violation of the NASD Rules of Fair Practice. Projections can be based on history only.

58. **D.** A custodian for an UGMA account cannot grant trading authority to a third party.

59. **A.**   A rep would always need to get permission from the firm before working for another firm.

60. **C.**   The RR must have prior written authority from the client and have received approval from a supervisory person before accepting discretionary authority. While a designated principal must frequently review the account, the branch manager need not initial each order before it is entered.

61. **D.**   A CFA is a securities analyst. Research reports are approved by a supervisory analyst.

15

Final Exam One

1. Treasury bills are

    A. issued at par
    B. callable
    C. issued in bearer form
    D. registered

2. If a bond is purchased at a premium, the yield to maturity would be

    A. higher than the nominal yield
    B. lower than the nominal yield
    C. the same as the nominal yield
    D. None of the above

3. A 12% corporate bond issued by the XYZ Company is due in ten years. The bond is convertible into XYZ common stock at a conversion price of $20 per share. The XYZ bond is quoted at 120. Parity of the common stock is

    A. $20
    B. $24
    C. $50
    D. $60

4. When a broker-dealer is holding money and/or securities in its own account, it is

    A. underwriting
    B. hypothecating the securities
    C. taking a position
    D. engaging in none of the above

5. If interest rates are increasing and the market price of bonds are decreasing, what would happen to the value of preferred stock during this same time period?

    A. The value would increase.
    B. The value would decrease.
    C. The value would remain the same.
    D. Interest rates and the value of bonds have no impact on the value of stock.

6. Which of the following would constitute a discretionary account?

    A. Trading account of the registered representative
    B. Trading account of the broker-dealer
    C. Account where the investor gives the broker-dealer the authority to buy or sell securities in the customer's account
    D. Mutual fund account allowing periodic withdrawals

7. Which of the following would be considered an unaffiliated person in a mutual fund?

    A. Member of the board of directors of the mutual fund who also is employed as the investment advisor
    B. Shareholder who owns 10% of the fund's shares
    C. Person who holds a position with the underwriter for the fund
    D. Member of the board of directors who cannot hold another position within the investment company

8. An investor purchasing a Treasury STRIP could be assured of

   I. a locked-in rate of return
   II. a lump-sum payment of principal and interest at maturity
   III. lower taxes because the returns would be taxed at the lower capital gains rate
   IV. little or no reinvestment risk

   A. I
   B. I, II and III
   C. I, II and IV
   D. I and IV

9. The ex-dividend date of a mutual fund would be

   A. the fourth business day prior to the record date
   B. seven calendar days after the declaration date
   C. seven business days after the declaration date
   D. whenever the board of directors stipulates the ex-dividend date to be

10. A client could be assured of federal government backing for an investment in which of the following agencies?

    A. Federal National Mortgage Association
    B. Inter-American Development Bank
    C. Government National Mortgage Association
    D. Federal Intermediate Credit Bank

11. In describing GNMAs to a potential investor, you would tell him that

    A. the certificates have the full faith and credit backing of the U.S. government
    B. each bond is backed by a pool of insured mortgages
    C. interest payments received by the investor are exempt from both local and federal income taxes
    D. a GNMA can be purchased for as little as $10,000

12. An investment company share normally goes ex-dividend

    A. on the record date
    B. the day after the record date
    C. five days after the record date
    D. seven days after the record date

13. An investor interested in monthly interest income should invest in

    A. GNMAs
    B. Treasury bonds
    C. stock of a utility company
    D. corporate bonds

14. Which of the following would be classified as an investment company?

    I. Closed-end company
    II. Open-end company
    III. Qualified plan company
    IV. Nonqualified plan company
    V. Fixed annuity company

    A. I and II
    B. II, II and V
    C. II
    D. III, IV and V

15. A teacher has placed money into a tax-qualified variable annuity over the past twelve years. The teacher has contributed $26,000, and the value of the annuity today is $36,000. If the teacher withdraws $15,000 today, what would be the tax consequences if the teacher is in the 30% tax bracket?

    A. $1,500
    B. $3,000
    C. $4,500
    D. There are no taxes due on this withdrawal.

16. The market price of a convertible bond will depend on

    A. the value of the underlying stock into which the bond can be converted
    B. current interest rates
    C. the rating of the bond
    D. all of the above

17. Where can closed-end investment company shares be purchased and sold?

    A. In the secondary marketplace
    B. From the closed-end company
    C. In the primary market
    D. All of the above

18. An investor has bonds maturing in two weeks. The investor plans to purchase new bonds with a 10% coupon rate. If interest rates decline in the period before the investor can purchase the new bonds, the investor would expect the income to be received from the new bonds to

    A. increase
    B. decline
    C. stay the same
    D. do none of the above

19. Under the provisions of an UGMA account, when the minor reaches the age of majority, the account

    A. should be turned over to the donee
    B. should be turned over to the donor
    C. remains an UGMA account
    D. None of the above will occur.

20. You would advise an investor interested in low volatility of interest rates to invest in a security that has a return tied to the

    A. passbook rate
    B. prime rate
    C. federal funds rate
    D. broker call rate

21. Federal funds are used primarily by

    A. large commercial banks
    B. mutual insurance companies
    C. independent broker-dealers
    D. savings and loans

22. One of the most important functions of a banker's acceptance is its use as a means of

    A. facilitating trades in foreign goods
    B. facilitating trades of foreign securities in the U.S.
    C. assigning previously declared distributions by foreign corporations
    D. guaranteeing payment of an international bank's promissory note

23. If a corporation wanted to offer stock at a given price for the next five years, it would issue

    A. rights
    B. warrants
    C. callable preferred stock
    D. put options

24. Which of the following withdrawal plans would an investor select if she wanted to receive a fixed payment monthly from the investment company?

    A. Fixed-time
    B. Fixed-share
    C. Fixed-percentage
    D. Fixed-dollar

25. Which of the following would come under NASD guidelines concerning sales literature or advertising?

    A. Giving a prepared presentation to the local Kiwanis Club
    B. Distributing a letter to all clients
    C. Distributing copies of an article from a magazine
    D. All of the above

26. In a nonqualified plan, all the following are true EXCEPT

A. the plan is a trust
B. contributions are made aftertax
C. the plan must be in writing
D. the plan can be discriminatory

27. All of the following would be considered typical of a money-market fund EXCEPT that

A. the underlying portfolio is normally made up of short-term debt instruments
B. most or all are offered as no-load investments
C. such funds have a high beta and are safest in periods of low market volatility
D. its net asset value normally remains unchanged

28. A customer indicates that she wishes to invest $50,000 in mutual funds. The investments are to be split into three different funds, each with its own management company. The registered representative should advise the customer that

A. this is an excellent idea because it spreads the risk of investing even more
B. she will pay greater commissions on the investment when the money is split between three funds than if she put the money into only one fund
C. she will be able to exchange shares from one fund to another as conditions change without incurring a new sales charge
D. she should buy individual stocks because mutual funds are only for smaller investors

29. The result of a client investing the same amount of money into a mutual fund over a long period of time is a lower

A. price per share than cost per share
B. cost per share than price per share
C. dollar amount invested
D. None of the above

30. A client calls up and orders 100 shares of XYZ Company. The agent sends the order in for 200 shares. The agent may effect

A. an excessive transaction
B. a discretionary transaction
C. an illegal transaction
D. all of the above

31. On February 14th an investor purchases 1,000 shares of the ABC Bond Fund, which has an objective of providing the highest possible level of income on a monthly basis. On February 15th, the investor informs his agent that he has changed his mind and wishes to exchange his bond fund shares for shares of a common stock growth fund with an objective of capital appreciation within the same family of funds. The investor's bond fund shares increased in value prior to the exchange. How will this increase in value be taxed?

A. As income because the bond fund's objective was to provide for current income on a monthly basis
B. As a short-term gain because the bond fund was held for less than six months
C. As a long-term gain because the exchange of the bond fund shares was made into a common stock fund with an objective of long-term capital appreciation
D. Because the shares were exchanged within a family of funds, the increase in value of the bond fund shares is not taxed, but it increases the cost base in the common stock fund investment.

32. A repurchase agreement is usually initiated by

I. the U.S. Treasury
II. the Federal Home Loan Bank
III. commercial banks
IV. the Federal Reserve Board

A. I and III
B. I and IV
C. II and IV
D. III and IV

33. What secures an industrial development revenue bond?

    A. State tax
    B. Municipal tax
    C. Trustee
    D. Net lease payments from the corporation

34. What organization or governmental unit sets economic policy?

    A. Federal Reserve Board
    B. Government Economic Board
    C. Congress
    D. Secretary of the Treasury

35. A registered representative of a member firm wishes to open an account with another member firm. The executing member shall take all the following actions EXCEPT

    A. notify the employer member in writing prior to the execution of the transaction of the intention to open or maintain the account for the representative
    B. immediately transmit to the employer member duplicate copies of confirmations or other statements with respect to the representative's account
    C. transmit duplicate copies of confirmations or other statements with respect to the representative's account upon request of the employer member
    D. notify the registered representative of the executing member's intent to notify the employer member

36. In its attempt to increase the money supply, the Federal Open Market Committee is purchasing T bills. This action should cause the yield on T bills to

    A. increase
    B. decrease
    C. remain the same
    D. fluctuate

37. Which of the following would not expose the investor to reinvestment risk?

    A. Treasury stock
    B. Treasury bonds
    C. Treasury STRIPS
    D. Treasury notes

38. Distributions to an employee from a profit-sharing plan after retirement are made

    A. from interest accumulating on the plan's assets
    B. only from the profits on the plan's assets
    C. from the amount allocated to the individual's account during the employee's participation in the plan
    D. only from the amount allocated to the individual's account plus accumulated earnings during the employee's participation in the plan

39. An individual calculating taxable income received from a municipal bond fund investment for this year would consider that

    A. part of the income distribution received as a dividend is taxable at ordinary income tax rates
    B. all of the income distribution received as a dividend is taxable at ordinary income tax rates
    C. any capital gains distributions received from the fund are taxable at ordinary income tax rates
    D. all distributions received from the fund, both income and gains, are exempt from federal income tax

40. If ABC Company's dividend decreases by 5% and its stock's market value decreases by 7%, the current yield of the stock will

    A. increase
    B. decrease
    C. remain at 5%
    D. not be affected

41. If a variable annuity has an assumed investment rate of 5% and the annualized return of the separate account is 4%, what would be the consequence?

    I. The value of the accumulation unit will rise.
    II. The value of the annuity unit will rise.
    III. The value of the accumulation unit will fall.
    IV. The value of the annuity unit will fall.

    A. I and II
    B. I and IV
    C. II and III
    D. III and IV

42. ABC, an open-end investment company, has the following financial information:

Dividend income	$2,000
Interest income	900
Short-term gains	1,000
Long-term gains	1,000
Expenses	900

    In order to qualify as a regulated investment company, ABC must distribute what amount to its investors?

    A. $1,800
    B. $2,700
    C. $3,510
    D. $3,600

43. Maggie Smith is 65. She had payroll deduction contributions into a tax-deferred annuity. Her contributions totaled $10,000, and the current value of her account is $16,000. For tax purposes, what is Maggie's cost basis?

    A. $0
    B. $10,000
    C. $16,000
    D. $6,000

44. If Mrs. Smith had payroll deductions totaling $10,000 placed into a tax-qualified deferred annuity and her current value in the account was $16,000, for tax purposes her cost base would be

    A. $0
    B. $6,000
    C. $10,000
    D. $16,000

45. An investor is looking into the purchase of Series EE bonds through payroll deduction at his place of employment. If the investor decides to purchase the Series EE bonds, he would receive the interest earned

    A. monthly
    B. semiannually
    C. annually
    D. at redemption

46. Which of the following insure that the principal and interest are paid when a municipal issuer is in financial difficulty?

    I. MBIA
    II. AMBAC
    III. SIPC
    IV. FDIC

    A. I and II only
    B. III only
    C. III and IV only
    D. I, II, III and IV

47. An investor is in the annuity stage of a variable annuity purchased 15 years ago. During the present month, the annuitant receives a check for an amount that is less than the previous month's payment. Which of the following events would have caused the annuitant to receive the smaller check?

A. The performance of the account was less than the previous month's performance.
B. The performance of the account was greater than the previous month's performance.
C. The performance of the account was less than the assumed interest rate.
D. The performance of the account was greater than the assumed interest rate.

48. A registered representative may arrange the purchase of an interest in a privately offered limited partnership only if the representative

I. informs her broker-dealer after the trade
II. informs her broker-dealer before the trade
III. provides all documents and information as required by her broker-dealer
IV. Because the sale is private, the representative does not have to do anything out of the ordinary.

A. I and II
B. II
C. II and III
D. IV

49. Which of the following statements is true of the expense ratio of an open-end investment company?

A. It is computed exclusive of the management fee.
B. It is computed inclusive of the management fee.
C. It is computed taking into account the management fee only.
D. It shows the extent of leverage in the fund.

50. A mutual fund paid $.30 in dividends and $.75 in capital gains during the year. The offering price at the end of the year is $6.50. The fund's current yield for the year is

A. 4.6%
B. 6.9%
C. 11.5%
D. 16.2%

51. Your customer buys a put. Prior to expiration, the put is exercised. What is your customer required to deposit?

I. Cash equal to the aggregate exercise price
II. Necessary margin for a short position
III. 100 shares of the underlying stock

A. I
B. I or II
C. II
D. II or III

52. The separate account funding a variable annuity that purchases shares in a mutual fund offered by the life insurance company is considered

A. a unit investment trust
B. a face-amount certificate company
C. a management investment company
D. none of the above

53. In a mutual fund, after opening an account an investor can generally make additional periodic investments in minimum amounts of

A. $50
B. $100
C. $500
D. The amount varies from fund to fund.

54. Which of the following characteristics describe stock rights?

    I. Short-term instruments that become worthless after the expiration date

    II. Most commonly offered in connection with debentures to sweeten the offering

    III. Issued by a corporation

    IV. Traded in the securities market

    A. I and II

    B. I and III

    C. I, III and IV

    D. II, III and IV

55. Marjorie and Harry Kellog are tenants in common in a joint account. Which of the following statements is(are) true?

    A. If one of them dies, the survivor will not automatically assume full ownership.

    B. They need not have equal interest in the account.

    C. They have an undivided interest in the property in the account.

    D. All of the above are true.

56. A prospectus for an individual variable annuity contract

    I. must provide full and fair disclosure

    II. is required by the Securities Act of 1933

    III. must be filed with the SEC

    IV. must precede or accompany every sales presentation

    A. I only

    B. I, III and IV only

    C. II and III only

    D. I, II, III and IV

57. In a mutual fund, the amount of increases and/or decreases in the NAV over the past years can be reviewed in the

    A. official statement

    B. customer account form

    C. prospectus

    D. tombstone

58. The NASD's Rules of Fair Practice prohibit members from

    I. lending a client's securities without prior authorization from the client

    II. inducing a client to purchase shares of a mutual fund by implying the client will profit from a pending dividend

    III. receiving discounts in securities transactions from another member

    A. I and II only

    B. II and III only

    C. III only

    D. I, II and III

59. The principal underwriter of an open-end investment company decides to give a $300 bonus to the registered representative from any other member firm who sells the most shares. This arrangement is

    I. unacceptable

    II. acceptable if the SEC approves

    III. acceptable if the underwriter is an NASD member

    IV. acceptable as long as it is not considered compensation

    A. I

    B. I and IV

    C. II

    D. II and III

60. Which of the following statements about sales charges is(are) true?

    I. Under NASD rules, mutual fund sales charges may not exceed 8.5% of the offering price.
    II. Under NASD rules, mutual fund sales charges may not exceed 8.5% of the share's net asset value.
    III. An investment company must offer rights of accumulation, breakpoints and reinvestment of dividends at NAV in order to charge an 8.5% sales charge.
    IV. Under the Investment Company Act of 1940, the maximum sales charge for purchases of mutual fund shares is 9%.

    A. I
    B. I and III
    C. I, III and IV
    D. II, III and IV

61. An owner of common stock has the right to

    I. determine when dividends will be issued
    II. vote at stockholders' meetings or by proxy
    III. receive a predetermined fixed portion of the corporation's profit in cash when declared
    IV. buy restricted securities before they are offered to the public

    A. I, III and IV
    B. II
    C. II, III and IV
    D. II and IV

62. Kim Filby is participating in a periodic payment plan. Fifty percent of her first year's payments are taken as a sales charge. What is the maximum the sales charge can average over the life of the plan?

    A. 8.5%
    B. 9%
    C. 16%
    D. 20%

63. In a mutual fund, a shareholder who elected not to receive share certificates can liquidate all or a portion of his holdings and receive payment from the fund if the fund receives which of the following?

    I. Written request from the shareholder
    II. Signed stock power from the shareholder
    III. Signature guarantee from the shareholder

    A. I only
    B. I and II only
    C. I and III only
    D. I, II and III

64. In order to get cash for an emergency that arose, Michael MacKay redeemed his mutual fund shares. Within how many days of redemption could he reinvest in the same fund without having to pay additional sales charges?

    A. 7
    B. 30
    C. 45
    D. 60

65. June Kaslov wants to buy $1,000 worth of an open-end investment company. She may buy them through

    I. the sponsor of the fund
    II. a brokerage firm
    III. the custodian of the fund
    IV. a bank acting as dealer

    A. I and II
    B. I, II and IV
    C. II
    D. III and IV

66. Contract holders must be given the right to vote on matters concerning separate account personnel at the

A. beginning of separate account operations
B. first meeting of contract holders within one year of beginning operations
C. meeting of contract holders after one year of selling the first variable life policy
D. Contract holders are not allowed to vote on separate account personnel according to federal law.

67. A separate account funding a variable life contract is considered to be a(n)

A. investment company issuing periodic payment plan certificates
B. insurance company issuing periodic payment plan certificates
C. investment company issuing variable annuity contracts
D. fixed annuity company issuing variable payment contracts

68. Separate accounts funding a variable life contract and certain personnel working for the account are required to be registered under which of the following securities acts?

I.   Securities Act of 1933
II. Securities Exchange Act of 1934
III. Investment Company Act of 1940
IV. Investment Advisers Act of 1940

A. I, II and III only
B. III only
C. III and III only
D. I, II, III and IV

69. Murray Murbles invests $3,000 in open-end investment company shares. After 60 days, he signs a letter of intent for a $10,000 breakpoint and backdates the letter two months. Six months later, he deposits $10,000 into the fund. He will receive a reduced sales charge on

A. the $3,000 investment only
B. $7,000 of the investment only
C. the $10,000 investment only
D. the entire $13,000 investment

70. *Limited liability* means that

I.   investors are not liable to the full extent of their investment in a corporation
II. creditors have recourse to the assets of the corporation but not to the personal assets of the individual owners
III. a business cannot go into bankruptcy
IV. the stockholder would lose only the amount of his or her investment in the corporation if it went bankrupt

A. I and II only
B. II and IV only
C. III only
D. I, II, III and IV

71. Some open-end investment companies offer their investors a conversion privilege, which permits investors to

A. exchange general securities for shares in the mutual fund's portfolio
B. delay payment of taxes on investment company shares that have appreciated in value
C. purchase additional fund shares from dividends paid by the fund
D. exchange shares of one mutual fund for those of another fund under the same management, at net asset value

72. Which of the following would be eligible for membership in the NASD?

    A. Bank organized under state and federal laws
    B. Closed-end investment company
    C. Broker or dealer whose regular course of business consists of transactions in securities or the investment banking business
    D. All of the above

73. Bernard Kalman uses the LIFO method to determine his capital gains. What does this mean?

    A. The IRS will assume a liquidation of the first shares that were acquired.
    B. Bernard will indicate the specific shares that were redeemed without regard to when they were purchased.
    C. The last shares purchased are the first shares to be redeemed.
    D. None of the above apply in this case.

74. Kirk Thomas is about to buy a variable annuity contract. He wants to select an annuity that will give him the largest possible monthly payment. Which of the following payout options would do so?

    A. Life annuity with period certain
    B. Unit refund life option
    C. Life annuity with ten-year period certain
    D. Life only annuity

75. Stan Baedecker has $350,000 in securities and $201,000 in cash with his brokerage firm. If the brokerage firm were forced to liquidate, how much of the account would be covered by SIPC?

    A. $250,000 of the securities and all of the cash
    B. All of the securities and $150,000 of the cash
    C. All of the securities and $100,000 of the cash
    D. All of the cash and $299,000 of the securities

76. If a customer submits a repurchase order to his broker-dealer after the close of the New York Stock Exchange, the customer will receive a price based on the net asset value computed

    A. the previous business day
    B. the same day regardless of when the order is received
    C. the next time the firm computes it
    D. within the next two business days

77. Mark Armitrage originally invested $20,000 into the NCA Fund and has reinvested dividends and gains of $8,000. His shares in NCA are now worth $40,000. He converts his investment in NCA to the DQ Fund, which is under the same management as NCA. Which of the following is true?

    A. He retains his cost basis of $28,000 in the DQ Fund.
    B. He must declare $12,000 as a taxable gain upon conversion into the DQ Fund.
    C. He retains a $20,000 cost basis in the DQ Fund because of the conversion privilege.
    D. He is not liable for taxes in the current year because he did not have constructive receipt of the money at conversion.

78. Which of the following statements about the underwriting of a new issue is(are) true?

    A. In a best-efforts offering, the underwriters will not be held financially liable for any unsold portion of the offering.
    B. In a firm commitment underwriting, the underwriters pay the issuer for the full amount of the offering and retain any unsold shares.
    C. In an all-or-none underwriting, the issuer agrees to cancel the offering if all the shares are not sold.
    D. All of the above are true.

79. Thomas Earl is the sole owner of a business. He earns $160,000 a year and makes the maximum contribution to a defined benefit Keogh plan. How much money may be contributed to his IRA?

    A. $0
    B. $2,000
    C. $15,000
    D. $30,000

80. The Securities Exchange Act of 1934 does which of the following?

    I. Requires registration of securities
    II. Requires registration of broker-dealers with the SEC
    III. Prohibits inequitable and unfair trade practices
    IV. Provides for regulation of the over-the-counter market

    A. I and II only
    B. II and III only
    C. II, III and IV only
    D. I, II, III and IV

81. A no-load fund sells its shares to the public

    A. through a network of underwriters and dealers
    B. through a dealer and its sales representatives
    C. by underwriter only
    D. by a direct sale from the fund to the investor

82. Tim Simmons owns a variable annuity contract, and the AIR stated in the contract is 5%. In January the realized rate of return in the separate account was 7%, and Tim received a check based on this return for $200. In February the rate of return was 10%, and Tim received a check for $210. To maintain the same payment Tim received in February, what rate of return would the separate account have to earn in March?

    A. 3%
    B. 5%
    C. 7%
    D. 10%

83. Which of the following statements about sales literature for mutual funds is(are) true?

    I. The material used to solicit the sale of mutual fund shares may require approval by a principal of the firm.
    II. All mutual fund sales literature must be approved by the NASD within three days of its first use.
    III. If the sponsor of the mutual fund has had the literature reviewed by the NASD in advance, no further approvals are required by the firm.

    A. I and III only
    B. II and III only
    C. III only
    D. I, II and III

84. When would an investor be liable for tax on reinvested distributions from an open-end investment company?

    A. When the shares purchased from the distribution are sold
    B. When the shares purchased with the distribution have been held for twelve months
    C. At the time the distribution is made
    D. None of the above

85. According to the NASD Rules of Fair Practice, a member firm may give certain selling concessions to

    A. the general public
    B. other NASD member firms
    C. nonmember broker-dealers
    D. all of the above

86. An investor who owns shares of a mutual fund actually owns

    A. an undivided interest in the fund's debt capitalization
    B. specific shares of stock in the fund's portfolio
    C. an undivided interest in the fund's portfolio
    D. certain unspecified securities among those owned by the fund

87. A municipal bond is quoted at 6 1/4%. Currently its yield to maturity is 6 3/4%. From this information it can be determined that the municipal bond is trading

    A. flat
    B. at par
    C. at a discount
    D. at a premium

88. The Securities Act of 1933 requires that which of the following be offered only by prospectus?

    I. Treasury bonds
    II. Mutual fund shares
    III. Variable annuities
    IV. Unit investment trusts

    A. I and II
    B. II and III
    C. II, III and IV
    D. III and IV

89. A customer decides to buy shares of an open-end investment company. When is the price of the shares determined?

    A. At the next calculation of net asset value the day the fund custodian receives proper notification from the client
    B. At the next calculation of net asset value the day the broker-dealer wires the custodian on behalf of the client
    C. Both A and B
    D. Neither A nor B

90. The Guardian Fund has prepared a piece of sales literature to be distributed to individuals who respond to Guardian's tombstone ad. If the fund sends the literature to a prospect, the literature must

    A. contain directions for obtaining a prospectus
    B. include the good points contained in the prospectus
    C. contain the SEC disclaimer
    D. be accompanied by a prospectus

91. Which of the following are characteristic of a mutual fund voluntary accumulation plan?

    I. Minimum initial purchase
    II. Minimum optional additional purchases
    III. Declining level sales charges as money accumulates
    IV. Obligatory purchase goal

    A. I and II only
    B. I, II and III only
    C. II and IV only
    D. I, II, III and IV

92. Your client tells you he wants a source of retirement income that is stable but that also could offer some protection against purchasing power risk in times of inflation. You should recommend

    A. a variable annuity
    B. a fixed annuity
    C. a combination annuity
    D. common stocks and municipal bonds

93. The NASD was established to

    I. set and standardize charges and commissions
    II. encourage just and equitable principles of trade
    III. adopt and enforce Rules of Fair Practice among brokers and dealers

    A. I only
    B. II and III only
    C. III only
    D. I, II and III

94. Which of the following characteristics describe(s) a contractual planholder?

    I. Receives unit trust certificates
    II. Owns an undivided interest in the mutual fund shares underlying the plan
    III. Owns an undivided interest in the portfolio of the underlying mutual fund

    A. I and II
    B. I and III
    C. II and III
    D. III

95. Which type of nonmarketable security pays semiannual interest?

    A. Series II bonds
    B. Treasury bonds
    C. Series HH bonds
    D. Agency issues

96. Which of the following statements about a straight-life variable annuity is(are) true?

    I. The number of annuity units a client redeems never changes.
    II. The number of accumulation units a client owns will never change.
    III. If the client dies during the annuity period, the remaining funds will be distributed to the beneficiary.
    IV. The monthly payout is fixed to the Consumer Price Index.

    A. I only
    B. I and II only
    C. I, II and III only
    D. I, II, III and IV

97. The Investment Company Act of 1940 requires that mutual funds pay dividends from their

    A. capital gains
    B. net income
    C. gross income
    D. portfolio earnings

98. Horace Horowitz is 61 years old. He would like to take a lump-sum distribution from his Keogh plan. What would be the tax treatment of this distribution?

    A. It is eligible for five-year income averaging.
    B. It will be taxed at long-term capital gains rates.
    C. There will be a 10% penalty.
    D. There will be a 50% penalty.

99. An NASD broker-dealer trading in shares of an open-end investment company is prohibited from buying shares of the fund

    A. to cover existing orders
    B. for the firm's own investment purposes
    C. at a discount
    D. for the purpose of resale at a later date

100. Which of the following has the authority to approve an investment advisor's contract with the investment company?

   A. NASD District Business Conduct Committee
   B. Board of directors of the fund
   C. Board of Governors of the NASD
   D. SEC

◆ Answers & Rationale

1. D. A registered security is one whose owner is designated on records maintained for this purpose. Even though T bills are book-entry securities and no certificates are issued, ownership records are maintained and therefore they are considered registered.

2. B. A bond purchased at a premium is purchased for an amount greater than the face amount of the bond at maturity. The premium paid reduces the yield of the bond if held until maturity.

3. B. The bond is quoted as 120; therefore, it is selling for $1,200. Parity of the stock in which the holder of the bond can convert is equal to $24 as follows. The bondholder would be able to convert the bond into 50 shares of stock (face amount $1,000 ÷ $20 per share = 50 shares), because the bond has a current price of $1,200; dividing this amount by 50 equals parity price of the underlying stock.

4. C. When a dealer is holding securities for its own account, it is considered to be taking a position.

5. B. Preferred stocks are interest rate sensitive as are other fixed-interest rate investment vehicles such as bonds. Because the dividend amount is fixed, if interest rates are increasing, the return provided by the dividend may be less than the return provided by other investments. The value of preferred stock will decrease.

6. C. A discretionary account is an account where a representative has been given authority to select the amount and type of investment for a client. The authorization must be written.

7. D. An affiliated person is defined as any person, officer, director, partner or employee directly or indirectly controlling, controlled by or under common control of the fund. Additionally, an affiliated person is defined as a person holding or controlling with the power to vote 5% or more of the outstanding securities of the fund. However, no person is considered an interested person solely by reason of membership as a director or just because he or she is an owner of securities.

8. C. Even though an investment in a Treasury STRIP does not yield a regular cash flow, paying all of its interest at maturity, the difference between the purchase price and the mature value is still taxed as ordinary income and must be accrued on a yearly basis.

9. D. The ex-dividend date for payment of dividends from a mutual fund is determined by the fund's board of directors. Normally for funds with regular dividend payment schedules, the ex-dividend date is set as the record date.

10. C. Only the Government National Mortgage Association (GNMA) issues securities backed by the full faith and credit of the U.S. government. The remainder are considered government agencies and, although their securities are considered second only to U.S. government issues in safety, they do not have direct U.S. government backing.

11. A. The certificates issued by the GNMA represent interests in government-insured mortgages pooled by mortgage brokers who guarantee the monthly cash flow, but it is the U.S. government that actually backs GNMA pass-through certificates. GNMA pass-throughs are issued in minimum denominations of $25,000, and all interest earned is subject to federal income tax.

12. B. An investor purchasing shares on the record date becomes a shareholder of record and is entitled to the dividend declared. Orders received after the pricing of shares or the record date would be processed the next day and would purchase shares ex-dividend.

13. A. The mortgages underlying GNMA modified pass-through certificates pay interest on a monthly basis. GNMA then passes this monthly income through to investors in GNMA pass-through certificates.

14. **A.** Open- and closed-end funds are classified as investment companies. Plan companies offer plans in which an investment company may be selected as an investment vehicle, but are not investment companies themselves. Fixed annuities are offered by insurance companies only.

15. **C.** Contributions to a tax-qualified annuity are taxable when withdrawn at ordinary income tax rates. Because in this case the teacher is withdrawing $15,000, that amount is subject to tax. 30% of $15,000 equals a tax liability of $4,500.

16. **D.** All of the factors listed affect the price of a convertible bond. The rating of a bond reflects the issuing company's health and therefore indirectly affects the value of the investment.

17. **A.** A closed-end company share is bought *and sold* in the secondary marketplace.

18. **C.** Fluctuations in interest rates may affect the price of a bond but will not affect the income payable from the bond. The percentage interest payable for use of money is stated on the face of a bond and is part of the bond indenture, a legal obligation on the part of the issuing company.

19. **A.** At the age of maturity, proceeds must be handed over to the child (donee) under the terms of the Uniform Gifts to Minors Act.

20. **A.** Using volatility or likelihood of changing as the benchmark, the passbook savings rate is the least volatile of the rates listed because it is usually fixed for long periods of time. All of the other rates fluctuate occasionally to frequently.

21. **A.** The federal funds rate is the rate of interest at which member banks of the Federal Reserve System can borrow excess funds from other members, usually on an overnight basis.

22. **A.** A banker's acceptance is a time draft typically used to facilitate overseas trading ven-

tures. It is guaranteed by a bank on behalf of a corporation in payment for goods or services.

23. **B.** A warrant is a purchase option for stock for a long period of time. The warrant allows the holder to purchase common stock for a set price. Rights and options have a short life.

24. **D.** A fixed-dollar plan is the only type of plan that fixes a definite dollar payment.

25. **D.** Sales literature is any public solicitation concerning securities.

26. **A.** Qualified plans, but not nonqualified plans, are trusts.

27. **C.** Money-market funds have no price volatility; the rate of interest on money-market funds fluctuates in conjunction with that of the instruments underlying the original money market certificates.

28. **B.** Because the funds are under separate management, the load charged on each separate investment will most likely be at the maximum. If the customer invested the entire sum within one fund or a family of funds, a reduced sales charge may have been available.

29. **B.** By investing a predetermined amount of money periodically for a long period of time, the investor is investing using the concept of *dollar cost averaging*. The result is to reduce the cost per share compared to the average market price.

30. **A.** Sending the order in for 200 shares when the client ordered only 100 shares is an excessive transaction.

31. **B.** Because the bond fund shares were held for less than six months, the gain is short term. An exchange privilege does not exempt the transfer of funds from taxation. The exchange is a taxable event.

32. **D.** Repurchase agreements, or repos, are entered into by a government securities dealer,

usually a bank, or by the Federal Reserve Board with an investor, usually a corporation.

33. **D.** IDRs are issued by municipalities to construct a facility that will be used by, or is being constructed for the benefit of a corporation. When this is done, the corporation is required to sign a long-term lease. Although classified as a municipal security, IDRs are backed by the revenues of the corporation participating in the project.

34. **C.** Congress sets fiscal policy, while the FRB sets monetary policy.

35. **B.** When an employee opens an account with another member, the employee will be notified by the executing member that the employing member will be notified that the account is to be opened, and copies of confirmations and other reports will be available upon request.

36. **B.** The purpose of the FOMC purchase is to increase the attractiveness of the market price of T bills. Because the price will be driven up by an increased market demand and a decreased supply, yields should decrease.

37. **C.** STRIPS are special bonds issued by the Treasury department and split into individual principal and interest payments, which are then resold in the form of zero-coupon bonds. Because zeros pay no interest, the investor realizes gains in the form of increased basis as the bond matures and there are no income payments to reinvest.

38. **D.** Distributions from a profit-sharing plan are made from the individual's account, reflecting the accrued amount of contributions and earnings on the contributions. Contributions to the plan are normally based on a predetermined percentage of profits.

39. **C.** Interest in the form of dividends paid from a municipal bond fund would be exempt from federal income tax. Gains from the sale of portfolio securities would be subject to ordinary income tax.

40. **A.** Because the dividend rate decreased at a rate less than the market value of the stock, the current yield will be greater.

41. **B.** The accumulation unit will increase in value because the portfolio earned 4%; however, the annuity unit value will decrease because actual return of the portfolio (4%) was less than the assumed interest rate of 5% necessary to maintain payments.

42. **A.** To qualify as a regulated investment company, at least 90% of net investment income (without regard to gains) must be distributed. Net investment income would equal dividend income ($2,000 in this case) plus interest income ($900) minus expenses ($900), to equal $2,000. Ninety percent of $2,000 is $1,800.

43. **B.** Contributions to a nonqualified annuity are made aftertax. The growth of the annuity is deferred, representing ordinary income when withdrawn. Cost base is $10,000.

44. **A.** If contributions are made into a tax-qualified annuity, the contributions are made before tax. The growth is deferred. Mrs. Smith has no cost base in this question. The entire $16,000 will be taxed as ordinary income.

45. **D.** Interest on Series EE bonds is received at redemption of the bonds.

46. **A.** The Municipal Bond Insurance Corporation (MBIA) and the AMBAC Indemnity Corporation (AMBAC) both insure municipal bonds. The Securities Investor Protection Corporation (SIPC) insures securities account holders from broker-dealer default; the Federal Depository Insurance Corporation (FDIC) insures bank account holders from bank default.

47. **C.** In the annuity stage of a variable annuity, the amount received will depend on the performance of the account compared to the assumed interest rate. If actual performance is less than the AIR, the value of the payout will decline.

48. **C.** In a private securities transaction the representative must obtain permission for the sale from his broker-dealer prior to the transaction. The transaction must be through the books of the broker-dealer, and any information requested by the broker-dealer must be supplied. The broker-dealer is still responsible for actions of the representative in this private transaction.

49. **B.** The expense ratio includes the expenses of operating the fund compared to fund assets. Expenses included in the ratio are management fees, administrative fees, brokerage fees and taxes.

50. **A.** Current yield of a mutual fund is current income ($.30 dividend in this case) divided by the net asset value ($6.50). Gains are not included in calculation of current yield; they are accounted for separately.

51. **D.** To exercise a put, an investor can either deliver the shares of the underlying stock or deposit the required amount of cash to sell short the stock.

52. **A.** A separate account purchasing shares of mutual funds to fund variable contracts does not actively manage the securities held; instead, the account holds the shares in trust for the contract holders. This account is classified as a unit investment trust under the act of 1940.

53. **D.** Minimum amounts are different from fund to fund, and an RR must refer to the prospectus for each fund.

54. **C.** Warrants are commonly used as a sweetener in debenture offerings. Rights are issued by the corporation, giving the subscriber the right to purchase stock within a short period of time at a reduced price from the stock's current market price. The right does not have to be exercised, but may be traded in the secondary market.

55. **D.** Under tenants in common, owners may have a fractional interest in the undivided ownership of an asset. The interest passes to the decedent's estate at death unlike JTWROS, wherein the survivor succeeds to the interest.

56. **D.** A variable annuity is a security and therefore must be registered with the SEC. As part of the registration requirements, a prospectus must be filed and distributed to prospective investors prior to or during any solicitation for sale.

57. **C.** Changes in NAV will be found in the prospectus for at least ten years if the fund has existed that long.

58. **A.** The Rules of Fair Practice prohibit unauthorized borrowing (theft) and selling dividends. Discounts are allowed to other NASD members if a dealer agreement has been signed.

59. **A.** Gifts in excess of $50 per person per year are not allowed.

60. **C.** The NASD limits sales charges to 8.5% of the POP as a maximum. If the fund does not allow for breakpoints, reinvestment of dividends at net or rights of accumulation, the maximum is less than 8.5%. Under the Investment Company Act of 1940, the maximum sales charge on mutual funds is deferred to the NASD rules, while a contractual plan specifically may charge 9% over the life of the plan.

61. **B.** The stockholder has the right to vote and the right to dividends if and when declared (although not a fixed dividend). A restricted security is one that has prescribed limits on resale generally requiring registration.

62. **B.** The maximum sales charge on a contractual plan whether front-end load or spread load is 9% over the life of the plan.

63. **D.** Orders for redemption without a certificate being issued requires a written request, signature guarantee and stock power.

64. **B.** Funds offering the reinstatement privilege allow the investor to redeem and reinvest shares within 30 days without an additional sales charge. The privilege can be used only once, and only the amount withdrawn can be reinstated.

65. **A.** The custodian does not sell the shares, but holds them for safekeeping. A bank cannot be a member of the NASD and therefore cannot act as a dealer (although subsidiaries independent of the bank may be set up as broker-dealers).

66. **B.** Contract holders must be given the right to vote on company personnel (directors, advisor, custodian, etc.) at the first meeting held within one year of the start of operations.

67. **A.** The Investment Company Act of 1940 defines an insurance company offering VLI contracts as an investment company offering periodic payment plan certificates. The separate account may be organized as either an open-end investment company or as a unit investment trust.

68. **D.** Companies offering VLI contracts must register under the Investment Company Act of 1940; the VLI contract must be registered under the Securities Act of 1933; representatives selling the contract must register under the Securities Exchange Act of 1934; and the advisor managing the separate account must register under the Investment Advisers Act of 1940.

69. **D.** The entire investment qualifies for the reduced load. A letter of intent covers purchases within a 13-month period and may be backdated 90 days. Murray Murbles actually had eleven months in which to make the additional investment.

70. **B.** Limited liability means that stockholders are liable only for amounts invested in the corporation; creditors cannot attach personal assets.

71. **D.** The exchange, or conversion, privilege allows an investor to exchange shares of one fund for another fund under the same management without paying an additional sales charge (although the exchange is still a taxable event).

72. **C.** Broker-dealers in the securities business may become members; banks cannot. A closed-end fund is an investment company and not a broker-dealer.

73. **C.** LIFO means last in, first out. Answer A describes FIFO; answer B describes share identification.

74. **D.** Generally a life only contract will pay the most per month because payments cease at the death of the annuitant.

75. **C.** SIPC covers cash and securities up to $500,000, but only $100,000 in cash.

76. **C.** Orders to redeem shares will be executed at the next computed price.

77. **B.** The exchange privilege offers exchange without an additional sales charge, but the exchange is still taxable. Mark is taxed on the gain of $12,000 ($40,000 − $28,000).

78. **D.** All of the statements listed are true. Firm commitment places the underwriter at risk; with best efforts the issuer is at risk; with all or none no sales are final unless the entire issue is sold.

79. **B.** The question asks what Thomas's IRA contribution may be; the maximum is the lesser of 100% earned income or $2,000.

80. **C.** The Securities Act of 1933 (paper act) requires registration of securities. The act of 1934 (people act) requires registration of people and exchanges transacting securities business in order to prevent manipulative and deceptive practices. The NASD is the SRO of the OTC market, but the SEC has final authority.

81. **D.** Because there is no load, there is no underwriter. The fund makes sales directly to the public.

82. **B.** If the actual rate of return equals the assumed interest rate, the check will stay the same. Recall that the payout is based on an accumulated value to be distributed over the life of the annuitant (like compounding). Therefore, for Tim to receive the $210 in March, the account must earn 5%.

83. **A.** Sales literature must be approved by a firm's principal prior to use. If the literature has been reviewed by the NASD, it need not be submitted by every broker-dealer intending to use it.

84. **C.** Reinvested income and gains distributions are taxable in the year they are received.

85. **B.** Members may give other members concessions, but must deal with the public and nonmembers at the public offering price.

86. **C.** Each shareholder owns an undivided (mutual) interest in the portfolio of the mutual fund.

87. **C.** The YTM is greater than the nominal yield, meaning the price must be less than par. The bond is selling at a discount.

88. **C.** Treasury securities are exempt from registration requirements as are municipal issues and do not require a prospectus.

89. **C.** The price for mutual fund shares is the next price calculated by the fund after receipt of the request. Answer B describes a repurchase transaction.

90. **D.** Any solicitation requires a prospectus to be delivered prior to or during the solicitation. (Sales literature is solicitation.)

91. **B.** A voluntary accumulation plan is voluntary, not binding. The company may require that the initial investment meets a certain minimum dollar amount. It may also specify that any additions meet set minimums (for example, $50). The sales charge is level, and the plan may qualify for breakpoints based on the accumulated value.

92. **C.** Because the investor wants the objectives provided by both a fixed and variable annuity, a combination annuity would be suitable.

93. **B.** The commissions charged are not set, but must be fair and reasonable for the service provided as enumerated in the NASD Rules of Fair Practice.

94. **A.** A contractual plan buys mutual fund shares to hold in trust. The planholder then owns an undivided interest in the mutual fund shares evidenced by the unit trust certificate(s).

95. **C.** Series EE bonds are sold at a discount and mature to face value; T bonds and agency issues are marketable debt. HH bonds are nonmarketable and pay interest semiannually.

96. **A.** Annuity units are fixed; their current value, when cashed in, determines the payout amount. A life only annuity ceases payments at the death of the annuitant. The company keeps any undistributed payments. Accumulation units will fluctuate in value and number during the accumulation period.

97. **B.** Dividends are paid from net income (interest plus dividends plus short-term gains when identified minus expenses).

98. **A.** The distribution would be taxed as ordinary income but would also qualify for five-year income averaging (TRA 1986). A 10% penalty would apply if Horace were under age 59 1/2; the 50% penalty would apply if he did not take the distribution according to his life expectancy by April 1st of the year following the year he turned 70 1/2.

99. **D.** A broker-dealer may purchase shares only to fulfill existing orders or for its own investment account, not for inventory.

100. **B.** The investment advisor's contract is approved by the board of directors of the fund and often a majority vote of the outstanding fund shares. An investment advisor must be *registered* with the SEC, not approved.

16 Final Exam Two

1. Equity ownership of a corporation is split into two types. These types are commonly referred to as

   A. stocks and bonds
   B. common stocks and preferred stocks
   C. preferred stocks and bonds
   D. common stocks and convertible bonds

2. Which of the following statements are true of Freddie Mac?

   I. It issues pass-through securities.
   II. It purchases student loans.
   III. It is restricted to purchasing conventional residential mortgages from financial institutions insured by an agency of the U.S. government.
   IV. It issues securities directly backed by the full faith and credit of the U.S. government.

   A. I and III
   B. I and IV
   C. II and III
   D. II and IV

3. A preferred stock that offers the new owner the privilege to receive any skipped or missed dividends is called

   A. straight preferred
   B. participating preferred
   C. convertible preferred
   D. cumulative preferred

4. Which of the following securities pays interest monthly?

   A. T bill
   B. Commercial paper
   C. Municipal general obligation bond
   D. Government National Mortgage Association pass-through certificate

5. The market value of a stock is determined by

   A. the board of directors
   B. what individuals are willing to pay for it
   C. a vote of the stockholders
   D. the company's financial condition

6. Which of the following Treasury securities allows an investor to lock in a yield for an extended period of time by minimizing reinvestment risk?

   A. Treasury bill
   B. Treasury STRIP
   C. Treasury bond
   D. Treasury note

7. Which of the following debt instruments pays no interest?

   A. T STRIP
   B. T note
   C. T bond
   D. T stock

8. The premium of an option is also known as the

   A. cost of the option
   B. profit on the option
   C. cost to exercise the option
   D. exercise price

9. Which of the following guarantees a listed option?

   A. OCC
   B. NASD
   C. NYSE
   D. SEC

10. Which of the following corporate bonds is usually backed by other investment securities?

    A. Mortgage bond
    B. Equipment trust certificate
    C. Collateral trust bond
    D. Debenture

11. Which of the following would be the best time for an investor to purchase long-term fixed-interest rate bonds?

    A. When short-term interest rates are high and are beginning to decline
    B. When short-term interest rates are low and are beginning to rise
    C. When long-term interest rates are low and are beginning to rise
    D. When long-term interest rates are high and are beginning to decline

12. Which of the following options would be used to protect against systematic risk?

    A. Stock
    B. Index
    C. Currency
    D. Interest rate

13. Interest rates have been rising for the past few days. What would happen to the price of bonds traded in the bond market during that period of time?

    A. Increase
    B. Decrease
    C. Stay the same
    D. Bond prices are not affected by interest rates.

14. Which of the following insure(s) municipal issues?

    I. FGIC
    II. BIGI
    III. AMBAC
    IV. FDIC

    A. I
    B. I, II and III
    C. II and III
    D. III and IV

15. Which of the following statements is(are) true of Treasury bills?

    I. They are sold at a discount.
    II. They pay a fixed rate of interest semiannually.
    III. They mature in one year or less.
    IV. They mature in ten years or more.

    A. I, II and III
    B. I and III
    C. II and IV
    D. III

16. The formula used to compare corporate return with municipal return is

    A. yield to maturity divided by 100% minus the investor's tax bracket
    B. current yield divided by 100% minus the investor's tax bracket
    C. nominal yield divided by 100% minus the investor's tax bracket
    D. coterminous yield divided by 100% minus the investor's tax bracket

17. The interest from which of the following bonds is exempt from federal income tax?

    I. State of California bonds
    II. City of Anchorage bonds
    III. Treasury bonds
    IV. GNMA bonds

    A. I and II only
    B. I, II and IV only
    C. III and IV only
    D. I, II, III and IV

18. Your clients would like to have $40,000 set aside when their child starts college, but do not want to invest in anything that could endanger their principal. In this situation, you would recommend

   A. zero-coupon bonds or Treasury STRIPS
   B. corporate bonds with a high rate of interest payment
   C. municipal bonds for their long-term tax benefits
   D. Treasury bills

19. Which of the following are money market instruments?

   I. Repurchase agreements
   II. Treasury bills
   III. Commercial paper
   IV. Treasury bonds maturing in six months

   A. I and II only
   B. I, II and III only
   C. II, III and IV only
   D. I, II, III and IV

20. When trading common stock, either at an exchange or over the counter, the typical size of the trading unit is how many shares?

   A. 10
   B. 50
   C. 100
   D. There is no standard unit.

21. When dealing with a market maker, he may tell you that the price of a stock is $22 bid—$23 ask firm. This means the market maker

   A. is ready to buy the stock at $23 and is willing to sell at $22
   B. is ready to sell the stock at $23 and is willing to buy at $22
   C. will always buy the stock at $23 regardless of the current price of the stock
   D. is sharing information about the current price of the stock but is not ready to trade

22. Which of the following is(are) the responsibility of an investment banker?

   I. Distributing large blocks of stock to the public and to institutions
   II. Buying previously unissued securities from an issuer and selling them to the public
   III. Raising long-term capital for corporations by underwriting new issues of securities
   IV. Lending money to corporate clients that require debt financing

   A. I, II and III only
   B. I, II and IV only
   C. III only
   D. I, II, III and IV

23. The federal funds rate is charged to banks for

   A. short-term bank loans from the government
   B. loans offered by major New York City banks
   C. loans from other banks and can change daily
   D. loans from broker-dealers

24. The over-the-counter market could be characterized as which of the following?

   A. Auction market
   B. Double-auction market
   C. Negotiated market
   D. None of the above

25. The ex-dividend date is the

   I. date on and after which the buyer is entitled to the dividend
   II. date on and after which the seller is entitled to the dividend
   III. fourth business day prior to the record date
   IV. fourth business day after the record date

   A. I and III
   B. I and IV
   C. II and III
   D. II and IV

26. Geographic diversification of municipal securities investments protects against all of the following EXCEPT

   A. adverse legislation in a certain area
   B. economic decline in a certain area
   C. a change in interest rates
   D. default by a particular issuer

27. John Jameson has $800 to invest in the XYZ Mutual Fund. If the shares are currently priced at $21.22 each, John will be able to purchase

   A. no shares because the minimum trading unit is 100 shares
   B. 37 shares and $14.85 in change
   C. 37.7 shares
   D. 38 shares

28. When examining the portfolio of a diversified common stock fund, you would most likely find

   A. all growth stocks within one particular industry
   B. stocks of many companies within many industries
   C. mostly convertible bonds and other debt instruments
   D. There is no telling what you would find.

29. A customer who watches the T bill auctions noticed that the average return to investors in the latest T bill auction fell to 4.71%, down from 4.82% at the previous week's sale. When he asks you for your interpretation, you tell him that

   A. the decline in yields indicates that the supply of short-term funds has decreased relative to demand
   B. investors who purchased bills at this auction paid more for them than purchasers over the last two months
   C. investors who purchased T bills twelve weeks ago paid less than purchasers since that time
   D. the federal funds rate and other short-term interest rate indicators are probably rising

30. The rate at which Japanese yen could be converted into American dollars, or British pounds into Swiss francs, would be set in which of the following markets?

   A. Exchange rate
   B. Interbank
   C. Secondary
   D. Fourth

31. Federal Open Market Committee activities are closely watched by Wall Street because of the effect of its decisions on all of the following EXCEPT

   A. money supply
   B. interest rates
   C. exchange rates
   D. money velocity

32. Which of the following statements describes a balanced fund?

   A. It has some portion of its portfolio invested in both debt and equity instruments at all times.
   B. It has equal amounts of common stock and corporate bonds at all times.
   C. It normally has equal amounts of common and preferred stock at all times.
   D. None of the above are true.

33. All the following are advantages of mutual fund investment EXCEPT

   A. the investor retains personal control of his or her investment in the mutual fund portfolio
   B. exchange privileges within a family of funds managed by the same management company
   C. the ability to invest almost any amount at any time
   D. the ability to qualify for reduced sales loads based on accumulation of investment within the fund

34. According to the Investment Company Act of 1940

    I. a company must have $1,000,000 in assets before it may begin operations
    II. at least 40% of the board of directors may not be affiliated or hold a position with the fund
    III. the fund must have at least 100 shareholders
    IV. the fund may not borrow more than 33 1/3% of its asset value

    A. I and III only
    B. II, III and IV only
    C. II and IV only
    D. I, II, III and IV

35. One of the members of the board of directors of the Ace open-end diversified investment company owns 3% of all the outstanding voting stock of the XYZ Company. Ace investment company

    A. can invest in XYZ as long as it purchases no more than 3% of the company's voting stock
    B. can invest in XYZ if the director sells off 2/3 of his holdings
    C. can invest as long as XYZ purchases an equal amount of Ace investment company shares
    D. cannot invest in the XYZ Company

36. The NAV of an open-end investment company

    I. is calculated seven days a week
    II. is calculated as stipulated in the prospectus
    III. takes into account cash held by the fund but not invested
    IV. when divided by the number of shares outstanding equals the net asset value per share

    A. I and IV
    B. II, III and IV
    C. II and IV
    D. IV

37. The net asset value per share of a mutual fund will fluctuate in value relative to the

    A. value of the fund's portfolio
    B. law of supply and demand
    C. number of shareholders
    D. S&P 500 market index

38. The net asset value per share will

    I. increase if the assets of the fund appreciate in value
    II. decrease if the fund distributes a dividend to shareholders
    III. decrease when shares are redeemed
    IV. increase if shareholders reinvest dividend and capital gains distributions

    A. I and II
    B. I and III
    C. II and III
    D. II and IV

39. Typically, no-load mutual funds are sold to the public in which of the following ways?

    A. The fund sells directly to the investor.
    B. The fund sells to a plan company, which in turn sells to the investor.
    C. The fund sells to a dealer, who in turn sells to the investor.
    D. The fund sells to investors through federal banks.

40. What organization or institution would insure a jumbo certificate of deposit issued by a bank?

    A. SIPC
    B. FRB
    C. FDIC
    D. FSLIC

41. The net asset value of a mutual fund is $9.30. If its sales charge is 7%, its offering price is

    A. $9.95
    B. $9.97
    C. $10
    D. $10.70

42. If a mutual fund charges an 8 1/2% sales charge, all of the following must be offered by the fund EXCEPT

    A. exchange privileges
    B. breakpoints
    C. rights of accumulation
    D. dividend reinvestment at NAV

43. If an investment company offers rights of accumulation and an investor wishes to get a reduced sales charge, the client must deposit the sufficient funds within

    A. 45 days
    B. 13 months
    C. There is no time limit.
    D. Each fund may have its own requirements.

44. Magnus Mutual Fund permits rights of accumulation. Gordon Dykstra has invested $9,000 and has signed a letter of intent for a $15,000 investment. His reinvested dividends during the 13 months total $720. How much money must Gordon contribute to fulfill the letter of intent?

    A. $5,280
    B. $6,000
    C. $9,000
    D. $15,000

45. You have decided to buy 100 shares of the BMK Mutual Fund, which prices its shares at 5:00 pm every business day. You turn in your order at 3:00 pm when the shares are priced at $10 NAV, $10.86 POP. The sales load is 7.9%. What will your 100 shares cost?

    A. $1,000
    B. $1,079
    C. $1,086
    D. 100 times the offering price, which will be calculated at 5:00 pm

46. When comparing definitions in the stock market and mutual funds, the bid price is similar to the NAV, and the ask price is similar to the

    A. net asset value
    B. sales load
    C. public offering price
    D. None of the above

47. John Jones is redeeming 1,000 shares of the HCW mutual fund. John has submitted his request for redemption, which HCW receives at noon. HCW prices its shares at the close of the NYSE each day, at which time the shares are priced at $12.50 NAV, $13.50 ask. HCW also charges a 1% redemption fee. John will receive what amount for his shares?

    A. $12,375
    B. $12,500
    C. $13,365
    D. $13,500

48. The ex-dividend date for shares of a mutual fund is

    A. four business days prior to the record date
    B. seven days prior to the record date
    C. the same day as the record date
    D. whenever the board of directors decides it will be

49. Paul Grumman buys shares of the Power Investment Company shortly before the ex-dividend date. Before he buys the shares, Paul should understand that

    A. the price of the shares will decline on the ex-dividend date by the amount of the distribution
    B. if he reinvests the dividend, he will not be liable for taxes on the dividend received
    C. there is a great advantage to his purchasing the shares immediately so that he can receive the dividend
    D. all of the above may occur

50. Which of the following makes up the net investment income of an open-end investment company?

    A. Net gains on sales of securities
    B. Dividends, interest and unrealized gains
    C. Income from dividends and interest paid by securities held by the fund minus the operating expenses
    D. Ninety percent of the net asset value of the fund

51. Which of the following are true of mutual fund dividend distributions?

    I. The fund pays dividends from net income.
    II. A single taxpayer may exclude $100 worth of dividend income from taxes annually.
    III. An investor is liable for taxes on distributions whether the dividend is a cash distribution or reinvested in the fund.
    IV. An investor is liable for taxes only if the distribution is received in cash.

    A. I and II
    B. I, II and III
    C. I and III
    D. II and IV

52. Mary Blackburn redeemed 200 of her 500 mutual fund shares. She has not designated which shares were redeemed. Which of the following methods does the IRS use to determine which shares have been redeemed?

    A. Identified shares
    B. Wash sale rules
    C. LIFO
    D. FIFO

53. ACE, an open-end investment company, operates under the conduit or pipeline tax theory. Last year it distributed 91% of all net investment income as a dividend to shareholders. Therefore ACE paid

    A. taxes on 9% of its net investment income last year
    B. taxes on 9% of its net investment income and capital gains last year
    C. taxes on 91% of its net investment income last year
    D. no taxes last year because it qualified as a regulated investment company under IRC Subchapter M

54. Your client has a $21,000 net capital loss this year. He plans to apply the maximum deduction towards his ordinary income for the year. After the year, he may

    A. carry $3,000 of the loss forward
    B. carry the loss forward for six years and deduct $3,000 per year
    C. carry the loss forward for seven years and deduct $3,000 per year
    D. not carry the loss forward

55. On January 10th, 1987, John Jones purchased 1,000 shares of the Delta open-end investment company. On January 22nd, 1987, Delta sells 25,000 shares of IBM at a profit. Delta originally purchased the IBM on June 24th, 1984. On February 15th, 1987, Delta distributes the gain from the sale of IBM to shareholders. How will John be taxed on this distribution?

    A. The income will be taxed as a long-term gain taxable as ordinary income.
    B. The income will be taxed as a long-term gain qualifying for the 60% exclusion.
    C. If John is using automatic reinvestment, he will not be taxed at all.
    D. John will not be taxed because he did not sell the IBM; Delta is liable for all taxes.

56. Which of the following is the usual source of a mutual fund's capital gains distribution?

    A. Net long-term gains resulting from the sale of the company's mutual fund shares
    B. Net short-term gains resulting from the sale of the company's mutual fund shares
    C. Net long-term gains resulting from the sale of securities in the fund's investment portfolio
    D. Net short-term gains resulting from the sale of securities in the fund's investment portfolio

57. Your open-end investment company client has decided not to take automatic reinvestment of dividend and capital gains distributions. This will

    A. not change the tax status of these distributions
    B. lower the client's proportionate ownership in the fund each time a distribution is made
    C. be the way individuals requiring income payments will often invest
    D. result in all of the above

58. Fenwick Jones has a large investment in the XYZ open-end investment company. He has selected a fixed-time withdrawal plan. The computation for the withdrawal plan will be based on the

    A. NAV each period
    B. NAV at the first payment
    C. POP each period
    D. POP at the first payment

59. A client is receiving funds from an open-end investment company under the provisions of a withdrawal plan. This means

    A. the client must continue to make investments into the fund
    B. the client will generally be discouraged from making further investments into the fund
    C. the client will always exhaust the plan within a predetermined period of time
    D. that if the client withdraws only dividend and gains distributions, the principal amount of the investment will always remain intact

60. A client chooses a voluntary accumulation plan and signs up for automatic checking account deductions of $100 a month. She tells the registered representative that she intends to continue the plan for ten years.

    A. Her decision to invest is binding, and she must continue to invest for ten years.
    B. She can terminate the plan at her option.
    C. She will be charged a late fee on investments not made in a timely fashion.
    D. She can terminate the plan if she agrees to pay the balance in lump sum.

61. Voting rights extended to contract holders of variable life insurance contracts funded by a separate account shall be one vote on company matters for each

    A. contract owned
    B. dollar of cash value credited to the contract
    C. $100 of cash value funded by the insurance company's general account
    D. $100 of cash value funded by the insurance company's separate account

62. The investment objective of a separate account funding variable life insurance may be changed

    A. with a majority vote of shares
    B. by order of the state insurance commissioner
    C. if either A or B occurs
    D. under no circumstances

63. A separate account registering as an investment company offering variable life contracts under the Investment Company Act of 1940 is required to have a minimum net capital of

    A. $100,000 before operations may begin
    B. $1,000,000 before operations may begin
    C. The separate account may operate if the insurer has capital of $1,000,000.
    D. both A and C

64. Under the Uniform Gifts to Minors Act, the owner of the securities held in the account is the

    A. custodian
    B. minor
    C. parent of the minor
    D. donor of the securities

65. John and his wife Linda own shares in the XYZ Mutual Fund as joint tenants with rights of survivorship. If John dies, what happens to the shares in the account?

    A. One half of the shares would belong to Linda, and the remaining half would be distributed to John's estate.
    B. Linda would own all the shares.
    C. Ownership of the shares would have to be determined by probate court.
    D. None of the above would occur.

66. Fred Jacobs has been investing $100 a month in the XYZ Mutual Fund over the past five months. His purchases are as follows:

Month	Price/Share	Quantity
1	10	10
2	20	5
3	25	4
4	5	20
5	10	10

What is the difference between Fred's average cost and the average price he paid for the shares?

    A. $3.80
    B. $7.14
    C. $10.20
    D. $14

67. The price of closed-end investment company shares is determined by

    A. supply and demand
    B. the New York Stock Exchange
    C. the board of directors
    D. the net asset value plus the sales charge

68. The offering price of the HQ Fund is $9, and its net asset value is $9.40. The offering price of the Shieko Fund is $23.80, and its net asset value is $19.45. From these quotes you know that

    I. HQ is an open-end fund
    II. HQ is a closed-end fund
    III. Shieko is an open-end fund
    IV. Shieko is a closed-end fund

    A. I and III
    B. I and IV
    C. II and III
    D. II and IV

69. Customers could pay a commission, rather than a sales charge, for shares of a(n)

    A. no-load fund
    B. mutual fund
    C. open-end investment company
    D. closed-end investment company

70. According to the NASD, the maximum sales charge on a variable annuity contract is

    A. 8.5% of the total amount invested
    B. 8.5% of the net amount invested
    C. 9% of the total amount invested
    D. unlimited

71. The value of a variable annuity separate account fluctuates in relationship to the

    A. general account maintained by the insurance company
    B. value of the separate account portfolio
    C. Consumer Price Index
    D. S&P 500 market index

72. At age 65, Fred Jacobs purchased an immediate variable annuity contract. Fred made a lump-sum $100,000 initial payment and selected a life income with ten-year period certain payment option. Fred lived until age 88. The insurance company made payments to Fred

    A. until his initial payment of $100,000 was exhausted
    B. for ten years
    C. for 23 years
    D. at a fixed rate for ten years and at a variable rate up until his death

73. The difference between a fixed annuity and a variable annuity is that the variable annuity

    I. offers a guaranteed return
    II. offers a payment that may vary in amount
    III. will always pay out more money than the fixed annuity
    IV. attempts to offer protection to the annuitant from inflation

    A. I and III
    B. I and IV
    C. II and III
    D. II and IV

74. The insurance company's separate account is

    I. used for the investment of moneys paid by variable annuity contract holders
    II. separate from the general investments of the insurance company
    III. operated in a manner similar to an investment company
    IV. as much a security as it is an insurance product

    A. I only
    B. I and II only
    C. I, II and III only
    D. I, II, III and IV

75. Similarities between a mutual fund and a variable annuity's separate account include which of the following?

    I. The investment portfolio is professionally managed.
    II. The client may vote for the board of directors or board of managers.
    III. The client assumes the investment risk.
    IV. The payout plans guarantee the client income for life.

    A. I, II and III only
    B. II and IV only
    C. III and IV only
    D. I, II, III and IV

76. If a client, age 35, invests $100 a month in a variable annuity for seven years and suddenly dies

    A. the client's beneficiaries will not receive any money until the year in which the client would have turned 59 1/2
    B. the insurance company gets to keep all the contributions made to date because the contract was not annuitized
    C. the client's beneficiaries will receive only the amount contributed
    D. if the contract were insured, the client's beneficiaries would receive the greater of the contributions or current value of the account

77. Your client is 68 years old, retired and in good health. She is concerned about budgeting funds. She needs funds for day-to-day living expenses starting now. As her representative, you might suggest that she purchase

   A. all the whole life insurance that she can afford
   B. a periodic-payment deferred variable annuity
   C. a single-payment deferred variable annuity
   D. an immediate annuity

78. An insurance company offering a variable annuity makes payments to annuitants on the 15th of each month. The contract has an assumed interest rate of 3%. In July of this year the contract earned 4%. In August the account earned 6%. If the contract earns 3% in September, the payments to annuitants will be

   A. greater than the payments in August
   B. less than the payments in August
   C. the same the payments in August
   D. less than the payments in July

79. Which of the following factors may determine the amount of payout from a variable annuity?

   I. Mortality experience of the company
   II. Age and sex of the annuitant
   III. Insurability of the annuitant
   IV. Rate of return of the separate account

   A. I, II and IV only
   B. II only
   C. II, III and IV only
   D. I, II, III and IV

80. Brad Smith has been investing in a non-qualified deferred annuity through a payroll deduction plan offered at the school system where he works. Brad has invested a total of $10,000. The annuity contract is currently valued at $16,000, and he plans to retire. On what amount will he be taxed if he chooses a lump-sum withdrawal?

   A. $6,000
   B. $10,000
   C. $16,000
   D. $26,000

81. If a client, age 52, chooses to cash in his or her annuity contract before payout begins, the client will

   I. be taxed at the ordinary income tax rate on earnings in excess of cost base
   II. have to pay a 10% penalty on the amount withdrawn that exceeds cost base
   III. have to pay a 5% penalty on the amount withdrawn that exceeds cost base
   IV. be taxed at ordinary rates on the amount withdrawn, which represents cost base, and will be taxed at capital gains rates on the amount withdrawn that exceeds cost base

   A. I
   B. I and II
   C. I and III
   D. III and IV

82. Which of the following characteristics describe a nonqualified deferred compensation plan

    I. Requires no approval from the IRS
    II. Does not allow the employer to deduct the cost of the plan
    III. Allows the employer to deduct the cost of the plan when the employee has constructive receipt of the benefits
    IV. Allows the employee to receive the benefit of deferral if she signs a contract stating that the funds are to be used for retirement and then abides by the contract

    A. I and III
    B. I, III and IV
    C. II and III
    D. II and IV

83. When a client withdraws money from an IRA after age 59 1/2, the

    A. amount withdrawn is subject to a 10% penalty
    B. amount withdrawn is subject to taxes at the capital gains rate
    C. entire amount in the IRA is subject to taxation at the ordinary rate, regardless of the amount withdrawn
    D. amount withdrawn is subject to taxation at ordinary income tax rates

84. When referring to employee retirement plans, the term *nonqualified* refers to plans

    I. not approved by the IRS
    II. which offer tax-deductible contributions and tax-deferred growth
    III. under which the employer may discriminate as to the inclusion of employees within the plan
    IV. where the employer may deduct contributions made on behalf of the employee as the contributions are made

    A. I and II
    B. I and III
    C. I, III and IV
    D. II and III

85. If an employer installs a Keogh plan, that plan must include all full-time employees with how many years of service?

    A. One
    B. Three
    C. Five
    D. None of the above

86. Keogh plans are retirement programs designed for use by nonincorporated businesses. These plans allow the self-employed individual to contribute on a tax-deductible basis

    A. the lesser of 25% of earned income or $30,000
    B. the lesser of 25% of all income or $30,000
    C. the greater of 25% of earned income or $30,000
    D. the greater of 25% of all income or $30,000

87. Karen Mayhew is a retired teacher participating in a qualified tax sheltered annuity. Contributions made on her behalf total $15,000. This year she received a lump-sum payment of $21,000. How would this payment be taxed?

   A. As a capital gains distribution
   B. As ordinary income
   C. $6,000 as capital gains and the remainder as ordinary income
   D. As ordinary income, except for the $15,000, which represents return of her contribution

88. The Norse Company, an NASD member, wants to buy shares in the ABC mutual fund from the fund's sponsor at a discount. This arrangement is possible if the sponsor of the ABC mutual fund

   A. is not an NASD member
   B. is also an NASD member and a sales agreement between the two firms is in effect
   C. has a sales agreement with the Norse Company
   D. meets any of the above restrictions

89. Under what conditions does the Investment Company Act of 1940 require a written statement disclosing the source of dividend payments?

   A. Whenever a dividend is paid
   B. Whenever net income is part of the dividend
   C. Whenever all or part of the dividend payment comes from a source other than current income or accumulated undistributed net income
   D. The Investment Company Act of 1940 does not require disclosure, only the Internal Revenue Code requires disclosure of the amount of the dividend.

90. When using the annual report as sales literature, the

   I. principal of the firm must approve its use as such
   II. prospectus must accompany the report
   III. figures contained in the report must be as of a specific date
   IV. report must contain the complete portfolio list

   A. I, II and III only
   B. I and III only
   C. II, III and IV only
   D. I, II, III and IV

91. In the sale of open-end investment company shares, the prospectus

   A. is not necessary
   B. must be delivered to the client either before or during the sales solicitation
   C. must be delivered before the sales solicitation
   D. must be delivered at or before the delivery of the fund share certificate

92. Which of the following persons would most likely become a member of the NASD?

   I. Person convicted of a crime involving fraudulent conversion in the securities business within the past ten years
   II. Person who transacts business for his own account and for others in the over-the-counter market
   III. Person acting as a specialist on the New York Stock Exchange only

   A. I and III only
   B. II only
   C. II and III only
   D. I, II and III

93. When deciding on the suitability of a particular investment for a client, that client's need for liquidity is

    A. not necessary to be determined
    B. only necessary to be determined if the individual is planning on retirement
    C. an important element to be considered when determining the suitability of an investment
    D. only important if the client has no other liquid investments

94. Which of the following individuals may not purchase shares of a hot issue of stock?

    A. General partner of a member firm
    B. Spouse of the person who is the managing underwriter of the issue
    C. Senior officer of a bank
    D. All of the above

95. A sale of securities in a dollar amount just below the point at which an investor could take advantage of a lower sales charge by making a larger purchase

    I. is called a breakpoint sale
    II. would not be a conflict of interest
    III. is contrary to just and equitable principles of trade
    IV. requires the approval of the District Business Conduct Committee

    A. I
    B. I and III
    C. I, II and IV
    D. II

96. NASD rules permit members to

    A. execute an order to sell shares of a customer's securities, knowing that delivery of these shares will be two weeks later
    B. continue to compensate a registered representative for sales that were made while the representative was working for the firm according to a previous contract
    C. arrange for a customer to receive $5,000 worth of credit in order to purchase mutual fund shares
    D. give a selling concession to a nonmember firm because of the large number of shares the nonmember is purchasing

97. While recommending the purchase of a security, a registered representative presented material indicating a possible upward move in the price of the recommended security. This recommendation to buy was probably

    I. fraudulent
    II. in violation of the Rules of Fair Practice
    III. not suitable for all investors
    IV. acceptable if the statements about prices and earnings were clearly labeled as forecasts

    A. I
    B. I and II
    C. III
    D. III and IV

98. An employee who is involved in the management of an NASD member's business, particularly in the supervision of business solicitation or in training, would have to be registered as a

    A. broker
    B. dealer
    C. partner
    D. principal

99. Which Federal Reserve Board regulation prohibits brokers and dealers from extending credit for the purchase of open-end investment company shares?

    A. Regulation A
    B. Regulation G
    C. Regulation U
    D. Regulation T

100. The NASD's Code of Procedure contains guidelines for

    A. handling violations of the NASD's Rules of Fair Practice
    B. reviewing and approving accounts, trades, correspondence and sales literature
    C. resolving disputes between two NASD members
    D. resolving disputes between NASD members and non-NASD firms

◆ Answers & Rationale

1. B.   Equity ownership comes with two types of securities. These are common and preferred stocks.

2. A.   Freddie Mac stands for Federal Home Loan Mortgage Corporation. Like Ginnie Mae, it issues mortgage-backed pass-through securities. Unlike Ginnie Mae, however, it deals only in conventional residential mortgages. Sallie Mae stands for Student Loan Marketing Association, which purchases student loans from originating financial institutions and provides financing to state student loan agencies.

3. D.   Preferred stock comes in all the listed types, but only cumulative preferred allows the holder the right to receive skipped or missed dividends.

4. D.   Government National Mortgage Association (GNMA) pass-through certificates pay investors interest and a return of principal on a monthly basis. Treasury bills and most commercial paper are sold on a discounted basis and mature for a par amount. The dollar difference between the discounted amount and par is the earned interest. Municipal bonds pay interest on a semiannual basis.

5. B.   Market value of stock is determined by supply and demand.

6. B.   This is actually a three-part question pertaining to locking in yield, a long period of time and reinvesting with minimum risk. The long time aspect is easily handled in that bonds are longer term securities than notes or bills. STRIPS (Separate Trading of Registered Interest and Principal of Securities) are T bonds with the coupons removed. The choice between bonds and STRIPS is simplified when reinvestment risk is considered. STRIPS don't pay interest; instead, they are sold at a deep discount and mature at face par value. Consequently, there are no interest payments to be reinvested and no reinvestment risk. This is also how the investor locks in a yield.

7. A.   STRIPS (Separate Trading of Registered Interest and Principal of Securities) are T bonds with the coupons removed. STRIPS don't pay interest; instead, they are sold at a deep discount and mature at face par value.

8. A.   The premium is the cost (or price) of the option. The profit on an option represents gain. Cost to exercise an option is the exercise or strike price. Premiums equal intrinsic value plus time value.

9. A.   The Options Clearing Corporation issues, guarantees and exercises options for the industry. It handles all of the clerical functions. The Options Clearing Corporation guarantees the performance of the option contract.

10. C.   Collateral trust bonds are backed by other securities, while mortgage bonds are backed by real estate. Equipment trust certificates are backed by equipment. Debentures are secured by the company's promise to pay.

11. D.   The best time to buy long-term bonds is when long-term interest rates have peaked. In addition to the high return, as interest rates fall the value of existing bonds will rise.

12. B.   Systematic risk is also called market risk. Index options allow the investor to protect against any decrease in the value of stocks due to market factors. This is different from nonsystematic or company specific risk, which can be hedged with equity options. All stocks have both types of risk—risk of what the market does and risk of what happens to the individual company.

13. B.   When interest rates rise, bond prices fall.

14. B.   The Financial Guaranty Insurance Corporation (FGIC), the Bond Investors Guaranty Insurance Co. (BIGI) and the AMBAC Indemnity

Corporation all insure municipal bonds, as do MGIC and MBIA.

15. **B.** T bills are sold at a discount and are for a duration of up to one year. Although they mature at face, it is not considered interest.

16. **A.** Because municipal securities are quoted in yield to maturity, that is the yield you have. This is the formula for tax equivalent yield.

17. **A.** Municipal bonds are exempt from federal income tax. Treasury bonds and GNMA bonds are both subject to income tax but would be exempt from state taxes.

18. **A.** Zero-coupon bonds represent the lowest risk coupled with the highest return of all the investments listed. They offer no current income.

19. **D.** Money markets are made up of short-term high-yield debt issues. All of the items listed here are considered short term—even the bonds because they will mature in less than one year.

20. **C.** Common stock trades in round lots of 100 shares each.

21. **B.** The bid price is the price at which the market maker is willing to buy the stock, while the ask price is the price at which he will sell. *Firm* means that the quote is good for a round lot of 100 shares.

22. **A.** *Investment banker* is another term for *broker-dealer*. Investment bankers do everything listed except lend money to corporate clients that require debt financing.

23. **C.** The federal funds rate is the rate of interest at which member banks of the Federal Reserve System can borrow excess funds from other members, usually on an overnight basis. The rate is subject to change and often does on a daily basis.

24. **C.** The New York Stock Exchange is an auction market, and the OTC market is a negotiated market.

25. **C.** Stocks sold on the ex-dividend date entitle the seller to the dividend. Stocks sell ex-dividend four business days before the record date.

26. **C.** If the interest rates change, geographic diversification will not help you. A change in interest rates will affect all of the yields.

27. **C.** John will be able to purchase 37.7 shares. Mutual fund shares may be sold in full or fractional amounts and do not trade in round lots of 100 shares.

28. **B.** A diversified common stock fund will have stocks from many companies and many industries.

29. **B.** As rates for T bills drop, T bill prices climb; T bill rates and prices have an inverse relationship. T bills are priced at their yield, so an investor who bids 4.71% is actually paying more for a T bill than one who bids 4.82%.

30. **B.** The foreign exchange rate for international currencies is determined by buying and selling interest in the interbank market.

31. **C.** The FOMC is one of the most influential committees in the Federal Reserve system, and its decisions affect money supplies, interest rates and even the speed at which dollars turn over (money velocity). The foreign exchange rate is set in the interbank market.

32. **A.** Balanced funds carry both equity and debt issues. An equal amount of these issues is not necessary to maintain.

33. **A.** The control of the investment is given over to the investment manager. All of the other items mentioned are considered advantages.

34. **B.** A company must have commitments for at least $100,000 in assets before it begins. All of the other items are true.

35. **D.** Because the director owns more than 1/2 of 1% of stock in XYZ Company, the investment company cannot invest in XYZ stock. Selling two thirds of his holdings will not get him down to this amount. XYZ Company could buy Ace if it decided to.

36. **B.** NAV must be calculated at least every business day but not on weekends or holidays. It takes into account all of the fund's assets and is arrived at by totaling the assets and dividing that amount by the number of shares outstanding.

37. **A.** Share prices fluctuate in relation to the assets held in the fund's portfolio.

38. **A.** Share prices will increase when assets in the portfolio increase in value. Share prices decrease when the fund distributes a dividend because the shareholder will receive either cash or additional shares. Redeeming or purchasing shares does not affect share prices, only total assets. Reinvesting dividends or capital gains has no effect on share prices either.

39. **A.** No-load funds sell directly to the investor through their own sales force.

40. **C.** The Federal Deposit Insurance Corporation guarantees money on deposit in banks that are members of the FDIC system.

41. **C.** To determine the selling price of the shares when given the NAV, you must divide the NAV by 100% minus the sales load:

$$\frac{NAV}{100\% - S.L.} = \text{Selling price}$$

or,

$$\frac{\$9.35}{100\% - 7\%} = \$10$$

42. **A.** Funds charging the full 8 1/2% sales load must offer breakpoints, rights of accumulation and dividend reinvestment at NAV. Exchange privileges are the exception.

43. **C.** Rights of accumulation are good forever, while the letter of intent has a 13-month limit.

44. **B.** Gordon must put in the full $15,000, an additional $6,000. Reinvested dividends and changes in the NAV do not affect the amount required.

45. **D.** Mutual funds use forward pricing. You will pay the offering price calculated at 5:00 pm.

46. **C.** Bid and NAV are similar in that they are both the price at which the customer sells shares. The ask price is similar to the public offering price (POP) because this is the price the customer pays for the purchase of shares.

47. **A.** John will receive $12.50 per share less a redemption fee of 1%; $12.50 times 100 shares is $12,500. A 1% redemption fee is $125, for a total of $12,375.

48. **D.** Mutual fund ex-dividend dates are dates set by the board of directors. Corporate stocks in the secondary market have the ex-dividend date of four business days before the record date.

49. **A.** Share prices decline on the ex-dividend date. Dividend distributions cause a tax liability, and the purchase of shares right before an ex-dividend date is not a good idea because of the tax liability.

50. **C.** Dividends and interest paid on the securities held in the portfolio make up investment income. From this the fund's expenses are paid before it becomes net investment income.

51. **C.** Funds pay dividends from net income, and the investor is liable for taxes on all distributions. The $100 annual exclusion was eliminated with the new tax code.

52. **D.** When a customer does not choose a method, the IRS uses FIFO.

53. **A.** ACE would pay taxes on any portion of income it does not distribute as long as it distributes at least 90%. ACE paid taxes on 9%.

54. **B.** Capital losses can be used to offset capital gains. A client can use $3,000 of capital losses per year to offset ordinary income. After using $3,000 this year, your client will have $18,000 to carry forward.

55. **A.** John owned shares of the mutual fund when it distributed the gain, and he is liable for the taxes. This is considered a long-term gain, which is currently taxed as ordinary income.

56. **C.** Capital gains come from the sale of securities held in the company's portfolio. Most of these gains will be the sale of securities held for long periods of time.

57. **D.** Reinvestment does not change the tax status, while taking distributions will lower proportionate ownership. An investment of this type will allow an investor to take distributions without touching the principal.

58. **A.** First, withdrawal of funds will be based on the NAV. Secondly, it will be determined each time a payment is made.

59. **B.** Taking money out of a fund at the same time a person is putting money into the fund is generally discouraged.

60. **B.** Voluntary accumulation plans allow for just that. The client can terminate at any time if she so chooses, and there is no penalty for doing so.

61. **D.** Contract holders receive one vote per $100 of cash value funded by the separate account. Additionally, if the insurance company votes the shares, the company must vote according to proxies received from the contract holders.

62. **C.** The insurance commissioner has the authority to change an investment objective if the objective is in violation of state law; otherwise, the objective may be changed only by majority vote of the separate account's outstanding shares.

63. **C.** According to the act of 1940, a separate account may begin operations as long as the insurance company offering the contract has a net worth of $1,000,000 or the account has a net worth of $100,000.

64. **B.** The minor is the owner of the securities in an UGMA account while they are held in the name of the custodian.

65. **B.** In a JTWROS account, securities pass on to the surviving owner.

66. **A.** Fred paid a total of $500 for 49 shares of stock, or $10.20 per share. The average price of the shares during this time was the total of the share prices ($70) divided by the number of investment periods (5), or $14. The difference between the two is $3.80.

67. **A.** Closed-end investment company shares trade in the secondary market; hence, price is determined by supply and demand.

68. **D.** HQ Fund is selling below its net asset value, so it must be a closed-end fund. Shieko is selling above its NAV by more than the 8 1/2% sales load allowed, so it also must be closed end.

69. **D.** Sales charges could be paid on all types of open-end funds, while commissions are paid on securities traded in the secondary market, such as a closed-end company.

70. **A.** NASD rules allow a maximum sales charge on a variable annuity contract of 8 1/2%.

71. **B.** The value of the separate account fluctuates in relation to the securities held in the account.

72. **C.**   An annuity with life and ten-year certain will pay for the greater of ten years or the life of the annuitant. Fred lived for 23 more years, which is more than the ten certain.

73. **D.**   Variable annuities are different from fixed annuities because the payments vary and they are designed to offer the annuitant protection against inflation.

74. **D.**   The separate account is used for the monies invested in variable annuities. It is kept separate from the general account and operated very much like an investment company. It is considered both an insurance product and an investment product.

75. **A.**   Both a mutual fund and a variable annuity's separate account offer professional management and a board of managers or directors, and the client assumes the investment risk. Only variable annuities have payout plans that guarantee the client income for life.

76. **D.**   The client's beneficiaries would receive the current market value, but if the contract were insured, they would receive the greater of the amount invested or the current market value.

77. **D.**   Your client needs immediate income. Of the options listed only the immediate annuity offers this.

78. **C.**   The contract earned 3% in September. The assumed interest rate for the contract is 3%. Payment size will not change from the payment made the previous month.

79. **A.**   Mortality experience, age, sex and rate of return all have a bearing on the size of payout. The insurability of the annuitant has no bearing.

80. **A.**   Payments into a nonqualified deferred annuity go in after taxes. Taxes must be paid on the earnings of $6,000.

81. **B.**   Cashing in an annuity will cause the annuitant taxation at the ordinary income tax rate on all earnings in excess of the cost base. Any withdrawal at age 52 is subject to a 10% penalty unless it is for death or disability.

82. **B.**   Nonqualified deferred compensation plans do not require the approval of the IRS. The plan does allow the employer to deduct the cost when payment is made to the employee. The employee must sign a contract stating that the funds are for retirement and must abide by the contract.

83. **D.**   Money withdrawn from an IRA after age 59 1/2 is subject to ordinary taxation on the amount withdrawn. There is no 10% penalty starting at 59 1/2 years of age.

84. **B.**   Nonqualified retirement plans do not require IRS approval. Nonqualified plans also allow the employer the right to discriminate as to inclusion in the plan. Contributions are not tax deductible and the employer can deduct contributions only when they are paid to the employee, not when they are made by the company.

85. **A.**   Keogh plans must allow for the inclusion of all full-time employees, age 21, with one year of service.

86. **A.**   Keogh plans allow contributions for the lesser of 25% of earned income or $30,000.

87. **B.**   Contributions into a TSA, as in all qualified plans, are made before taxes. Payments from these plans require the payment of taxes at the ordinary income tax rate.

88. **B.**   This arrangement is possible if both firms are NASD members and there is a sales agreement in effect.

89. **C.**   The Investment Company Act of 1940 requires disclosure when all or part of the dividend payment comes from a source other than current income or accumulated undistributed net income.

90. **D.**   The principal of the firm must approve the use of the annual report as sales literature, and

the figures contained must be current and complete. A prospectus is always required.

91. **B.** The sale of mutual fund shares requires that the client get the prospectus before or during the sales solicitation.

92. **B.** A person conducting business in the over-the-counter market needs to be a member of the NASD. Transacting business on the exchange requires membership with the NYSE.

93. **C.** Liquidity is very important when determining suitability for a client.

94. **D.** None of the people listed may purchase hot issues.

95. **B.** This is called a breakpoint sale and is contrary to just and equitable principles of trade.

96. **B.** Registered reps may continue to be compensated for sales that were made while working for the firm and were in accordance with the contract.

97. **D.** No investment is suitable for all investors. Statements about future prices and earnings may be used if they are clearly labeled as forecasts.

98. **D.** Supervision of business solicitation or training requires being registered as a principal.

99. **D.** It is Regulation T that regulates the extension of credit by brokers and dealers for investment company shares.

100. **A.** The Code of Procedure contains the guidelines for handling violations of the NASD Rules of Fair Practice.

1. During a recessionary period, which of the following funds would have done better: a growth fund or a balanced fund?

   A. Growth fund because its objective is to grow regardless of the economic environment
   B. Balanced fund because of the downside protection that the bonds and other debt securities held by the fund would provide
   C. Growth fund because stocks of growth companies typically fare well during recessionary periods
   D. Balanced fund because any convertible securities held by the fund would increase

2. The exchange privilege offered by some mutual funds that are in a family of funds managed by the same company refers to the right of the shareholder to

   A. convert mutual fund shares to securities listed on the New York Stock Exchange
   B. reinvest dividends and capital gains without a sales charge
   C. convert shares to a different investment company within the family of funds on a dollar-for-dollar basis
   D. switch shares to an investment company within the family of funds and defer the taxes on any capital gains due to the exchange

3. An annuity is purchased with a life contingency offering a fully paid contribution to the annuity in the event of the owner's death. This life contingency applies during

   A. the accumulation period
   B. the annuity period
   C. both A and B
   D. neither A nor B

4. Failure by a shareholder to provide or verify her Social Security number to the investment company will result in which of the following taxes?

   A. Surtax
   B. Alternative minimum tax
   C. Noncertification tax
   D. Withholding tax

5. John Dobson deposits $21,000 in a mutual fund that offers rights of accumulation. John's account is currently valued at $20,000. For John to get a break on sales charges at the $25,000 breakpoint, he must deposit

   A. $4,000
   B. $5,000
   C. $21,000
   D. $25,000

6. An annuity that offers the annuitant a designated payment amount will have what type of payout?

   A. Fixed amount, variable time
   B. Fixed time, variable amount
   C. Variable amount, variable time
   D. Fixed amount, fixed time

7. A mutual fund previously invested in bonds with a medium-length maturity. As the bonds matured, the fund reinvested the proceeds and purchased long-term bonds with maturities of up to 20 years. What would have happened to the fund if the reinvestment had occurred during a period when interest rates were rising?

    I. Decrease in yield
    II. Decrease in income
    III. Increase in yield
    IV. Increase in income

    A. I and II
    B. I and IV
    C. II and III
    D. III and IV

8. A company that has paid its common stockholders a dividend would be required to also have made distributions to which of the other securities issued by the company?

    I. Bonds
    II. Convertible bonds
    III. Preferred stock
    IV. Convertible preferred stock

    A. I and II only
    B. I and III only
    C. II and III only
    D. I, II, III and IV

9. Where can you purchase shares of a closed-end investment company?

    A. Directly from the investment company
    B. From other shareholders through a broker-dealer
    C. From either A or B
    D. From neither A nor B

10. What is the minimum percentage of disinterested board members a mutual fund must have?

    A. 40%
    B. 60%
    C. 80%
    D. 100%

11. The last day a client can purchase shares of a mutual fund and still be entitled to a dividend is

    A. the day after the record date
    B. the record date
    C. seven days after the declaration date
    D. four days before the payment date

12. The rules that a company has regarding who may participate in a retirement plan are covered by which of the following types of requirements?

    A. Funding
    B. Participation
    C. Vesting
    D. Beneficiary

13. The provision that a company has to ensure that money will be available in the retirement plan is covered by which of the following types of requirements?

    A. Funding
    B. Participation
    C. Vesting
    D. Beneficiary

14. Based on the following figures, what are XYZ Mutual Fund's total assets at the year's end?

Assets	
Beginning of the year	$87,000,000
Net income	1,500,000
Dividends paid to shareholders	1,500,000
Realized capital gains	16,500,000
Capital gains paid to shareholders	16,500,000
Unrealized capital gains	5,000,000

    A. $82,000,000
    B. $87,000,000
    C. $88,500,000
    D. $92,000,000

15. Which of the following best describes a cause of inflation?

   A. Too much money chasing too few goods
   B. Too little money chasing too many goods
   C. Average of wage increases are below the Consumer Price Index (CPI).
   D. Money center banks reducing the prime lending rate by .5%

16. The maximum contribution to a TSA, including catch-up provisions, is

   A. the lesser of the participant's exclusion allowance, or 25% of compensation plus $4,000, or $15,000
   B. the lesser of $30,000 or the amount that could have been contributed, but was not, during the employee's last ten years or less of service
   C. the lesser of 25% of compensation or $30,000 in lieu of the regular allowance
   D. any of the above

17. If XYZ Company's dividend increases by 5% and its stock's market value increases by 7%, the current yield of the stock will

   A. increase
   B. decrease
   C. remain at 5%
   D. not be affected

18. Which of the following statements best describe warrants?

   I. They are short-term instruments that become worthless after the expiration date.
   II. They are most commonly offered in connection with debentures to sweeten the offering.
   III. They are issued by a corporation.
   IV. They are traded in the securities market.

   A. I and II
   B. I and III
   C. I, III and IV
   D. II, III and IV

19. An owner of preferred stock has which of the following rights?

   I. Right to determine when dividends will be issued
   II. Right to vote at stockholders' meetings or by proxy
   III. Right to a predetermined fixed portion of the corporation's profit in cash when declared
   IV. Right to buy restricted securities before they are offered to the public

   A. I, III and IV
   B. II, III and IV
   C. II and IV
   D. III

20. The interest from which of the following bonds is exempt from federal income tax?

   I. State of California bonds
   II. City of Anchorage bonds
   III. Treasury bonds
   IV. GNMA bonds

   A. I and II only
   B. I, II and IV only
   C. III and IV only
   D. I, II, III and IV

21. Baa rated bonds may yield more than Aaa rated bonds because

   A. Baa rated bonds are more secure than Aaa rated bonds
   B. Baa rated bonds are debentures, whereas Aaa rated bonds are secured by collateral
   C. Aaa rated bonds are less marketable
   D. Baa rated bonds carry more investment risk than Aaa rated bonds

22. Which of the following are money-market instruments?

    I. Repurchase agreements
    II. Treasury bills
    III. Commercial paper
    IV. Treasury bonds maturing in six months

    A. I and II only
    B. I, II and III only
    C. II, III and IV only
    D. I, II, III and IV

23. When you accept an order to sell stock, that order

    A. must be in writing
    B. must be approved by the NASD or the DBCC
    C. shall be reviewed by the branch manager, or partner
    D. is cancelable at any time

24. A client buys 500 shares of Amalgamated Horse Manure at $50 per share. He deposits with his broker $23,500, leaving a $1,500 balance, which he intends to pay on the fifth full business day following the trade date. But one day after the trade date, the market price drops to $40 per share. This change

    A. increases his equity by $5,000
    B. increases his debt balance by $5,000
    C. will cause a margin call
    D. does not change the balance due the broker-dealer

25. The ex-dividend date of a stock is Tuesday, January 13th. When is the record date?

    A. Wednesday, January 7th
    B. Friday, January 9th
    C. Saturday, January 17th
    D. Monday, January 19th

26. The NAV of mutual fund shares is priced

    A. daily
    B. monthly
    C. annually
    D. whenever the number of shares outstanding increases

27. Which of the following statements about sales charges is(are) true?

    I. Under NASD rules, mutual fund sales charges may not exceed 8.5% of the offering price.
    II. Under NASD rules, mutual fund sales charges may not exceed 8.5% of the share's net asset value.
    III. An investment company must offer rights of accumulation, breakpoints and reinvestment of dividends at NAV in order to charge an 8.5% sales charge.
    IV. Under the Investment Company Act of 1940, the maximum sales charge for purchases of mutual fund shares is 9%.

    A. I
    B. I and III
    C. I, III and IV
    D. II, III and IV

28. If a customer submits a repurchase order to his broker-dealer after the close of the New York Stock Exchange, the customer will receive a price based on the net asset value computed

    A. the previous business day
    B. the same day regardless of when the order is received
    C. the next time the firm computes it
    D. within the next two business days

29. A customer decides to buy shares of an open-end investment company. When is the price of the shares determined?

   A. At the next calculation of net asset value the day the fund custodian receives proper notification from the client
   B. At the next calculation of net asset value the day the broker-dealer wires the custodian on behalf of the client
   C. At both A and B
   D. At neither A nor B

30. Doris Ack is planning for retirement. She wants to be assured of a minimum income per month, and she wants some protection from inflation. Doris should consider a plan with

   A. installments for a designated amount
   B. period certain
   C. a combination fixed and variable payout
   D. installments for a designated period

31. A variable annuity contract guarantees a

   I. rate of return
   II. fixed mortality expense
   III. fixed administrative expense

   A. I and II only
   B. I and III only
   C. II and III only
   D. I, II and III

32. Bob Barrett, a registered representative, is discussing variable annuities with a client. He explains that under the contract the annuitant receives payments for life. Bob is describing a(n)

   A. payment guarantee
   B. insurance protection
   C. expense guarantee
   D. mortality guarantee

33. Which of the following persons may set up a Keogh plan?

   A. Accountant who works for a large corporation
   B. Single proprietor who owns a hardware store
   C. Chemical engineer employed by Dow Chemical Co.
   D. Doctor who is employed by Humana Hospital and who has no outside practice

34. Distribution of funds from a Keogh plan may be made without penalty if the

   A. investor becomes disabled
   B. IRS is notified within 60 days
   C. investor makes a major purchase, such as a car
   D. investments in the account decrease in value

35. Bob Madden is 67 and has just retired. He has $56,000 in his Keogh plan, to which he has contributed for eight years. None of his payments were voluntary nondeductible contributions. If Bob requests a periodic payment of $1,000 per month, how will the distribution of his payments be taxed?

   A. Part as ordinary income, part as long-term gains
   B. Ordinary income on the amount exceeding cost basis
   C. Ordinary income
   D. No taxes will be paid on the distribution because Bob is older than 59 1/2.

36. Broker A has an order to sell stock at 23 1/2, broker B has an order to sell at 23 and broker C has an order to sell at 24 1/4. Which broker would sell the shares first?

   A. Broker A
   B. Broker B
   C. Broker C
   D. This cannot be determined with the information given.

37. A stock is quoted at 97 1/8 bid—97 7/8 ask. Disregarding commissions, a purchaser of this stock would pay

    A. $97.12 1/2
    B. $97.75
    C. $97.87 1/2
    D. $97.87 1/2 plus the difference between the prices

38. When checking the newspaper for the daily bid and ask prices of over-the-counter stocks, you notice that two stocks in which you are interested have dramatically different spreads. You conclude that

    A. typically, the stock with the narrower spread is more active than the stock with the wider spread
    B. typically, the stock with the wider spread is more active than the stock with the narrower spread
    C. the stock with the narrower spread will always be less expensive in the long run
    D. No conclusion may be drawn from this information.

39. An example of a secondary distribution would be

    A. the sale of authorized stock
    B. the placement of a block of newly issued securities with one buyer
    C. the distribution of a new issue by an underwriter
    D. a large block of outstanding securities being redistributed in smaller blocks

40. When referring to the third market, transactions occur in

    A. major stock exchanges (New York, American, etc.)
    B. the over-the-counter market
    C. over-the-counter trading of listed securities
    D. the government bond market

41. Excessive activity in a customer's account primarily for the purpose of generating excess commissions to the registered representative is referred to as

    A. twisting
    B. churning
    C. whirling
    D. all of the above

42. Over the years, stockbrokers have been known to get themselves into hot water by overinvesting. Hence, any trade made by an NASD registered representative must be approved by the

    A. NASD
    B. SEC
    C. DBCC
    D. branch manager of the representative's office

43. The NASD rules regarding sales literature apply to which of the following?

    A. NASD registered representative putting on investment seminars which are open to the public
    B. Registered representative appearing on a TV show to discuss investments
    C. Registered representative sending to 300 of his clients a form letter that refers to the purchase of ABC Fund shares
    D. All of the above

44. The District Business Conduct Committee is an arm of

    A. the SEC
    B. the NASD
    C. the New York Stock Exchange
    D. all of the above

45. The NASD Code of Procedure

    A. handles trade practice complaints regarding violations of the Rules of Fair Practice
    B. is the application for and the granting of extensions of time
    C. is the processing of applications for registrations of representatives
    D. handles over-the-counter transactions and new stocks

46. In a mutual fund, a shareholder who elected not to receive share certificates can liquidate all or a portion of his holdings and receive payment from the fund if the fund receives from him which of the following?

    I.   Written request
    II. Signed stock power
    III. Signature guarantee

    A. I only
    B. I and II only
    C. I and III only
    D. I, II and III

47. Clifford Jones purchased a variable life contract last year. Of the initial premium of $1,000, $300 was deducted as a sales charge. Of the second year's premium of $1,000, $100 was deducted as a sales charge. Currently, the cash value of the contract is $1,000. If Clifford terminates the contract today, he would receive

    A. $0
    B. $400, being the sales charges only
    C. $1,000, being the cash value
    D. $1,400, being the cash value plus all sales charges

48. According to federal law, the insurance company must allow a variable life policyholder the option to convert the policy into a whole life contract for a period of

    A. 45 days
    B. 12 months
    C. 18 months
    D. 24 months

49. If within a two-year period, a variable life contract holder terminates the policy, the contract holder must receive as a refund the current cash value

    A. of the contract and forfeits sales charges
    B. of the contract plus 10% of the sales charges deducted
    C. of the contract plus 30% of the sales charges deducted
    D. of the contract plus all sales charges deducted in excess of 30% of the premium in the first year and 10% of the premium in the second year

50. Cash value does NOT have to be determined if

    A. changes in the value of the separate account do not affect the contract's cash value
    B. no request for redemption or payment is made to the separate account
    C. the day is a regularly scheduled holiday
    D. all of the above occur

51. In order to get cash for an emergency that arose, Michael MacKay redeemed his mutual fund shares. Within how many days of redemption could he reinvest in the same fund without having to pay additional sales charges?

    A. 7
    B. 30
    C. 45
    D. 60

52. Murray Murbles invests $3,000 in open-end investment company shares. After 60 days, he signs a letter of intent for a $10,000 breakpoint and backdates the letter two months. Six months later, he deposits $10,000 into the fund. He will receive a reduced sales charge on

    A. the $3,000 investment only
    B. $7,000 of the investment only
    C. the $10,000 investment only
    D. the entire $13,000 investment

53. Some open-end investment companies offer their investors a conversion privilege, which permits investors to

A. exchange general securities for shares in the mutual fund's portfolio
B. delay payment of taxes on investment company shares that have appreciated in value
C. purchase additional fund shares from dividends paid by the fund
D. exchange shares of one mutual fund for those of another fund under the same management at net asset value

54. Which of the following are characteristic of a mutual fund voluntary accumulation plan?

I. Minimum initial purchase
II. Minimum optional additional purchases
III. Declining level sales charges as money accumulates
IV. Obligatory purchase goal

A. I and II only
B. I, II and III only
C. II and IV only
D. I, II, III and IV

55. The record date is the

A. date on which a transaction is made between two parties
B. day on and after which the buyer of a common stock is not entitled to the dividend previously declared
C. day on which a list is compiled of stockholders who will receive dividends from a corporation
D. day on which a dividend is paid

56. An investor buys 100 shares of stock for $100 per share. The total value of the outstanding stock is $10,000,000. The company loses $6,000,000 a year for three years. What is the investor liable for?

A. His original $10,000
B. The full $10,000,000
C. The full $18,000,000
D. It is necessary to see the balance sheet to answer this question.

57. If the current dividend distribution of a company stock has increased by 5% while the offering price has increased by 7%, the current yield of this stock has

A. increased
B. decreased
C. stayed the same
D. More information is needed to answer this question.

58. A cumulative preferred stockholder could have all the following rights EXCEPT the right to

A. receive skipped dividends
B. receive a stated dividend
C. vote on the issue of more preferred stock
D. vote on the issue of more common stock

59. When the underlying stock price increases, the premium of a call option will generally

A. increase
B. decrease
C. remain the same
D. fluctuate rapidly

60. Which of the following investors will purchase stock if the option is exercised?

    I. Owner of a call
    II. Owner of a put
    III. Writer of a call
    IV. Writer of a put

    A. I and II
    B. I and IV
    C. II and III
    D. III and IV

61. Which of the following securities are backed by the full faith and credit of the U.S. government?

    A. Savings bonds
    B. Treasury bills
    C. Treasury bonds
    D. All of the above

62. Joan Clausen owns several Series EE bonds. If she wishes to redeem them after three years, she will

    I. pay federal income tax on the interest she has earned
    II. sell them through her broker
    III. receive the same rate of interest as she would had she held the bonds to maturity

    A. I only
    B. I and II only
    C. II and III only
    D. I, II and III

63. Interest earned on U.S. Treasury bills is subject to

    A. local tax
    B. state tax
    C. federal tax
    D. all of the above

64. Which of the following statements about general obligation municipal bonds are true?

    I. They are second only to U.S. government bonds in safety of principal.
    II. They are backed by the taxing power of the municipality.
    III. They are nonmarketable.
    IV. They pay higher interest rates than corporate debt securities.

    A. I and II
    B. I, II and IV
    C. II and III
    D. II, III and IV

65. Colleen Boyle is in the 33% tax bracket and is considering investing in a 6% municipal bond. What yield would she need on a corporate bond for the investment to yield an equivalent return?

    A. The corporate yield would have to be higher than the municipal yield of 6%.
    B. The corporate yield would have to be less than the municipal yield of 6%.
    C. The corporate yield would have to be the same as the municipal yield of 6%.
    D. Equivalent yields between corporate and municipal securities depend on the par value of the bonds.

66. The annuity unit of a variable annuity changes in value in a manner that corresponds most closely to changes in the

    I. Dow Jones index
    II. cost of living index
    III. value of the securities held by the insurance company
    IV. value of the securities kept in a separate account

    A. I and III only
    B. I, III and IV only
    C. IV only
    D. I, II, III and IV

67. In a nonqualified variable annuity, which of the following best describes the risk borne by the annuitant?

   A. The annuitant must pay taxes on the earnings in the current period.
   B. Mortality risk
   C. Interest rate risk
   D. Operating expense risk

68. When recommending a variable annuity to a prospective purchaser, which of the following should you take into account?

   A. Savings account
   B. Amount of purchaser's insurance
   C. Employer's pension plan
   D. All of the above

69. In calculating the investment performance of a separate account, you would take into account

   A. realized capital gains
   B. unrealized capital gains
   C. dividend income
   D. all of the above

70. The capital gains tax rate that an individual pays on appreciation in the reserves held for his variable annuity in a separate account while the contract is in the accumulation period is

   A. 0%
   B. 10%
   C. 25%
   D. 50%

71. Which of the following would be considered an unaffiliated person in a mutual fund?

   A. Member of the board of directors of the mutual fund who also is employed as the investment advisor
   B. Shareholder who owns 10% of the fund's shares
   C. Person who holds a position with the underwriter for the fund
   D. Member of the board of directors who cannot hold another position within the investment company

72. Clyde Baedecker has $350,000 in securities and $201,000 in cash with his brokerage firm. If the brokerage firm were forced to liquidate, how much of the account would be covered by SIPC?

   A. $250,000 of the securities and all of the cash
   B. All of the securities and $100,000 of the cash
   C. All of the securities and $150,000 of the cash
   D. All of the cash and $299,000 of the securities

73. The Securities Exchange Act of 1934

   I. requires registration of securities
   II. requires registration of broker-dealers with the SEC
   III. prohibits inequitable and unfair trade practices
   IV. provides for regulation of the over-the-counter market

   A. I and II only
   B. II and III only
   C. II, III and IV only
   D. I, II, III and IV

74. The Securities Act of 1933 requires that which of the following be offered only by prospectus?

    I. Treasury bonds
    II. Mutual fund shares
    III. Variable annuities
    IV. Unit investment trusts

    A. I and II
    B. II and III
    C. II, III and IV
    D. III and IV

75. Which of the following are true of the Securities Act of 1933?

    I. The act applies only to listed securities traded over the counter.
    II. One chief purpose of the requirements for registration and prospectuses is to provide full disclosure of pertinent information to the public.
    III. The act is designed to prevent fraud in the sale of newly issued securities.

    A. I and II only
    B. I and III only
    C. II and III only
    D. I, II and III

76. Which of the following situations would be governed by the Securities Act of 1933?

    I. Cosmopolitan Securities buys 3,000 shares of Amalgamated stock for its own account from a client.
    II. Hubert Gillian Investment Corporation is underwriting a primary distribution of stock.
    III. Gleason Investment Corporation is the distributor of Gleason Growth Fund shares.

    A. I and II only
    B. I and III only
    C. II and III only
    D. I, II and III

77. An announcement of a new issue of a security that gives the name of the issuer, the price and the name of the underwriter is called a(n)

    A. offering statement
    B. tombstone
    C. red herring
    D. prospectus

78. The Securities Exchange Act of 1934 was designed to

    I. maintain orderly markets
    II. control the regulation of new issues
    III. provide liquidity for securities holdings
    IV. regulate securities trading

    A. I, II and IV only
    B. I and IV only
    C. II and III only
    D. I, II, III and IV

79. One of the main objectives of the Investment Company Act of 1940 is to

    A. protect an investment company's investors from loss
    B. regulate the over-the-counter market
    C. require registration of investment companies with the SEC
    D. ensure that all investors are fully informed about all types of securities

80. Corporate bonds are considered safer than corporate stock issued by the same company because

    I. bonds represent equity in the corporation
    II. the company is more likely to back the original investors
    III. bonds are senior to common stock
    IV. the holder of a corporate bond is a debtor to the company

    A. I and II
    B. II, III and IV
    C. III
    D. III and IV

81. Which of the following securities is(are) issued with a fixed rate of return?

    I.   Bonds
    II. Preferred stock
    III. Common stock
    IV. Convertible preferred stock

    A. I, II and IV only
    B. III only
    C. IV only
    D. I, II, III and IV

82. Which of the following are characteristics of a municipal revenue bond?

    I.   Interest is exempt from federal income taxes.
    II. Interest is payable only from the revenue of the facility being financed.
    III. It does not have to carry a legal opinion of counsel.
    IV. The principal is backed by the full faith and credit of the issuing municipality.

    A. I and II only
    B. I, II and IV only
    C. I and IV only
    D. I, II, III and IV

83. John Jones is in the 30% tax bracket and is earning 7% interest on a municipal bond. What rate of interest would he have to earn on a corporate bond to receive the same return?

    A. 6.7%
    B. 7%
    C. 10%
    D. 15%

84. The standard denomination of a corporate bond is

    A. $100
    B. $500
    C. $1,000
    D. $5,000

85. Cities and states issue both revenue bonds and general obligation bonds. Which of the following characteristics are true of a revenue bond?

    I.   Interest from a revenue bond is exempt from federal income taxes.
    II. Interest is payable only from the revenue of the facility being financed.
    III. It does not carry a legal opinion of counsel.
    IV. The principal is payable only from the revenue of the facility being financed.

    A. I and II only
    B. I, II and IV only
    C. I and IV only
    D. I, II, III and IV

86. George has $300,000 worth of securities with ABC brokerage, his wife has $300,000 in securities and they have a joint account with $400,000 in securities. ABC filed for bankruptcy. What is the couple's SIPC coverage?

    A. $300,000
    B. $600,000
    C. $700,000
    D. $1,000,000

87. An investor in a low tax bracket wishes to invest a moderate sum in an investment that will provide him with some protection from inflation. Which of the following would you recommend?

    A. Municipal unit investment trust
    B. Specialized mutual fund
    C. Money market mutual fund
    D. Ginnie Mae fund

88. If the Federal Reserve Board changes the reserve requirement, the effect of the change on the economy will most likely be

    A. regressive
    B. nonregressive
    C. multiplied
    D. insignificant

89. An economic downturn that lasts for six months is called

    A. a recession
    B. a depression
    C. progressive
    D. regressive

90. Which of the following best describes the federal funds rate?

    A. The average rate for short-term bank loans last week
    B. The rate charged by major New York City banks
    C. A rate that changes daily and that banks charge each other
    D. The rate major New York City banks charge broker-dealers

91. Each of the following terms would be associated with an underwriting of corporate securities EXCEPT

    A. stabilization
    B. matched orders
    C. blue-sky
    D. due diligence

92. The settlement for a government bond trade in a cash account is

    A. the same day
    B. the next business day
    C. five business days after the trade date
    D. seven business days after the trade date

93. Under the SEC customer protection rule, broker-dealers must deliver to other broker-dealers no later than

    A. 5 business days after the trade date
    B. 10 business days after the settlement date
    C. 30 calendar days after the settlement date
    D. 30 business days after the settlement date

94. A customer is buying 800 shares of OTC stock. The trader responds to the firm's request for an 800-share quote with 15 bid—15 1/2 ask. The trader must sell

    A. 100 shares at 15
    B. 100 shares at 15 1/2
    C. 800 share at 15
    D. 800 shares at 15 1/2

95. The federal funds rate has been increasing for a long time. Which of the following is likely to occur?

    A. The FRB will increase bank reserve requirements.
    B. Member banks' deposits at Federal Reserve Banks will decrease.
    C. Money market interest rates will decrease.
    D. The prime rate will decrease.

96. An improvement in the business cycle is indicated by an increase in all of the following EXCEPT

    A. industrial production
    B. inventory
    C. the S&P index
    D. consumer orders

97. An investor's portfolio includes ten bonds and 200 shares of common stock. If both positions increase by 1/2 point, what is the gain?

    A. $50
    B. $105
    C. $110
    D. $150

98. Which of the following statements is true of a Treasury STRIP bond?

   I. The rate of return is locked in.
   II. There is no reinvestment risk.
   III. The interest is taxed as a capital gain.
   IV. The interest is realized at maturity.

   A. I
   B. I and IV
   C. I, II and III
   D. I, II and IV

99. Securities issued by which of the following are backed by the federal government?

   A. Federal National Mortgage Association
   B. Federal Home Loan Mortgage Securities
   C. Government National Mortgage Association
   D. Federal Intermediate Credit Bank

100. Which of the following statements is true of GNMA mortgage-backed securities?

   A. They are backed by the Federal National Mortgage Association, which may borrow from the Treasury to pay principal and interest.
   B. They are backed by a pool of mortgages.
   C. Interest payments are exempt from federal income taxes.
   D. The minimum purchase is $25,000.

◆ Answers & Rationale

1. B. A balanced fund's objective is to offer stability of return. Typically, a balanced fund will be invested in both common stock and debt securities. During market advances, the common stock portion of the portfolio will show superior returns. During down markets, the debt portion of the portfolio will offer returns that are greater than common stock. The value of convertible securities is linked in part to the value of common stock into which the security can be converted. As a result, the convertible security will offer some downside protection, but not as much as a straight debt instrument would.

2. C. The exchange privilege allows a shareholder to exchange shares from one fund to another within a family of funds under the same management without paying an additional sales charge (dollar for dollar). The shareholder is liable for any tax on gains as a result of the exchange.

3. A. An annuity with a life contingency (death benefit) promising a full contribution amount applies to the annuity during the accumulation stage. A guaranteed payout to a beneficiary in the event of an annuitant's death applies to the annuity period.

4. D. Failure to provide a Social Security or federal tax identification number results in an automatic withholding tax of 20% on the account.

5. A. Under rights of accumulation, the shareholder qualifies for a reduced sales charge on the additional investment, if the additional investment plus the greater of the amount previously invested or current value of the account exceeds the breakpoint. In this case, John's original investment ($21,000) plus the $4,000 additional investment qualifies for the $25,000 breakpoint.

6. A. An annuity guarantees payment for the life of the annuitant. If the annuitant elects a fixed-amount payout, the payout amount is guaranteed (the annuity must be a fixed annuity). Because the annuitant's life expectancy is variable, the length of time the annuity is paid depends on how long the annuitant lives.

7. D. The longer the maturity of a bond, the greater the risk to the investor. As a result, long-term bonds pay higher interest rates than medium- or short-term bonds. If the fund replaces medium-term bonds with long-term bonds, you would expect the long-term bonds to pay higher interest rates and thus more income. Additionally, as interest rates increase, so do yields. For example, the fund has a medium-term bond paying 8%. The income from the bond is $80 annually. The bond matures and the fund receives $1,000 as a return of principal. The fund is purchasing a long-term bond paying 9%, or $90, annually (income to the fund will increase by $10). Additionally, if interest rates are rising, price is declining. Thus, the 9% long-term bond will not cost $1,000, but say $950. Therefore, the current yield of the 9% bond will be 9.47% ($90 ÷ $950)—yield is up.

8. D. Because common stock is paid last (most junior), other securities issued by the firm will receive distributions (interest payments on debt securities and dividends on senior equity securities).

9. B. Closed-end investment company shares are traded in the secondary marketplace (OTC or exchange). Therefore shares are purchased from other shareholders through broker-dealers. Closed-end funds (unlike open-end funds) cannot issue shares directly to shareholders.

10. A. The board of directors of an open-end investment company must have, as a minimum, disinterested persons (nonaffiliated) comprising 40% of the board's membership.

11. B. Because transactions with a mutual fund settle on the day the order is received by the fund, an investor will become a shareholder of record if the transaction occurs on the record date.

12. **B.** The description of who qualifies to participate in a company's retirement plan must be in the participation requirements of the plan. A company may exclude certain employees through eligibility standards; however, any eligibility requirements for participation cannot discriminate in favor of a select group of employees.

13. **A.** ERISA mandates minimum funding standards for plans. These minimums ensure that benefits will be available for payment upon retirement of the participant.

14. **D.** The fund earned $1.5 million in income, but paid out this amount as a dividend. The fund also realized $16.5 million in capital gains, but again paid out this amount to shareholders. Unrealized capital gains is the value of appreciation in the fund during the year, and as a result the year-end asset value of the XYZ Fund is $92 million ($87 million plus $5 million).

15. **A.** Too much money chasing too few goods is the textbook definition of demand-pull inflation. As the economy attempts to purchase an inadequate supply of goods, the price of those goods will rise until an equilibrium between demand and cost is achieved. Cost-push is another textbook definition for inflation. Wages and raw material prices increase, and as a result end-product prices for goods increase.

16. **D.** The catch-up provisions allow employees who have not contributed to the plan's full potential to "catch up" on contributions under any of the answers, A, B or C. The restriction that applies is that once the method of additional catch-up contributions is selected, the participant must stay with the selected method.

17. **B.** Because the dividend rate increased at a rate less than the market value of the stock, the current yield will be less.

18. **D.** Warrants are commonly used as a sweetener in debenture offerings and carry a long life. Rights are issued by the corporation, giving the subscriber the right to purchase stock within a short period of time at a reduced price from the stock's current market price. The warrant does not have to be exercised but may be traded in the secondary market.

19. **D.** The preferred stockholder generally has no right to vote, but carries a prior right to dividends if and when declared. A restricted security is one that has prescribed limits on resale generally requiring registration.

20. **A.** Municipal bonds are exempt from federal income tax. Treasury bonds and GNMAs are both subject to income tax but would be exempt from state taxes.

21. **D.** Baa bonds carry a greater investment risk, so they will most likely pay greater interest to induce investors to purchase them.

22. **D.** Money markets are made up of short-term high-yield debt issues. All of the items listed are considered short term—even the bonds because they will mature in less than one year.

23. **C.** All orders received by a registered representative shall be reviewed by a principal of that firm.

24. **D.** As of the trade date, the terms of a transaction are fixed. Regardless of what events occur before settlement, the terms of the trade remain as stipulated at the time of the trade.

25. **D.** The record date is four business days after the ex-dividend date.

Wed	Thur	Fri	Sat	Sun	Mon	Tues
EX-	2	3	X	X	4	RECORD

26. **A.** The NAV of a mutual fund is calculated according to a formula described in the prospectus, but under no circumstances may calculation occur less frequently than once per business day.

27. **C.** The NASD limits sales charges to 8.5% of the POP as a maximum. If the fund does not allow for breakpoints, reinvestment of dividends at

NAV or rights of accumulation, the maximum is less than 8.5%. Under the Investment Company Act of 1940, the maximum sales charge on mutual funds is deferred to the NASD rules, while a contractual plan specifically may charge 9% over the life of the plan.

28. **C.** Orders to redeem shares will be executed at the next computed price.

29. **C.** The price for mutual fund shares is the next price calculated by the fund after receipt of the request.

30. **C.** Doris wants a fixed payment and protection from inflation. She wants to combine the objectives of a fixed and variable annuity.

31. **C.** A variable annuity does not guarantee an earnings rate; however, it does guarantee to make payments for life (mortality) and normally guarantees that expenses will not increase above a specified level.

32. **D.** The company assumes the mortality risk by guaranteeing payments for life.

33. **B.** Keogh plans are for unincorporated self-employed businesses.

34. **A.** Premature distribution is allowed without penalty if the participant dies or becomes disabled.

35. **C.** Distributions from any qualified plan are taxed as ordinary income.

36. **B.** The lowest offer and highest bid price prevail in the marketplace. Therefore, broker B's order would go first because it represents the lowest price at which the security can be purchased.

37. **C.** The purchaser of a stock buys at the offering price. The price quoted is 97 7/8, or $97.875.

38. **A.** Generally the narrower the spread between bid and ask in an over-the-counter security, the greater the marketability of the issue. Issues with a high degree of marketability are typically more active.

39. **D.** A secondary transaction is the redistribution of *outstanding* securities; the company does not receive the proceeds of the sale. The sale of authorized stock or a new issue is a primary offering.

40. **C.** A third market transaction is the sale of exchange-listed securities in the over-the-counter market.

41. **B.** Excessive activity in an account for the purpose of generating commissions is called *churning*.

42. **D.** The securities laws regulate the activities of associated persons. One of those regulations stipulates that the company is responsible for the conduct of its representatives. Hence, all correspondence and sales by the representative must be approved by a branch manager.

43. **D.** Any written communication such as seminar and TV scripts, form letters and so on fall under the NASD guidelines of sales literature or advertising.

44. **B.** The District Business Conduct Committee is an arm of the NASD. The DBCC is the first body to hear and judge complaints.

45. **A.** The Code of Procedure prescribes the method for handling trade practice complaints and sets the standards for fines and other actions.

46. **D.** Orders for redemption without a certificate being issued require a written request, signature guarantee and stock power.

47. **C.** Under the act of 1940, an insurance company must refund the cash value of a VLI contract plus all sales charges deducted in *excess* of 30% of the first year's premium and 10% of the

second year's premium. Because in this question sales charges did not exceed these amounts, only the cash value will be refunded.

48. **D.** Although state law may allow for periods other than 24 months, federal law requires a two-year conversion privilege.

49. **D.** The law requires a full refund of cash value plus a return of sales charges in excess of 30% in year 1 and 10% in year 2. After two years, only cash value need be refunded.

50. **D.** The separate account must be valued at least daily (the days the NYSE is open for business). The cash value of a contract must also be valued during regular business days unless activity in the separate account is such that cash value is not affected.

51. **B.** Funds offering the reinstatement privilege allow the investor to redeem and reinvest shares within 30 days without an additional sales charge. The privilege can be used only once, and only the amount withdrawn can be reinstated.

52. **D.** The entire investment qualifies for the reduced load. A letter of intent covers purchases within a 13-month period and may be backdated 90 days. Murray Murbles actually had eleven months in which to make the additional investment.

53. **D.** The exchange or conversion privilege allows an investor to exchange shares of one fund for another fund under the same management without paying an additional sales charge (although the exchange is still a taxable event).

54. **B.** A voluntary accumulation plan is voluntary, not binding. The company may require that the initial investment meet a certain minimum dollar amount. It may also specify that any additions meet set minimums (for example, $50). The sales charge is level, and the plan may qualify for breakpoints based on the accumulated value.

55. **C.** The record date is the day stockholders are listed in the company's record books as owners.

Shareholders of record may receive dividends when declared.

56. **A.** A stockholder of a corporation, although an owner, is liable only for the amount of money contributed to the corporation (limited liability).

57. **B.** The price of the stock has increased to a greater extent than the distribution. Price up, yield down, the current yield on the stock has decreased by 2%.

58. **D.** Only common stockholders have the right to vote on the issuance of common stock.

59. **A.** As the price of the underlying stock increases, so does the premium of a call option. The more the market price exceeds the exercise price, the more intrinsic value the option has. Because intrinsic value is part of premium (Premium equals Intrinsic value plus Time value), the premium goes up with the intrinsic value.

60. **B.** A call owner has the right to purchase stock from a call writer. A put writer has the obligation to purchase stock if a put buyer chooses to exercise the option.

61. **D.** Treasury securities (bills, notes and bonds) and U.S. savings bonds (EE and HH) are backed by the full faith and credit of the U.S. government.

62. **A.** A Series EE bond is a nonnegotiable instrument. The bond is redeemed by the government (usually through a bank). The interest received by the bondholder will be less if the bond is redeemed prior to maturity. The difference between purchase price and redemption value represents interest, which is taxable at the federal level.

63. **C.** Direct government debt is taxable only at the federal level. Direct debt includes Treasury debt and savings bonds.

64. **A.** General obligation bonds are backed by the general taxing authority of the municipal issuer. As such, they are often considered very safe investments. Municipal issues are marketable and are bought and sold in the secondary marketplace. Because interest received on municipal debt is exempt from federal taxation, yields offered on municipal debt are lower than yields offered on corporate debt.

65. **A.** Because a corporate yield is taxable at the federal level and because Colleen is in a 33% tax bracket, to receive the same aftertax yield as offered by the municipal issue the corporate yield would have to be at least 33% higher than the 6% offered by the municipal bond.

66. **C.** The value of an annuity unit will reflect changes in the assets held in the life insurance company's separate account.

67. **C.** In a variable annuity, performance of the account is not guaranteed; the investor accepts the risk the account will not perform at the assumed interest rate.

68. **D.** When recommending any investment to a prospective client, suitability of the investment must first be determined.

69. **D.** Performance of a separate account will depend on increases and decreases of the securities held in the portfolio. Whether gains are realized or unrealized, the account will reflect the gain or loss.

70. **A.** Gains in a separate account are tax deferred. The annuitant will pay ordinary income tax on the distribution upon receipt.

71. **D.** An affiliated person is defined as any person, officer, director, partner or employee directly or indirectly controlling, controlled by or under common control of the fund. Additionally, an affiliated person is defined as a person holding or controlling with the power to vote 5% or more of the outstanding securities of the fund. However, no person is considered an interested person solely by reason of membership as a director or just because he or she is an owner of securities.

72. **B.** SIPC covers cash and securities up to $500,000, but only $100,000 in cash.

73. **C.** The Securities Act of 1933 (paper act) requires registration of securities. The act of 1934 (people act) requires registration of people and exchanges transacting securities business in order to prevent manipulative and deceptive practices. The NASD is the SRO of the OTC market, but the SEC has final authority.

74. **C.** Treasury securities are exempt from registration requirements as are municipal issues and do not require a prospectus.

75. **C.** The Securities Act of 1933 applies to all newly issued securities and requires a registration statement and prospectus to be filed with the SEC. The purpose of filing and distributing the prospectus is to provide full disclosure of the offering and thus deter the sale of fraudulent securities.

76. **C.** The Securities Act of 1933 requires registration of newly issued securities. The purchase of the Amalgamated stock is a secondary transaction and thus regulated by the Securities Exchange Act of 1934. The underwriting of a primary distribution (also the sale of mutual fund shares because they are a continuous primary offering) is subject to the reporting and filing requirements under the Securities Act of 1933.

77. **B.** A tombstone announces the sale of a primary offering; it tells the price of the security, where a prospectus may be obtained and where the security may be purchased.

78. **B.** The Securities Exchange Act of 1934 was enacted to regulate the trading of securities and individuals effecting transactions of securities in the secondary market.

79. **C.** Under the Investment Company Act of 1940, companies in the business of investing or reinvesting in securities are required to register

with the SEC as a face-amount company, a unit investment trust or a management company.

80. **C.**   A bond represents a legal obligation to repay principal and interest by the company. The holder of a corporate bond is a *creditor* of the company.

81. **A.**   Bonds and preferred stock are typically issued with a stated payment, either in interest or dividends. Common stockholders are entitled to receive a variable distribution of profits if and when a dividend is declared.

82. **A.**   All municipal bonds must carry a legal opinion of counsel affirming that the issue is a municipal issue and that interest is exempt from federal taxation. Interest and principal of a revenue bond will be paid only if the facility financed produces the revenue necessary to pay. A GO is a municipal issue backed by the full faith and credit of the municipality.

83. **C.**   First of all, because a corporate yield is taxable and the interest rate would have to be greater than 7%, answers A and B can be eliminated. Answer D is more than twice the yield of 7%, and because John is only in a 30% bracket, the answer is too high, leaving answer C as the answer. The formula would be municipal rate (7%) divided by the complement of the tax bracket (100% − 30% = 70%), or 7 divided by 70 equals 10%.

84. **C.**   The majority of corporate bonds are issued with a face amount (principal) of $1,000.

85. **B.**   A revenue bond is a municipal issue sold to raise funds for the purpose of constructing a revenue-producing facility. All municipal bonds require an opinion of specialized bond counsel stating that the issue does indeed represent a municipal obligation and that interest payments are exempt from federal taxation. The interest and principal payments are backed to the extent that the facility produces enough revenue to make payments.

86. **D.**   SIPC insurance is figured by account ownership. George is covered for his $300,000 in securities, and his wife is covered for her $300,000 in securities. The joint account would be treated separately and would be covered for the $400,000 in securities. The total securities coverage for the two of them and their three accounts is $1,000,000. Insurance coverage per account is $500,000, no more than $100,000 of which can be in cash.

87. **B.**   The growth fund will give the investor some protection from inflation, and we must assume that the specialty fund is a growth fund (historically common stock is a better inflation hedge than fixed-income instruments). The other three answers are income-oriented funds.

88. **C.**   Whenever the Federal Reserve changes a national policy or requirement (such as reserve requirements, margin requirements or the discount rate), the effect tends to be multiplied throughout the economy. If the reserve requirement is raised, money will be tightened because banks have to hold more in reserve, thus causing interest rates to rise; in turn, companies that borrow will have to raise prices.

89. **A.**   When the economy is bad for six months (or two consecutive quarters) we are in a *recession*; if it continues we would go into a *depression*.

90. **C.**   The federal funds rate is what banks charge each other for overnight loans. It can fluctuate hourly.

91. **B.**   Matched orders refer to orders of the same size being executed on the floor of the exchange (instead of a partial fill). The underwriter must exercise diligence in ensuring that the information in the prospectus is correct. The issue must be registered in a state (blue-sky) to be sold within the state. Stabilization is the process of supporting the price of a new issue in the secondary market to ensure a normal and systematic issue of the securities in the primary market.

92. **B.** Be careful to distinguish between a cash account and a cash transaction. Regular way settlement for a government bond is the next business day. Most other securities settle regular way on the fifth business day.

93. **C.** The SEC says that broker-dealers must reconcile any dispute as it relates to settlements within 30 calendar days. This is part of SEC Rule 15c3-3 of the Securities Exchange Act of 1934.

94. **D.** The trader has responded to a quote for a specific size.

95. **B.** If the cost of borrowing funds is increasing, members will need to keep more of their own funds available.

96. **B.** If inventories are going up, it is generally taken as an indication that sales are going down.

97. **D.** The gain would be $50 for the bonds (1/2 point for one bond is $5 times ten bonds) and $100 for the common stock (1/2 point is $.50 times 200 shares).

98. **D.** A STRIP has no reinvestment risk because there are no interest payments to have at risk in regards to reinvestment. Because there is no reinvestment risk, the total rate of return is locked in, or set at issuance. The interest in the bond is paid at maturity, but it is taxed as interest income over the life of the bond.

99. **C.** GNMAs are guaranteed by the government. These are the only agency issues backed directly by the government. The other answers listed are indirect federal debt.

100. **D.** GNMAs are issued in minimum denominations of $25,000.

Notes

Notes

Notes

Notes

Notes

Profits are a Quick Read with Dearborn's Library of Money Makers!

Securities	Unit Price
Financial Instruments Overview Video Get all the basic facts on profitable financial investments – securities markets, mutual funds, variable contracts and more. **Order No. 3901.01**	$ 89.00
Financial Products Manual Put financial product information at your fingertips. Our ready-reference guide answers all your financial product questions quickly and in plain English. Covers over 30 investment topics. **Order No. 3904.02**	$ 25.00
Managing Investments, Equity Strategies Set up powerful financial plans for your clients with this book of key strategies. **Order No. 3909.01**	$125.00
Know-How for Sales Assistants Generate more sales by making your sales assistant knowledgeable and efficient. (15-hour self-study course) **Order No. 3921.01**	$ 75.00

Insurance	Unit Price
Survey of Advanced Sales Build the skill and confidence you need to market yourself in advanced sales interviews. **Order No. 5408.11**	$ 26.95
Investment Planning Come up a winner in today's economy and tax environment with a thorough knowledge of 16 types of investment risk. **Order No. 5205.03**	$ 45.95
Income Tax Planning Avoid the pitfalls of tax planning. In clear and simple terms, this book explains Federal income tax facts, theory and new tax law application. **Order No. 5206.15**	$ 49.95
Business Insurance Break into the profitable business market with a course designed for aggressive, professional life underwriters. **Order No. 5412.05**	$ 49.95
Estate Planning Sell big premium cases in the estate planning market with this comprehensive guide. **Order No. 5414.09**	$ 49.95
Common Sense Selling: **No Smoke...No Fluff...No Mystique** Get the edge in today's competitive market by using Joe Casales' common-sense techniques. **Order No. 2401.25**	$ 16.95

Order information and additional selections on reverse

Dearborn
Financial Publishing, Inc.

Where Experts Begin

Dearborn Financial Publishing, Inc.

Where Experts Begin

Business Professional	Unit Price

The 100 Best Stocks to Own in America
Put your decision making on target. Get over 4,000 facts on America's 100 most successful publicly-traded corporations. **Order No. 5608.13** — $ 19.95

Diversify: The Investor's Guide to Asset Allocation Strategies
Create a strong and resilient portfolio. This easy-to-read guide explains diversification, asset allocation and how different assets correlate to one another. **Order No. 5608.22** — $ 22.95

The Global Investor: How to Buy Stocks Around the World
Expand your investment horizons with this fact-filled book on the international market. **Order No. 5608.24** — $ 29.95

Winning with Your Stockbroker in Good Times and Bad
Make money and build net worth by learning how successful investors select brokers and use them to the best advantage. **Order No. 5608.02** — $ 19.95

The Mutual Fund Encyclopedia (Fall 1990)
Tap into money-making opportunities in the mutual fund market. Our one-volume, quick-reference guide details over 1,110 mutual funds, including load, no-load and low-load funds. **Order No. 5608.23** — $ 27.95

ORDER FORM

Place your order today!
Call toll-free 1-800-621-9621, ext. 650
In Illinois, call 1-800-654-8596, ext. 650

Or, mail payment and this completed form to: **Dearborn Financial Publishing, Inc., Order Department, 520 North Dearborn Street, Chicago, IL 60610-4975**

Shipping Address (please print):

Name _____

Address _____

City _____ *State* _____ *Zip* _____

Telephone No. (_____) _____

Account No. _____ *Exp. Date* _____

Signature _____
(All charge orders must be signed)

30-Day Money-Back Guarantee
Please send me the book(s) I have indicated. If I return any book within the 30 day period, I'll receive a refund with no further obligation.

Payment must accompany all orders
(Please check one)

☐ Check or money order payable to Dearborn
☐ Credit card charge **(circle one)**
   VISA   MasterCard   AMEX

Item	Order No.	Quantity	Unit Price	Amount Due

☐ Please send Dearborn's Catalog for Securities Professionals

Subtotal	
Sales Tax	
Shipping & Handling	
Total	

SHIPPING AND HANDLING					
Total Purchase	$0.00-24.99	$25.00-49.99	$50.00-99.99	$100.00-249.99	$250.00-499.99
Shipping & Handling Charges	$4.00	$5.00	$6.00	$8.00	$11.00

Orders shipped to the following states must include applicable sales tax: **CA, CO, FL, IL, MI, MN, NY, PA, TX, WI.**

RUSH delivery using UPS overnight, add **$25.00**
RUSH delivery using UPS 2nd-day delivery, add **$16.00**

Please allow 2-3 weeks for delivery. Orders will be shipped by UPS unless requested otherwise. All prices subject to change without notice.

900501